Essays in
ANCIENT & MODERN
PHILOSOPHY

Essays in
ANCIENT & MODERN
PHILOSOPHY

By
H. W. B. JOSEPH
M.A., F.B.A.
Fellow of New College, Oxford

OXFORD
AT THE CLARENDON PRESS
1935

OXFORD
UNIVERSITY PRESS
AMEN HOUSE, E.C. 4
London Edinburgh Glasgow
New York Toronto Melbourne
Capetown Bombay Calcutta
Madras Shanghai
HUMPHREY MILFORD
PUBLISHER TO THE
UNIVERSITY

PRINTED IN GREAT BRITAIN

PREFACE

FOUR of the following papers have appeared before. That on 'Aristotle's Definition of Moral Virtue and Plato's Account of Justice in the Soul' is reprinted, with some additions and alterations, from the issue of *Philosophy* for April 1934. That on 'Purposive Action' was published in two parts in the *Hibbert Journal*, January and April 1934, and 'A Comparison of Kant's Idealism with that of Berkeley' was delivered as the Annual Philosophical Lecture on the Henriette Hertz Trust at the British Academy in 1929; slight changes have been made in both of these. The Essay on 'The Concept of Evolution' was delivered as the Herbert Spencer Lecture in the University of Oxford in 1924, and is reprinted almost exactly as published then. I have to thank respectively the Editors of *Philosophy* and of the *Hibbert Journal*, the Council of the British Academy, and the Delegates of the Oxford University Press for permission to reprint them. The remaining seven are new. But the first five develop theses which formed part of a course of Lectures on Plato's *Republic* which I used to give at New College, Oxford, and I fear that the argument of III is to some extent drawn upon again in VI; while the two on Kant's *Kritik of Pure Reason*, work out, *inter alia*, the line of thought suggested in the British Academy Lecture.

H. W. B. J.

OXFORD, 1935.

CONTENTS

I

PLATO'S *REPUBLIC*: THE ARGUMENT WITH POLEMARCHUS

I REMEMBER being much puzzled and dissatisfied with the first book of Plato's *Republic*, when I first read it; and I do not suppose the experience to be uncommon. The writing is brilliant, the dramatic interest greater than anywhere later in the work. But the argument is elusive, and in places has an appearance of being scarcely serious, or even unfair. Yet the book is one on which, if we may judge by the story of his having rewritten the opening of it ten times, Plato spent great care, and we can hardly suppose that he cared only about the style; he must have thought that the arguments which Socrates is made to bring against what he (Socrates) thinks are false doctrines about Justice and Injustice, before developing his own, were sound arguments; why else, in a dialogue of such importance, should they have been allowed to stand? The book may be earlier in date than those which follow. This view about it has strong support from 'stylometric' investigations, besides being suggested by obvious differences between it and the rest, and obvious resemblances of it to dialogues of the so-called 'Socratic' group, like the *Charmides* or *Laches*. One may even say that it could have stood alone as a 'dialogue of refutation'. But these dialogues are serious, and surely not consciously unfair. And if it had been written and laid aside, Plato, when he came to take up again the problem of Justice, was not so poor that, if he did not think what he had already written adequate, he could not write something else by way of opening. We must, therefore, if we are puzzled and dissatisfied, believe nevertheless that Plato was content. Are we then to suppose that he was incapable of seeing how weak the arguments which he put into the mouth of Socrates were? Or are we dissatisfied

with them because we misunderstand them? Those who
have read their Plato longest will, I think, be most inclined
to the second alternative.

At any rate, I myself have come to believe that my
original dissatisfaction was merely due to misunderstanding; that the discussion in this book is of great value both in
itself, and in relation to what follows. And I should like to
make an attempt to set forth the grounds for my belief.

The problem of the *Republic* may be said to be, how a
man should live. Socrates himself gives that as the subject
on which Thrasymachus and he are arguing.[1] Now one
way of settling that problem is by giving a list of duties;
and many men, in many ages, live by such lists uncritically,
or at least accept them as what they ought to live by. Yet
sometimes they ask, Why these duties? and sometimes,
Are there any duties? Is it not wise to please oneself, so
far as one can, without regard to others?[2]

In the argument between Polemarchus and Socrates,
Plato is dealing with the first of these questions; and he
shows, indirectly, that the problem what a man should do
cannot be settled by giving a list of duties. In the argument between Thrasymachus and Socrates, he is dealing
with the second; and he shows that the implications of
'acting wisely' are inconsistent with such a rule of action
being wise. The remainder of the dialogue develops and
justifies these conclusions. We are given a picture of the
organization of a perfect commonwealth and an account
of the constitution of the human soul, in order that we

---

[1] i. 352 d 6: περὶ τοῦ ὅντινα τρόπον χρὴ ᾖν.

[2] It may be objected that the second of these two questions is wrongly
put; there are duties, and a man ought not merely to please himself; if 'Why
not please oneself?' means 'Why ought I to do my duty?', the question is
absurd; if it means 'Shall I do my duty, and not rather please myself?', this
is not a question, but an expression of the thought involved in deciding.
But to Plato it seemed that a wise man would endeavour to attain what is
good, i.e. to make himself, or his soul, or his life good; and that what we
ought to do is what contributes to this. Cf. *infra*, pp. 129–31.

may see how *what* any man ought to do depends on his nature and powers, and his place in the commonwealth of which he is a member; therefore it cannot be laid down in general rules. And we are given also an account of what wisdom is, that we may see how the very notion of living wisely, implied in asking how a man *should* live, involves distinguishing between what is really good and what seems so, and how to seek what is really good is to subordinate our chance desires.

This is, of course, a very summary statement, and only of the main outline. Some critics may object to it on the ground that Plato never does attempt to show that there is anything a man ought to do, but merely what it is in his interest to do.[1] These critics, however, are accusing Plato of mistaking one question for another, passing from one to another without seeing the difference between them, not of explicitly denying that a man has any duties. As a statement therefore of the outline plan of the *Republic*, and the relation of the first book to the rest, what I have said may still be correct; I am not concerned here with the justice of the critics' accusation. Of course there are many points in the arguments of the first book which any so summary a statement must ignore, many anticipations in it of later discussions that connect it with the rest. Some of these will appear as we proceed. But the above is the general thesis that I desire to justify.

We need not spend long over the first few pages, before Cephalus retires, leaving the argument to Polemarchus; though we may notice how there appears in them the subject of the life after death, and the lots awaiting in it those who have lived justly or unjustly here, to which the dialogue returns at its close; and also how in Cephalus himself we have a picture of a man living rightly of custom and without understanding:[2] a way of life which at the close is

---

[1] Cf. Prof. H. A. Prichard, *Duty and Interest*, pp. 5–21.
[2] ἔθει ἄνευ φιλοσοφίας ἀρετῆς μετειληφότα, x. 619 c 7.

indicated not to be sufficient, and with which indeed the
effort of the whole dialogue shows that Plato was not
content. The conversation gives Socrates opportunity to
raise the question whether what justice is can be told
by giving a list of duties: 'this thing, justice, shall we say
that it is thus simply to speak truth, and to restore anything one may have taken from another, or may these
deeds themselves be sometimes justly done, sometimes
unjustly?'[1]

This question, or rather the wider question it implies,
viz. whether any list of duties can tell us what justice is,
whether justice can be defined by specifying the ἔργα
Ξικαιοσύνης,[2] is handed over by Cephalus to Polemarchus,
and I have suggested that it is Plato's main purpose, in the
discussion which follows between him and Socrates, to
show that the answer is No. Incidentally we may remind
ourselves how in other dialogues Plato proceeds similarly,
in the *Laches* with courage, in the *Charmides* with temperance. Each virtue may be thought to require of us its own
definite acts; and yet there are shown to be situations in
which a man thus virtuous should act differently from how
it seemed that the virtue in question would make him
act. And for discriminating these situations knowledge is
necessary: not any knowledge, but knowledge of good and
evil. But what the relation of this knowledge is to all those
different knowledges required for doing well the different
kinds of action which a man has to do, remains a problem.
The same problem is before us here. Plato would have us
see that it is not co-ordinate with those specialized knowledges. The occasions for applying them exclude each
other; the occasion which calls for the knowledge of a
physician does not call for that of a sailor. But to act
justly or rightly, to live as one should, needs some other

---

[1] i. 331 c 1.
[2] The phrase is from Xen. *Mem.* iv. ii. 12. The whole of §§ 1–20
there should be compared with *Rep.* 1. 331 e 1–334 b 7.

sort of knowledge called for on all occasions and in which the requirements of all particular virtues are somehow comprehended. Of this knowledge two things may be said, that distinguish it from those specialized knowledges. It cannot be discriminated from them, as they can from one another, by assigning its particular field, specifying its ἔργα. And its possession is bound up, as theirs is not, with what we should call qualities of character, that may depend partly on nature, φύσις, but must be developed by a proper nurture, παιδεία. All this we are shown as the dialogue proceeds. What is sometimes called the Socratic paradox, that virtue is knowledge, probably never meant that the difference between a good and a bad man is a merely intellectual difference, like that between men who do and who do not understand economic theory. Certainly Plato in the *Republic* never teaches that. He does indeed teach that if a man really knew good and evil, he must ensue one and eschew the other; and that without knowledge, or in default true opinion, about good and evil no man can live as he should. But that much every one must allow who is not prepared to accept 'What you think you ought to do' as a sufficient answer to the question 'What ought I to do?' or to the question 'What is good?', 'What you think good'. No doubt Plato denied that a man can deliberately reject what he thinks good; οὐδεὶς ἑκὼν ἀδικεῖ. But that is not to hold instruction enough to make any one a virtuous man, as it is enough to make him a doctor. The knowledge (Plato thought) required for living a good life is differenced from that required for being a doctor, or for doing well any specialized work, in another way than merely by not being specialized; it involves the whole soul in a way in which they do not.

The argument with Polemarchus falls into two main parts, (*a*) from 331 d 4 to 334 b 9, (*b*) from there to 336 a 8. In the first it is shown that what justice requires

of a man towards others is not restricted to any special
occasions of his intercourse with them; in the second, that
the 'others' towards whom it places him under obligation are not some men only. If justice then must inform
his actions towards all persons on all occasions, clearly its
nature and requirements cannot be shown by giving a list
of duties.

But whereas (*b*) is a straightforward argument, reaching
the conclusion which Socrates would have Polemarchus
accept, (*a*) is indirect, proceeding by *reductio ad absurdum*.
This may make the reader suppose that it is a piece of
quibbling, in which Socrates merely entangles his opponent, without interest in the truth. But absurdity may
be reached either by bad argument or by proceeding from
false assumptions. Was Plato taken in by quibbles put
into the mouth of Socrates that any freshman can detect?
If not, and if he knew them for quibbles, why should he
have introduced them? Is it not possible that the absurd
conclusion is reached fairly from false assumptions which
were clearer to him than they are at first sight to a modern
reader?

I believe this to be so, and that the false assumptions are
so many forms of a single error, that of supposing that the
practice of justice (or righteousness) consists in the performance of specifiable acts. It is the error of those who
believe in 'the righteousness which is of the law', and has
been common enough at all times. The Pharisee who said
'I fast twice in the week; I give tithes of all that I possess'
entertained it. But we are apt to think the error lies merely
in overlooking the spirit in which the acts should be done.
'The letter killeth, but the spirit maketh alive.' This is not
Plato's point, though he certainly did not think the spirit
in which a man acted irrelevant, as may be seen notably in
Rep. iv. 443 c 9–444 a 2. Polemarchus, in the passage we
have to consider, imputes to a just man the purpose to
help his friends; but so equally does Socrates. It is not

by slipping in the unfair assumption that justice is a mere matter of skill without regard to purpose that Socrates develops his argument. There is another side of the error of the Pharisee which Plato would bring out. In whatever spirit a man may fast and give alms, when he has done that, he has not done all that is required of him. Or, to use the list of duties in our text, though he speak truth and pay what he owes out of love of his friends or because he thinks he ought, he need not be just; for sometimes justice requires that he should not act thus, and it requires very much besides.

We need not, therefore, charge Plato with letting Polemarchus confuse the statement that to pay one's debts is just with the definition that justice is to pay one's debts (331 d 2–e 4). For his case is more than that this definition incorrectly specifies the works of justice; it is that justice cannot be defined that way at all. Simonides, whom Polemarchus quotes, in support of the definition he takes over from his father, as saying that to pay one's debts is just, might have mentioned other acts, which, together with this, would have made up such a definition of justice; but the argument could proceed just in the same way from such definition as from the saying of Simonides.

For Socrates' first step is to show by instances (as he had already suggested to Cephalus) that sometimes a man ought not to restore to another what is owed to him; whereupon Polemarchus glosses the saying, and declares that I owe to another not what is his in the sense of a thing he had lodged with me, but good if he is a friend, and evil if he is an enemy (331 e 5–332 c 4). What is owing to any one is what is fitting. This is a much more elastic term, and indeed Samuel Clarke tried to find in the notion that what is right is what is fitting to the given situation, a means of showing that morality is a matter of demonstration. But he failed, because there are no principles from which we can deduce conclusions in detail about the conduct fitting on each occasion. And just as little can we set it out in lists, stating it without deducing it. If to treat a man justly is to treat him as is fitting, there is no intercourse of a man with others which is not an occasion for justice; a man may not sometimes practise justice and sometimes medicine, as he may sometimes practise medicine and sometimes seamanship.

But how then is practising justice related to practising medicine or seamanship? If justice is to be defined by naming its works, it will not serve to name the works of medicine or seamanship, for that would be to indicate not what a just man but what a doctor or a seaman does. Socrates, however, puts questions to Polemarchus which imply that justice is to be defined by naming its works, because Polemarchus has started from that position. We are not told that this assumption is the source of all the trouble. We are left to discover it.

Socrates takes the statement that justice is to render to each what is fitting, and shows that for rendering to certain subjects certain things fitting, a man is called a doctor or a cook. For rendering to what subjects what that is fitting is he to be called just? For doing good to friends and evil to enemies, replies Polemarchus. But is it in virtue of justice that he can do this? In what concerns their health and sickness the doctor is best able so to act; when they are at sea, the seaman. When and for what is it the just man who is best able to help his friends and harm his enemies (332 c 5–e 4)? Polemarchus should have refused to name any special occasions; but that would have been to abandon the assumption that governs his thought; and he replies, in fighting on their side or against them. But what when there is no fighting? A man's justice must be of use also in peace. Yet so are husbandry and shoemaking, for different purposes; for what is justice useful? Again he specifies a particular sort of purpose—in matters of contract. But a contract is an undertaking in which men engage together, and according to the nature of the undertaking different kinds of men will be useful. For what undertaking is it a just man that is required? For those concerning money, Polemarchus suggests; and again he ought to have suggested no special undertaking. For if money is to be used, as in buying or selling a horse or a boat, it is knowledge of horse-flesh or of boat-building or sailing that is required; and the question occurs once more, when is it justice that is required? Polemarchus replies, when money is to be deposited and kept safe; and no doubt it is highly important that those to whom money is entrusted should be honest. But if justice is required when money is to be kept in safety, not when it is to be used—and the same would apply to anything else, as well as to money—it will result that in the use of anything justice is useless, and useful only when anything is not in use (332 e 4–333 d 12). This, as Socrates observes, does not make justice a very fine thing; and he might have added that it brings Polemarchus back to the position from which he started, and which he had endeavoured to amend, that it is in virtue of his justice that a man restores what has been lodged with him. And Polemarchus has been driven back to it because at every turn he accepted from Socrates questions implying his own assumption that for the practice of justice, as for that of medicine or seamanship or any other art, there are special occasions.

It is often said that Plato makes false analogies between conduct and the arts. But if we read this book carefully we shall see that he thinks conduct in some ways differs from the arts, and in some shares their nature. It differs in not having, as every art has, a special field or subject-matter. It shares with them that it can be either right or wrong, correct or faulty. The part of the argument between Socrates and Polemarchus which we have so far considered is intended to bring out this difference. In the argument between Socrates and Thrasymachus, Plato endeavours to show what is involved for conduct by that which it shares with the arts. It is not accurate to say even there that he argues from the analogy of the arts. What he does is to make us see what a character acknowledged to be common to them and conduct involves in them, and to ask us to admit that this is involved for conduct also.

Since in carrying on any art, and also in conduct, a man may proceed correctly or faultily, rightly or wrongly, an art and conduct are so far the same. But if we went on to say that conduct is one of the arts, it should then, like them, have its special field or subject-matter; and justice, which is what a man's conduct should show, would be shown precisely in that field or subject-matter. But the consequence would be to exclude it from all action in which a man exercises any art commonly so called, for these arts are delimited from each other by having different fields or subject-matters. That is what Socrates has so far shown. If then there is an art of conduct, or of living, as in a sense Plato thinks there is, the practice of it must somehow coincide with or inform that of all the special arts. But how it can is no easy question.

Socrates now turns (333 e 6–334 b 6) to a fresh point, arising out of the conclusion that justice is of use merely to safeguard what is out of use. That conclusion is anyhow absurd, but it is to be shown so even more glaringly by this ensuing argument: one which is apt to arouse what I think is ill-considered hostility. On the assumptions so far made, however, it is a fair *reductio ad absurdum*.

He applies the principle, formulated later by Aristotle, that contraries fall under the same capacity.[1] Those who can best deliver can best ward off a blow; those who can best guard against can best secretly convey disease, and so forth. If then the use of a just man were for safe-keeping, it should also be for circumventing the precautions of

---

[1] e.g. τῶν ἐναντίων ἐστὶ μία ἐπιστήμη, *Anal. Pri.* I. xxxvi. 48 b 5; Δύναμις μὲν γὰρ καὶ ἐπιστήμη Δοκεῖ τῶν ἐναντίων ἡ αὐτὴ εἶναι, *Eth. Nic.* v. i. 1129 a 13.

others to keep things safe; he will be able not only at guarding but at thieving, and so turn out to be a sort of thief—κλέπτης τις.

The obvious retort is that to possess a power is not to have the will to use it; that justice is a matter of character and purpose, not of skill. But Plato is not forgetting this. Ever since Polemarchus' statement to that effect at 332 d 5, it is assumed that a just man's purpose is to help his friends and harm his enemies. The question has been how precisely justice qualifies him to do this. In one situation seamanship, in another a knowledge of horse-flesh will do it, and so forth; and if justice has a restricted field, alternative to theirs as theirs are to each other, that field has been reduced to safeguarding what is not in use. Granted that his justice is such a special power which the just man possesses, and that he uses it to help his friends, if the same power enables him to circumvent others' safeguarding, why should he not use it that way to help his friends also? It is not suggested that he will steal for himself any more than that he will keep for himself what is lodged with him. That is why Socrates says he will be κλέπτης τις, a *sort* of thief; the common thief steals for himself. If justice, though to be shown by a man in helping his friends and harming his enemies, is not to inform all that a man does, but is required only on special occasions, we naturally ask why those are the occasions on which it is required; presumably because on those occasions, and not on others, it is by justice that a man can help his friends or harm his enemies. If that is so, justice must be a specialized ability, which it is reasonable he should use for the purpose in question in all ways in which it admits of being used. And one way would be to steal (perhaps from their enemies) and give to one's friends. This consequence is, no doubt, absurd. But the moral is, that justice is not to inform a man's conduct only on special occasions, and so cannot be defined by any list of a just man's ἔργα or works.

We come now to (*b*) the second main part of the discussion, 334 c 1–336 a 8. This is not a *reductio ad absurdum*, but proceeds directly to a conclusion we are meant to accept. We have been shown indirectly that there is no restriction on the occasions when justice must inform a man's action; we are now to see that there is no restriction on the persons towards whom it places him under obligation. The formula that distinguishes the 'rendering of what is fit' which is justice from other 'rendering of what is fit' said that a just man should help his friends and harm his enemies; but this implies not so much that he has a duty to his enemies to harm them, as that he has no duties to them, and is therefore at liberty to show his manhood in their despite.[1] The spirit in which he will act towards his enemies is that expressed in an oath which Aristotle tells us was taken in some oligarchies: 'I will be of evil mind towards the people and devise against them any ill I can.'[2] Hitherto Socrates has developed the assumptions underlying Polemarchus' account of how a man's justice will manifest itself, so far as his purpose is to help his friends. Now he examines them so far as a man has to deal with those who are not his friends.

Socrates begins (334 c 1–335 a 10) by pointing out that to distinguish men as one's friends and enemies is not the same with distinguishing them as good and bad. It cannot be just for me to harm the good, who themselves do not act unjustly, merely because I happen to be at enmity with them. He assumes that any one would be on terms of friendship or of enmity with others according as

[1] Cf. Xen. *Mem.* ii. iii. 14: καὶ μὴν πλείστου γε δοκεῖ ἀνὴρ ἐπαίνου ἄξιος εἶναι, ὃς ἂν φθάνῃ τοὺς μὲν πολεμίους κακῶς ποιῶν, τοὺς δὲ φίλους εὐεργετῶν: ibid. vi. 35 ἔγνωκας ἀνδρὸς ἀρετὴν εἶναι νικᾶν μὲν τοὺς φίλους εὖ ποιοῦντα, τοὺς δ'ἐχθροὺς κακῶς: Isocr. *ad Demonicum* 7 c. ὁμοίως αἰσχρὸν εἶναι νόμιζε τῶν ἐχθρῶν νικᾶσθαι ταῖς κακοποιίαις καὶ τῶν φίλων ἡττᾶσθαι ταῖς εὐεργεσίαις.

[2] *Pol.* vii (v). ix. 1310 a 9: καὶ τῷ δήμῳ κακόνους ἔσομαι καὶ βουλεύσω ὅτι ἂν ἔχω κάκον.

they seem to him good or bad. This accords with the Socratic and Platonic conviction that at bottom every one desires what is good. But the assumption is not crucial to the argument. What is crucial is the admission that the formula about helping one's friends and harming one's enemies must be amended by saying that it is just to help one's friends when they are good men, and harm one's enemies when they are bad men. And Polemarchus admits this because he sees that justice requires of me to treat others according to what they are and on some principle, not according to my liking and capriciously.

But the question now arises whether it can be just to harm anybody: whether even their being bad men therefore can make it just for me to harm my enemies. Others besides Gomperz[1] have said that in this passage (335 b 2– e 5) Plato confuses two senses of the word βλάπτειν, to harm or injure. But the charge is unjustified. Socrates asks if a horse or a dog, if harmed, will not be made worse in respect of its specific excellence. This being granted, surely a man if harmed will be made worse in respect of a man's specific excellence, and that is justice. But it is impossible that by justice I should make others less just, for the spread of justice would then defeat itself. Gomperz thinks there is an undoubted confusion here between harming or injuring in the sense of rendering unserviceable and in the sense of causing pain or unhappiness. But Plato is not saying that to a man no more than to a horse or dog is it ever just to cause pain. Pain may be justly inflicted by way of punishment, but that would be for a man's benefit, and not to harm him.[2] So pain may be used in the training of an animal and not harm it in respect of its specific excellence. But if you knock an animal about, because of its faults, venting on it your ill temper, you will make it worse. And if you treat bad men that way, they

---

[1] *Greek Thinkers*, E.T., iii. 55–6.
[2] Cf. *Rep.* ii. 380 b 1: οἱ δὲ ὠνίναντο κολαζόμενοι.

will become worse too. A merely vindictive (which is not
the same as a retributory) penal system may be fortunate
enough to have only bad men consigned to it; it will not
be fortunate enough to make them better. The injunction
or even the permission to 'harm' the bad means that one
may treat them as having no rights; and a man treated as
having no rights will be led to deny or disregard rights in
others. A just man may treat others differently according
as they are good or bad, as he may be entitled to treat
differently in some respects his friends and his enemies.
But the principle of justice does not permit that against
any one he should devise whatever ill he can: no more
against a bad man than against a personal enemy.

Justice then cannot be what Polemarchus thinks it. It is
a principle that must inform all a man's actions towards
all with whom he is brought into intercourse. What that
involves, and how, while no definition of justice by naming
its works is possible, we may yet give an elucidation of its
nature that another sort of definition can enshrine, Plato
endeavours to show in the long discussion from ii. 368 e 2
to the end of the fourth book. But in the remainder of
Book i he examines a very different view. Polemarchus at
any rate thought that, in distinguishing just acts from unjust, men acknowledged obligations that could conflict
with their desires, rights in others no less than their own
rights. Thrasymachus in effect rejects rights and obligations altogether. The only right is the right of the
stronger, which in a moral sense is no right. The only
obligation is that which Paley admits, 'a violent motive
resulting from the command of another'[1]—a motive, that
is, furnished by somebody who commands under penalty
for disobedience some action contrary to one's inclination.

---

[1] *Principles of Moral and Political Philosophy*, bk. ii, ch. ii.

II

PLATO'S *REPUBLIC*: THE ARGUMENT WITH THRASYMACHUS

THE argument between Thrasymachus and Socrates shows high dramatic power, and besides its philosophical has historical interest in its picture of a famous sophist and rhetorician. With the question whether Plato's portrait is unjust we need not concern ourselves, though Grote's contention, that Thrasymachus would not have talked about justice in the way in which Plato makes him talk, if he had desired to give any satisfaction to an Athenian audience, is unconvincing;[1] and it is scarcely accurate to say[5] that we have no evidence to inform us how far the present portrait is a copy of the real man.[2] For we happen to have some independent testimony to the two most notable features of the portrait, Thrasymachus' combativeness and his fondness for his fees. Aristotle in the *Rhetoric*, illustrating the device of making a point against your opponent by reference to his name, tells us how Herodicus said to Thrasymachus αἰεὶ θρασύμαχος εἶ—'you are always spoiling for a fight'.[3] And Athenaeus[4] quotes from Ephippus the line Βρυσωνοθρασυμαχειοληψικερμάτων, which ascribes to Bryson and Thrasymachus an unwillingness to forgo small gains. But Grote was perhaps influenced by the view he took of the merits in the issue between Plato and the Sophists. In identifying Socrates' contention (*Rep.* i. 337 c 3–10), that a man should hold to what his own consideration makes him think true, with the Protagorean

---

[1] *History of Greece*, ed. 1883, viii, 194, ch. lxvii; but the passage from Antiphon in the *Oxyrhynchus Papyri*, vol. xi, no. 1364, pp. 92–104, shows that such views of justice were taught by sophists.

[2] Id., *Plato*, iv, p. 7.

[3] ii. 23, 1400 b 19.

[4] xi. 509 c: the reference for Ephippus is 14. 3. An alternative reading omits Bryson from the indictment.

principle that man is the measure of all things, he shows
that he hardly appreciates Plato's distinction between
knowledge and true opinion.[1] And he thinks that 'the
substantive opinion ascribed to Thrasymachus, apart from
the brutality with which he is made to state it, does not even
countenance the charge of immoral teaching made against
him'.[2] 'That which offends in the language ascribed to
Thrasymachus is . . . the presentation of the just man as
weak and silly, and of injustice in all the *prestige* of triumph
and dignity.'[3] And he argued that Thrasymachus would
not really have so offended his audience. But the Sophists'
teaching would not have been less immoral, if expressed
with less brutality, as it is by Glaucon and Adeimantus in
the next book. If injustice owes its reputation of base-
ness only to convention and opinion,[4] Thrasymachus was
merely honest. Grote thinks that a better superstructure
can be built on Thrasymachus' foundation, and that is the
question which we have to consider.

Justice, says Thrasymachus, is the interest of the
stronger—οὐκ ἄλλο τι ἢ τὸ τοῦ κρείττονος συμφέρον (338 c 2).
To explain his meaning, he points out how the laws of any
state, or city, are in the interest of those who make them:
of the despot or τύραννος, of the aristocracy, or of the people
according as tyranny, aristocracy, or democracy is the form
of the State. But always what is just is what serves the
interest of those in power, that is, of the stronger.

In reply to a question from Socrates, he admits that to
obey those in power is just. Whereupon Socrates asks
whether they are not capable of error, and in making
laws may sometimes do so rightly, sometimes not: to do
so rightly being to enact what is in their own interest, and
wrongly to enact what is not. To this also Thrasymachus

[1] See *Plato*, iv, p. 8, n. 1 and iii, pp. 116–26.
[2] *History of Greece*, cap. lxvii, ed. 1883, vol. viii, p. 196.
[3] Id., ibid., p. 195.
[4] *Rep.* ii. 364 a 4: Δόξῃ Δὲ μόνον καὶ νόμῳ αἰσχρόν.

assents, and Socrates at once pounces upon him and points out that he has involved himself in a contradiction (339 d 1). For when laws are wrongly made, obedience is not in the ruler's interest; yet we have been told both that to obey is just and that the just is what is in the ruler's interest.

At this point Cleitophon makes his only incursion into the conversation (340 a 3–b 8); by the interest of the stronger, he says, Thrasymachus meant what the stronger conceived to be in his interest. Jowett unkindly describes this escape from the contradiction as an 'unmeaning evasion'.[1] It is in fact precisely what Thrasymachus should have said. For he holds, like Hobbes, that every man acts only with a view to his private interest—if he makes laws, as thinking them in his own interest; if he obeys them, as thinking it in his interest rather to obey than to pay the penalty of disobedience, though the act itself required of him brings benefit not to him but to the ruler. Laws have come into being and their observance is maintained because certain persons, thinking the observance of such laws by others would be to their—the makers'—advantage, are also strong enough to enforce it. That explains the existence of laws and the observance of them, without its being necessary to suppose that they should be really to the advantage of their makers. They were made and are enforced because they are thought to be so.

Whether in fact laws are thus imposed is here irrelevant. Glaucon in the next book suggests that they have arisen by agreement of the many, who impose them on one another and on the more powerful few. But collectively the many are still the stronger; and between this view and that of Thrasymachus there is no difference of principle. Either way, laws are made in the interest of those who make them; either way they are obeyed in the interest—so long as the alternative is to suffer the sanctions attached—of those who obey them. Either way there is no motive of

---

[1] *The Republic of Plato translated into English*[3], p. xx.

moral obligation, and no one recognizes any but a private interest. At bottom every man is egoistic, and in competition with his neighbours; and though it may be in his interest to let others have things he would like for himself, lest in default they should take both them and what he already has, his and their interests are competitive. The enforcement of law may be in the interest of the majority, as those think for whom Glaucon speaks. But if a man could disregard it against others, without their disregarding it against him, that would be for his advantage.

But Thrasymachus rejects the help of Cleitophon. The contradiction between the statements that what is just is in the interest of the stronger and that to obey the stronger is just only arises if the stronger commands what is not in his interest. Provided the stronger makes no mistakes, the same action will be just by both accounts. This, of course, is not a satisfactory defence. Socrates had shown by appeal to a possible case that two general statements were inconsistent. Thrasymachus merely suggests that in an ideally ordered state such a case would not arise. So Henry Sidgwick, in his *Methods of Ethics*, first admits that it is reasonable for a man to seek his own greatest happiness, and then that is reasonable for him to seek the greatest happiness of the greatest number; and that the conduct demanded on the first ground may be forbidden on the second. His tentative solution is to suggest a system of rewards and punishments hereafter which should make what is demanded on the second ground coincide with what is demanded on the first.[1] But this also is only to show that on a certain assumption the case which exposes the inconsistency would not arise. And in the argument before us Thrasymachus' line of defence has, from his standpoint, a further defect. It introduces a contrast between the actual and the ideal which is ultimately fatal to his position.

In its first form, this appears in the notion of an art of

[1] Op. cit., *Concluding Chapter.*

ruling, or of a ruler in the strict sense of the term, κατὰ τὸν ἀκριβῆ λόγον (340 e 1). Ruling is an art, like medicine or computation, or any craft a man may practise. There is a way in which it ought to be practised, and if he does not practise it thus, in strictness he is no ruler or craftsman.

To speak of the way in which an art ought to be practised is not to allege a moral obligation to practise it in that way. Thrasymachus admits no moral obligation, though he finds it difficult at places to divest his mind of sentiments based on its admission. When he says that to obey the law is just, or that it is just to do what is the interest of the stronger, he does not think himself to be informing persons who know what they mean by 'just' what actions have that character. 'Just' is no more than a name given to actions that are in the interest of the stronger or that conform to law, by which they are designated without implication of any further character than that of advantaging the stronger or conforming to law. It is really very difficult to believe this, or to bring oneself to the way of speaking that it demands. It is like what Bernard de Mandeville said, that virtues 'are the political offspring which flattery begot upon pride'. Politic rulers, he meant, took advantage of men's pride or love of praise to induce them to actions in the politicians' interest by calling those who did them virtuous. But if to be virtuous only signifies to do actions in the interest of one's rulers, it is hard to see why men should be flattered by being called virtuous. Only if the word already signifies the possession of some character that a man would be proud to possess, could the device be effective. And when we are told that to obey the law is just, we are not less disposed to think the word 'just' already signifies a character, for the sake of which a man should do the acts to which it belongs. We must, however, sedulously put from our minds that interpretation of Thrasymachus' language. No moral obligation to live thus or thus exists, according to him. He does, nevertheless, think that a man may live wisely or unwisely; and what Plato endeavours to show is that on his view of how a wise man should live, there could be no art of life, no wisdom of living.

To this end, Plato makes Thrasymachus reject Cleitophon's emendation, and put forward in defence the notion of an art of ruling, which if a man practised he would make no mistake, so that obedience to his laws could not fail to be also in his interest. In the passage 341 c 2–342 e 11 the implications of the conception of an art are examined. The conclusion reached, that if ruling is an art the ruler in the strict sense must seek the interest of his subjects, is not really proved; and Plato knows that. Nevertheless, something very important in itself and to the next stage of the argument is proved.

To every art (or craft) there is a purpose, and to each different art a different purpose. The purpose is, of course, the man's who practises the art, and the same man may practise many, but Plato means that for each art that he may practise there is a work of a definite sort on which he is set. Thus the purpose of medicine is to heal the sick, not to make money. Socrates describes the purpose of an art as seeking and providing what is advantageous for that whereon it is practised, not, he insists, for itself. In itself, he explains, it needs nothing except to be as perfect as possible (341 d 10). The point of that remark may be understood if we remember that our question is how a ruler would act who possessed in perfection the art of ruling. A man possessing any art imperfectly may practise it to improve his art; but that is the only service he can render to his art itself, and if it is already perfect, his purpose must be to improve not his art but something else, on which his art is exercised, or over which it has control, and which is subject to it, τὸ ἧττον καὶ ἀρχόμενον ὑπὸ ἑαυτῆς. To this it sees and labours for its advantage, a physician for his patients' health, the captain of a ship for his passengers' safety; and likewise the ruler for his subjects' weal.

Thrasymachus, having been brought step by step to this conclusion, bursts out into a passionate and by no means wholly unreasonable protest. It is obvious that a shepherd or a herdsman thinks of the benefit to accrue from his craft not to his sheep or cattle but to himself or his master. So it is with a ruler; and Thrasymachus expatiates on the advantages that a tyrant may gain for himself by injustice—that is, disregard of law. To do justice is to work for the benefit of another: to do injustice, for one's own; and if one can do it on a large enough scale, as a tyrant can, he will get what he works for, neither will men reproach him. Small injustices, by burglars, thieves, temple-robbers, and such like, are profitable if undiscovered, but if discovered are punished and denounced. It is to injustice in its supreme form that we must look, and to what men say of its supreme practitioners, if we are to see that it, not justice, is profitable to a man and advantageous, more powerful and free and masterful than justice, and admitted to be so (343 a 1–344 c 8).

Whether or not we must accept Thrasymachus' conclusion, he was rightly persuaded that Socrates had not established his. But he was unable to show, as Socrates in effect presently does, where the argument was defective. What Socrates did show is that, if ruling is a particular art, it must have a particular purpose, the execution of which may require the man who practises it to forgo the execution of some other particular purpose, or the satisfaction of some desire, even though he thinks that to satisfy the desire or execute the other particular purpose is more to his advantage than to execute the purpose which he has as a ruler. But all this might be true, though the purpose of ruling were not to benefit one's subjects. If it is not that, indeed, it will be a little difficult to suggest any other particular purpose by which to distinguish it from other arts; so that Thrasymachus found no way to refuse assent when Socrates asked if its purpose were not to benefit the subjects. But we may consider the question a little more closely.

The instances which Socrates took to illustrate how each art had a special purpose were of arts whose purposes are to benefit others over whom the practitioner of the art is in charge or command—medicine and navigation. But there are arts of which this cannot be said. The dancer exercises his art upon his own body; the violinist not over other persons or even animals at all; the hunter over game, but not for its benefit. Of all these it is, indeed, true that they have a special purpose of which the execution may conflict with what the artist thinks his interest. To give a perfect exhibition of a dance, the dancer may have to strain his muscles or injure his health; the violinist may know that if he plays faultlessly his master will be jealous and work against his promotion; the hunter may be in a position where he can only save his life by running away, and supreme skill will be in vain. We cannot, therefore, identify the perfect practice of an art with the pursuit of one's interest. But neither can we identify it with the promotion of the interest of others, if there be others on whom the art is exercised. A man may cultivate an estate with the labour of slaves; his efficiency in his craft will be shown in producing the best crops at the least outlay. If he has no other purpose than that—and no other belongs to the art of estate-management with slave labour—he will no doubt consider their health and contentment so far as these are necessary to securing the best results, but he will not rule them with a view to their advantage. Nevertheless, here too, even if any profits of cultivation are his own, the pursuit of his art is not identical with the pursuit of his interest. For a time may come when, however perfectly he practises it, the cultivation can only be carried on at a loss; his interest would be served by abandoning the cultivation; his art could not be displayed in so doing. Or his slaves may revolt, and place him in a position like that of a hunter exposed to wild beasts at bay. The most skilful conduct in the capacity of slave-master may then be incapable of securing his safety; and to secure this, rather than to exercise his art any further, appears to be what his interest requires.

Socrates then was justified in saying that, if there is an art of ruling, it must have a purpose distinguishable from the pursuit of the ruler's interest. But he has not proved either that its purpose must be to benefit the ruled, or that even the most perfect ruler need carry it on without any regard to his own interest. And Thrasymachus was entitled to point out that a shepherd or herdsman looks beyond the interest of his sheep or cattle. But he was not entitled to go back upon what he had admitted, when he said that the physician as such is not a money-maker but a healer of the sick (341 c 8), as Socrates points out (345 b 8). If the shepherd or if the ruler (supposing he, too, practises an art) is looking for gain, he has therein another purpose besides that of his art; to identify the two would be to abolish the distinction between the purposes of the several arts, and therefore between the several arts themselves, by making the getting of gain the purpose of them all. We must distinguish then an art of gain, μισθαρνητικὴ τέχνη, from the ruler's or the shepherd's or any other particular art, and still assign to each of these the task of securing the advantage not of him who practises it but of that over which it is set (345 b 8–346 e 7).

It appears by what was said in the last paragraph but one that Socrates is still in part only reiterating what he has not proved. For a ruler might be conceived to show his art in running the State as a slave-owner shows his in running an estate, i.e. so as to realize the largest profit in the most efficient way. Whether the profit realized is to be his or another's makes no difference to what his art requires; but such a purpose is not the advantage of the ruled. That the genuine ruler will look to the advantage not of himself but of the ruled (347 d 4) is not a necessary consequence of the principle that an art seeks not its own advantage but that of its subject-matter. For the subject-matter of an art, as we have seen, may mean the work in which it is displayed, the dancer's or violinist's perform-ance, the carrying on the cultivation of an estate. In making this as perfect as possible one may be said to look to its advantage or συμφέρον, just as much as the advantage of an art may be said (341 d 10) to be, that it should be as perfect as possible.

Yet in relegating the getting of gain to a distinct art, and denying that, because a man hopes to make a living by carrying on his art, therefore the purpose of his art is barely to get gain, Socrates is absolutely right, as we may see by asking what would follow from the contrary assump-tion. A man shows his mastery of a craft or art by the suc-cess with which he achieves his purpose in it. If then the physician's purpose were to get gain, he who made most money out of his work would prove himself to be the best physician. He might make more money by keeping trustful patients ill and in need of attendance than by curing them outright; and expectant heirs might pay him far larger sums for hastening, in ways that would not excite suspicion, the death of those whose inheritance they coveted, than the latter would ever pay for medical treat-ment. Yet it would be ridiculous to suggest that the acquisition of greater gain in ways like these would show that a man was a better doctor than those whose gains were less. To take another example, it will hardly be denied that any one in charge of the police of a great city carries on a difficult art. Is its purpose to secure the safety and good order of the citizens, or his own profit? If we say the latter, he is a better Prefect or Chief Constable, supposing he amasses a large fortune by taking bribes from racketeers for his connivance with them and so forth, than if he suppressed their practices and had only his official salary.

The notion of an art of gain may seem far-fetched. In reality, as will shortly appear, Plato has in mind something which we should describe differently, but the recognition of which is profoundly important. Taking the phrase in its most meagre sense, we might perhaps say that to contract for wages or a salary hardly seems worthy of being described as practising an art. Nevertheless we must agree with Socrates that the payment of a wage or salary is evidence that a man is not expected to make a profit for himself from the practice of the art, or discharge of the occupation, for which it is paid. Pay is no inducement to a man who has no desire of money; but a man who does desire money needs no monetary inducement to engage in work that should itself bring it him. To offer pay for work implies therefore that the work itself is not to bring in money or is not itself money-making.

But Socrates indicates that other inducements than money may be offered, and this throws light on what he means by the art of gain or μισθαρνητικὴ τέχνη. Some men can be induced by the prospect of honour to undertake the labour of ruling; but to the best men neither money nor honour is a sufficient inducement. The gain they look for is that of not being ruled by worse men than themselves. Could there be a city in which all men were good, not office but escape from office would be the object of their competition.

We might have expected Socrates to say that to the best men the reward for their pains in ruling is the consciousness of so greatly serving others. And I think he would admit that in so greatly serving others a man secures for himself a better life than he could live under evil rule. But it is implied, I also think, that the speculative life is higher than this life of service. The same conviction is expressed in the seventh book, where we are told of those who, after having most excelled both in practical tasks and in the tasks of learning, are at the age of fifty permitted to see the vision of the good, that they will spend the remainder of their lives for the most part in the pursuit of philosophy, but will labour when their turn comes at affairs of state and government for the city's sake, not as at a noble but as at a necessary work (540 a 4–b 5).

With these various examples before us of the gain, with a view to earning which a man may practise an art whose purpose is not his own advantage, we can better understand the importance of the notion of a μισθαρνητικὴ τέχνη. It is really the same as that of what Aristotle afterwards called ἀρχιτεκτονικὴ τέχνη[1]—the art of so ordering one's life as to secure happiness, or realize for oneself in it—so far as that can be realized in one man's life—good. These ways of stating its purpose raise many difficult questions. Some of them emerge at once when we consider the difference between the ways in which Thrasymachus and Socrates conceived the practice of the art to be related to what it seeks to achieve. In Thrasymachus' view, the μισθός, to get which men act, some wisely and successfully and some foolishly and unsuccessfully, is material goods; or, if he had been asked whether what men want is the possession of these, and not rather the pleasures which their possession commands, he would at least have said that it is these pleasures, not a man's activities, that are good. He is of the number of those who reason as if, in Bishop Butler's language, property were 'itself our happiness or good';[2] something of which if one man gets more, others must have less. This is true of material goods, at any given moment; and those who think that happiness depends upon (even if it does not consist in) the possession of material goods easily suppose that it is true of happiness. In Socrates' view, the reason for living wisely is the goodness of the life so lived. The ἀρχιτεκτονικὴ τέχνη is the art, or power that springs from wisdom, so to order one's life

---

[1] *Eth. Nic.* I. ii. 4, 1094 a 26.
[2] Sermon XI, last paragraph but two.

that it may be really good. To order one's life is to select
the occupations in which it is to be spent, to assign to them
their several times and relative precedence. In whatever
occupation a man may engage, there is an art or τέχνη
whereby he will do the work belonging to it well. These
are the particular τέχναι, such as medicine and navigation,
dancing and hunting. But whether he should be practising
some particular art at all is not a problem which supremacy
in that art enables him to decide. And yet at any moment,
if he is to order his life well, he needs to know not only
how to carry on the work in which he may be engaged, but
also whether to be engaged in it. The proper exercise of
the art requires that he do thus or thus: so treat a patient's
body, or so tend sheep. How, if he occupy himself as a
physician or a shepherd, he should proceed has nothing to
do with the question whether he should occupy himself as
a physician or a shepherd. But both questions need an
answer; and the knowledge how to answer a question of
the first sort belongs to a different τέχνη than the knowledge
how to answer the second. I say 'the second', and not 'a
question of the second sort', because whereas the particular arts are many, the architectonic is one. It belongs to the
same consideration, whether I should engage in this particular occupation or in another, whether if I do I should
subordinate all else to doing perfectly the work belonging
to it or not, whatever the particular occupation may be;
and these are the problems of the art of life, the ἀρχιτεκτονικὴ τέχνη.

Now if in this consideration I am to take account of
nothing but of how my engaging in some occupation, or
my greater or less effort to do the work of it perfectly, will
affect the amount of a reward that consists in money or
material goods (or at any rate not in the nature of the
life which my occupations constitute), then this controlling
and ordering art of life is the art of gaining the rewards
attached to the practice of those particular arts. That is

how Thrasymachus conceives it, and therefore Socrates
describes it, from his opponent's point of view, as the art
of getting gain, μισθαρνητικὴ τέχνη.[1] When he goes on to
say that the reward of ruling may be not to live subject to
worse men than oneself, he is stretching μισθός beyond its
usual meaning. Later Adeimantus distinguishes the μισθοὺς
καὶ 2όξας, the rewards and reputation, which the practice
of justice or injustice may bring from the benefit or harm
which either, purely of itself, αὐτὴ 2ι' αὐτήν, does to the
man possessed of it (367 d 2–5); and Socrates accepts the
distinction. Whether he finally succeeds in showing that in
all stations and circumstances a man is happier as well as
better for being just than if he were unjust, may be
questioned.[2] And many have denied the propriety of
demanding that this should be shown; whether I ought
to do some action, they urge, is a question altogether
independent of whether I am any way benefited in doing
it; benefit arising purely through thus acting and reward
accruing from another's action are equally irrelevant.
That issue is not before us now. What we must realize
in order to understand Plato's thought in this part of
the argument between Thrasymachus and Socrates is that
what is called the μισθαρνητικὴ τέχνη is nothing less than
the art of conducting one's life as a whole; whether one
adds, so as to make the largest gain, or so as to be happy,
or so as to live well, will indicate differences in how one
may conceive the purpose of life, but not in how one conceives the relation of that purpose to those of particular
arts.

That is why, in respect of the difference between the
shepherd's or physician's or ship's captain's or ruler's art
and the so-called μισθαρνητικὴ τέχνη, Socrates will not, so to
say, let Thrasymachus off. Whether he realizes it or not,

---

[1] Or μισθωτικὴ τέχνη, 346 b 1, 8. Jowett infelicitously translates it
'the art of pay'.

[2] This question is discussed later in Essay V.

Thrasymachus is making the same distinction which he himself makes. But in regard to what the purpose of the μισθαρνητικὴ τέχνη, the art of conducting one's life, is he and Thrasymachus differ profoundly. And this difference is the heart of their controversy.

'I do not by any means agree with Thrasymachus', says Socrates, 'that what is just is what advantages a superior. But this we will examine by and by. What he now says seems to me far more serious, viz. that the unjust man lives a life superior to the just man. . . . Come then, Thrasymachus: tell it us *de novo*. Do you say that perfect injustice is more profitable than justice which is perfect?'[1]

And Thrasymachus assents.

Socrates proceeds to get from Thrasymachus the admission that injustice is an excellence and a wisdom, ἀρετὴ καὶ σοφία, justice the contrary; though Thrasymachus jibs at saying in so many words that justice is a vice, κακία; he calls it a fine folly. We must suppose that Plato means by this touch in the picture to indicate the difficulty of ridding one's mind altogether of the conviction that there are moral distinctions, or at least to indicate the air of paradox attaching to statements that such riddance would require. But Thrasymachus ought not to have hesitated to say that justice is a vice or κακία, since the only sense of vice that his doctrine admits is that in which we speak of a vicious argument; one man is not morally better or worse than another; all equally seek a private gain by means they judge most fruitful; but one judges more wisely than another. The unjust man, says Thrasymachus, is a wise man and a good; the just is a foolish man.[2] He should have been ready to say, a foolish man and a bad.

Thrasymachus has now committed himself to maintaining that injustice is superior to justice (κρείττω, 347 e 4, cf. ἰσχυρόν, 348 e 10), more profitable (λυσιτελέστερον, 348 b

---

[1] 347 d 8–e 4 . . . 348 b 8–10. I have translated by 'superior' κρείττων.
[2] 348 b 8–e 4.

10), and better and wiser (ἐν ἀρετῆς καὶ σοφίας μέρει, 348 e 2, ἐν ἀρετῇ καὶ σοφίᾳ, 349 a 2). And Socrates attacks him on all three counts. But the first and crucial conflict is over the question whether to live a life of injustice is to live one of excellence and wisdom. 'Excellence', ἀρετή, here does not mean specifically moral excellence, as those conceive this who say, with Kant, that nothing is unconditionally good but a good will. It means something in respect of which different men's performances in medicine or music can be rated, as well as in the conduct of their lives. For Plato is trying to show that there is intellectual, not moral, error in the theory of Thrasymachus. We speak of a good doctor or a good musician, meaning one with such intelligence and understanding of the problems of his particular art as to make his practice in it perfect. And we may similarly mean, in speaking of a good man, one having such intelligence and understanding of the problems, not of any particular art, but of the general conduct of life, as to make his practice perfect in that. And Socrates wishes to show that, on Thrasymachus' view of what perfect practice consists in, there could be no such goodness and intelligence.

It is obvious that this is an important issue; but we must be careful not to misunderstand what Plato is doing. He is not undertaking to prove the fact of moral obligation. He is accepting, perhaps one may even say as an hypothesis, that, as in work of any specific kind we properly distinguish between good work and bad work, what is correct or right and what is incorrect or wrong, so it is in the conduct of life as a whole. Words like *art* and *craft* and *skill* are evidence that we recognize the distinction in the one case; and we may speak correspondingly of an art of living. Thrasymachus makes this hypothesis from the outset, when he insists that there is an art of ruling; for he thinks of the ruler's job as being to do the best for himself in life. Socrates has shown that the ruler's is a specific job; and that not ruling but the conduct of life is that in which his opponent should have said that a man really κρείττων or superior will not err. But that only substitutes for the question, whether the ruler who makes no mistakes in ruling will perfectly achieve at the expense of the ruled his own advantage, the question whether the man who makes no mistakes in the conduct of his life will perfectly achieve it at the expense of other men. And to this, in Plato's judgement, we cannot answer yes, because in such competition among men the very notion of perfection is inapplicable. You may, if you like, accept this conclusion, and say that the life of men is a competition in which sometimes one man and sometimes another gets more, but we are not entitled to say that any one proceeds correctly. Of this position Plato offers here no refutation; he merely assumes its falsehood. So far as any refutation of it is offered in the *Republic*, we must look for it in Book vi, where the notion of the αὐτὸ ἀγαθόν, the form of good, is declared to be that in the light of which itself and everything else, and therefore human life, becomes intelligible.

After this discussion of the nature and importance of the issue, we may now return to the text of the argument upon it (348 c 2–350 c 11). Many readers, I believe, on first acquaintance see little in it; yet I also believe that it is absolutely convincing, and that the whole positive doctrine of justice in the *Republic* is in accordance with the principle of it.

Injustice is conceived as πλεονεξία—the attempt to get more than anybody else. Thrasymachus has always so conceived it.

'You must look at it this way, O most simple Socrates: everywhere a just man has less than an unjust. When they have dealings with one another, you will never find that at the close the just man has more than the unjust, but less. In their dealings with the city, the just contributes more from the same resources, the unjust less, or if there is anything to be had, the just takes nothing, the unjust

makes great gains. In office, the just man suffers by having to
neglect his own affairs, and makes nothing out of the public estate;
with the unjust it is precisely contrary'.[1]

A just man, on the other hand, Socrates says, does not try
to get more than everybody else; he tries to get more than
the unjust, not than the just man; or, as Socrates also puts
it, he tries to get more than the unjust, not than the just,
action. By putting it also in this way, Socrates shows that
he does not mean that a just man would be prepared to
swindle an unjust, though not another just, man. He
would endeavour to get more than what an unjust man
would try to let him get, because the unjust man would not
'play fair'; but not more than what is just to be done, the
Δικαία πρᾶξις. An unjust man, on the contrary, would
endeavour to get more both than what another unjust man
would try to let him get and than what a just man would;
he would try to overreach both. When he needs a verb to
express the action of a man inspired by πλεονεξία, Socrates
sometimes says πλεονεκτεῖν, sometimes πλέον ἔχειν ἐθέλειν
or βούλεσθαι; but the first, which we may translate 'overreach', expresses the principle of the action, the second the
form that it takes when one man overreaches another in
their efforts after material goods.

Now these two procedures are two ways of conducting
one's life; and as Thrasymachus maintains, it is the unjust
man who conducts his life aright and wisely. The right
and wise procedure, then, in the art of life, is to overreach
all one's competitors, unjust and just alike—that is, those
who also are conducting their lives aright and wisely, and
those who are not. Socrates urges that this is contrary to
the nature of an art, and that we shall see it to be so if we
consider how the practitioners of any art proceed. The
argument is not one from the analogy of the arts, in that
sense in which an argument from analogy is no more than
inferring, from some ascertained resemblance between two

[1] 343 d 1–e 7, abridged.

subjects, that a further character of one belongs to the other. It lays bare, by the help of examples where all men agree which procedure is right and wise, which wrong and foolish, the principles of the two procedures, and shows that the master of any art, he whose procedure is right and wise, acts on the principle whereon the just man acts in the conduct of his life: while he who in the practice of an art acts on the principle on which the unjust man acts in the conduct of his life is an ignoramus, and without understanding of his art, so that if there is an art of life, the unjust man cannot be the master of it.

For if we consider competitors in the practice of music or of medicine, we shall find that one who knows his job does not try, when another has done rightly, to overreach or go beyond him. One musician, seeking a right progression of notes, gives to the strings of his lyre a certain tension. If the first is a good musician, another good musician will give to the strings of his lyre the same tension; only if the first is a bad musician will the second overreach or go beyond him in tightening or slackening the strings. In medicine, one man prescribes a certain dose, or so much food; a rival doctor, if the first has prescribed correctly, does not seek excellence by prescribing more. In every art, competition consists in trying to get nearer than others to that in achieving which all alike recognize that their success would consist; so that a perfect artist or craftsman does not endeavour to overreach or surpass his like, who are perfect, but only those who are not, his unlike. And if wisdom or art can be shown in the conduct of life as a whole, as well as in its component special occupations, the same must be true there. It cannot, therefore, be shown in the mere attempt to overreach all others. As R. L. Nettleship has said, that is to make into a principle 'the denial that there is any principle at all'.[1]

---

[1] *Lectures on Plato's 'Republic' (Philosophical Lectures and Remains of Richard Lewis Nettleship,* vol. i, p. 36).

In Lowes Dickinson's book, *A Modern Symposium*, one of the speakers, recently returned from the United States, is 'inclined to think . . . that the real end which Americans set before themselves is Acceleration. To be always moving, and always moving faster, that they think is the beatific life; and with their happy detachment from philosophy and speculation, they are not troubled by the question, Whither?'[1] The point is the same with Plato's here, and no one is more likely than the author to have noticed it. An art must have a purpose; there must be that which it would achieve, or at least approach. And the fact that several persons practise the same art cannot of itself make it impossible that they should all achieve this, when each, had he been the sole practitioner, could have done so. Yet if the purpose of life is to get the better of all one's neighbours, only one man can achieve it. What was perfect practice in me ceases to be so not because my practice alters, but because another man comes along and over-reaches me. How then can it ever have been perfect practice? Perfection is qualitative; and excess is not a quality.

We are so accustomed to competitions, and not least of speed, that we may be slow at first to see that Socrates must be right. But a little reflection will show that even in competitions of speed we take the winner's performance as evidence of a qualitative superiority in a field where the moving body, whether animal or machine, admits of a qualitative perfection that prescribes a limit to its velocity. The winning horse is best only because of its build, muscles, heart, stamina. If there were no limit to attainable speeds, a record would lose its interest. In competitions of skill, we easily recognize the absurdity of merely quantitative considerations. When Peleus bade his child αἰὲν ἀριστεύειν καὶ ὑπείροχον ἔμμεναι ἄλλων,[2] the first part of his precept set before Achilles an ideal; the second did not.

---

[1] J. M. Dent & Sons, 1912, p. 104.   [2] *Iliad*, vi. 208.

Yet popular biology assures us that the perfection of species is secured by the struggle for existence. It is not true. That only secures that characters in members of a species which unfit them to defeat their rivals, whether of the same or other species, will not persist in subsequent generations. Whether a modification of the specific form necessary to survival is in the direction of greater perfection or of less is quite irrelevant. We cannot define perfection as what gives success in the struggle for existence without reducing the allegation to a triviality: the struggle for existence secures that only what can succeed in the struggle shall exist. Perfection, or the approximation to it, must be judged by something else than survival; and we may then discover that under some conditions the more perfect but under others the less will have an advantage in the struggle for existence.

The notion of adaptation to environment is workable enough, so long as we consider only one species and a fixed environment; we may then say that increase in numbers is evidence of a species becoming better adapted to its environment, though even so it is not evidence of its becoming better. But if its environment consists of members of other species, whose adaptation to theirs is to be conceived in the same way, species cannot all become better adapted to their environment. It has been suggested that the increase of steam-trawling is negligible to the herring supply; that the fluctuations in the numbers of herring depend upon those in the numbers of sharks, but also vice-versa. For when herrings are very plentiful, the food-supply of the sharks is increased; and these survive in such numbers as to deplete the stock of herrings; whereupon the number of sharks dwindles, until from comparative immunity that of herrings begins to rise again. The period has been submitted to mathematical calculation; but it cannot be said that there is better adaptation in one phase of it than in another. To a stable environment a species might be perfectly adapted in virtue of what it is qualitatively; and a number of species whose perfection is fixed qualitatively might be better adapted to live together, according as they or some of them were more or less perfect. But if perfect adaptation consists in ability to spread at the expense of others, the species can never all be perfectly adapted: there is no perfect state for that community. The biologist does not suppose that the spread of a species is carried on designedly, or the modifications which assist it designedly acquired. But the argument would be the same if they were; and the most consummate art in such design exercised by every species would leave them as far as ever from the perfection that was to consist in each advancing in numbers at the expense of the rest.

Yet wisdom is justified of her children, and cannot lose her nature because her children are many. If there is something which she enables her possessor to achieve, it cannot be what only one among her possessors can achieve. That nevertheless is the nature of what Thrasymachus assigns for task to the wisdom of the unjust. It is no wonder that when Socrates showed this up, at last Thrasymachus blushed.

Life may be nothing but a scene of restless desire, where men may pursue perfection in this or that activity of some particular kind, but no one choice and combination of activities is better or worse than another for what it excludes or contains, nor for the activities contained in it being carried on better or worse. If it be so, the just man will not be good and wise; but neither will the unjust. Thrasymachus, however, does not so regard life; and herein at least he surely thinks as we are all inclined to do. But if in so thinking he is right, he must be wrong in holding the unjust man to be good and wise, for achieving his own advantage at the expense of every one else.

The remainder of the argument is of less importance. Socrates endeavours to show secondly that injustice does not make those who practise it more powerful than the just (350 e 11–352 d 2), and thirdly that it does not make them happier (352 d 2–354 a 4): so that on all counts we must deny that injustice is more profitable than justice. As to the second count, men acting together are only strong in combination if at least they can trust each other. However they may treat their common enemy, if each of them at every moment was trying to get the better of his fellows, no effective concerted action would be possible to them. The proverb says that honesty is the best policy; Plato is pointing out that this is only so because it is really honesty. The value to the gang of honour among thieves lies in the fact that each man can be relied upon to keep faith beyond the point to which it pays him individually. But if he were completely unjust, κομιδῇ ἄδικος, he could not be so relied on. Hobbes, who thought, as Thrasymachus does, that men are purely egoistic, looked to the power of the sovereign to force them to keep faith; and Thrasymachus, by his definition of justice as the interest of the stronger, suggests that the power of the ruler is what makes subjects obey the law. But perhaps what else he says implies some reliance on their folly too; the just, he thinks, are the foolish. Some evolutionary writers, who have believed with Thrasymachus that intelligent or reasonable action is egoistic, but have seen that, if this is so, and all men always acted reasonably, society would not get on as it does, have suggested that altruistic impulses, arising by way of spontaneous variation, are valuable to the group in any of whose members they appear, though not to those members; yet that through the victory of this group some of the altruistically-minded individuals will be preserved, and so such impulses will not be eliminated. But with Thrasymachus they have regarded the conduct inspired by these impulses as irrational.

One other observation must be made on this section of the argument. At 352 a 5 Socrates asks whether, as their injustice would render ineffective any body of men, so it will not also render ineffective any individual—setting him at discord with himself and making him his own enemy. This is the first emergence in the *Republic* of the notion that there is a constitution in the soul of any man comparable to what may exist in any community of men, so that justice and injustice are the same in a man and in a community, and according to the degree in which either prevails in them different and corresponding types of man and of community arise. But at this stage the justification of Socrates' question is hardly clear. Perhaps the simplest way of bringing out his meaning is this: we saw that the principle of injustice was the very absence of any principle; the man who acts on no principle will be at discord with himself and never of one mind.

The third and last count in this argument[1] concerns the alleged happiness of an unjust life. In this alone can it be said with some plausibility that Socrates is guilty of equivocation; yet perhaps Plato wished us to notice that the very fact of the ambiguity in the phrase 'to live well' is significant. But there are other weaknesses in the passage.

Socrates starts from the conception of things that have a work or function, ἔργον, like a sword or knife or sickle, or a living thing such as a horse, or the organs of a living thing, such as eye and ear.[2] If we ask how one may know what is the function of some particular thing, the answer is that one should consider what it only or it best can do. And if a thing has a function or work to do, plainly it may do it well or ill; and to do it well it must possess a corresponding ἀρετή or excellence. He then proceeds to say that the soul is such a thing; only a soul can take care or counsel or can rule; these, therefore, belong to its function; but we may say, too, that to live is its function. It will not perform any of this work well without it be possessed of a soul's excellence; and that has been shown to be justice.

[1] i. 352 b 5 ad fin.   [2] Cf. Arist., *Eth. Nic.* I. vii. 9–15, 1097^{b}22–1098^{a}18.

The just soul, therefore, and the just man will live well; and he who lives well is blessed and happy.

The equivocation is here, at the end. The notion of life as a function of the soul, and of an excellence possessed of which the soul will discharge that function well, is clearly akin to the notion that there is an art of life and that he who understands and practises it will have in living and will achieve some purpose. But neither notion tells us in what living well consists, though we have seen that it must be such that men, so far as they alike possess the appropriate excellence or understand the art, will not prevent each other from living well. To live well has, however, a popular sense in which it means to enjoy the pleasures which riches can buy; and it is in this sense that those who think with Thrasymachus would allow that to live well is to be happy. Whether to live well in the other sense is to be happy is a very different question, which indeed Plato would say we cannot settle till we have discovered how that life would be lived.

But, apart from this, the whole position developed in this section stands in need of justification. We cannot argue from what we know to have been made by man, and therefore presumably with a purpose which it is its function to serve, to a horse or a man, unless we think that they have been created with a purpose. That there is what a man ought to achieve or realize in his life may be true; but it cannot be shown by such analogies. Again, if care and counsel and rule are the function of the soul because only a soul is capable of them, yet a soul is as much the only thing capable of counselling or ruling badly as it is of counselling or ruling well. Other arguments than this section contains are needed to show that its function is to do these things well. And the transition from describing its function as care and counsel and rule to describing it as to live, though necessary if the final equivocation is to be possible, has much to be said against it. For life is common to man with animals and plants, to neither of which would Plato or Aristotle deny ψυχή, or soul, *anima*. But justice is not the excellence whereby a soul discharges the function of living, as one shared by men with plants and animals. To live well, in that sense, would be to be physiologically vigorous; we should be perilously near to taking survival as our standard of excellence. Whether his soul is that in a man whereby he is capable of living well or ill in a moral sense, or that whereby he is capable in the biological sense of living well or ill, and how the one capacity is connected with the other, are questions here not considered. Moreover, we may note that in the tenth Book Plato uses an argument for the soul's immortality vitiated by the same uncertainty whether soul is the principle of physical life, ζωή, or of conscious and moral life, βίος.[1]

We cannot therefore rate this section very highly. Yet there may be conceptions and assumptions in it capable of better justification, by a fuller development, than they get here. And that indeed may be said of the whole conception, running through the book, of living well, or of rightly conducting one's life, or of carrying out in life that purpose which a wisdom wherein all might conceivably share would enable those that practised it to attain. To justify this conception by a fuller development is the task of the rest of the dialogue.

[1] x. 608 c 9–611 a 2. So here he shifts from εὖ βιώσεται, 353 e 10, to εὖ ζῶν, 354 a 1.

III

PLATO'S *REPUBLIC*: THE NATURE OF THE SOUL

It is the doctrine of Plato in the *Republic* that the corporate acts of a State or city are really the acts of its citizens, or of some of them, co-operating in the prosecution of some common purpose. Therefore whether these corporate acts are just or unjust depends on whether the citizens, or those who determine what the purpose of their co-operation shall be, are just or unjust; and if we would know what these words, *Justice* and *Injustice*, mean, we must know what the characters are in the souls of individuals. Though Socrates is made to look for them first on the larger scale of their manifestation in States, whose form and order we call just and unjust, he makes it clear that these manifestations of them proceed from the form and order in the souls of men. When he says that of man's way of life there must be as many types as there are of constitutions, he gives as reason that constitutions do not spring from a tree or a stone, but from the citizens' characters that preponderate in the city and draw after them the rest.[1] The types of constitution indicate and are a clue to, they do not in the first instance produce, those of individual lives.

What holds of the justice or injustice ascribed to States is, of course, equally true of the happiness or misery ascribed to them. A State is only to be called happy or miserable through the happiness or misery of its citizens. Plato did not think otherwise. He is sometimes accused of sacrificing the individual to the State. If this means that the interests of no man or set of men are so sacrosanct that nothing may be done against them, no matter what therefore befalls the rest, the charge is justified;[2] but it may be borne with equanimity. If it means that there is a State whose interests can and should be promoted even at the

[1] viii. 544 d 6; cf. iv. 435 e 1–3.   [2] See iv. 420 b 3–421 c 6.

sacrifice of those of every citizen, Plato would have rejected such a notion altogether. It is true that in his opinion the welfare of the State is not a mere sum of individual welfares, any more than its purpose is a mere sum of individual purposes. It is an identical factor in the welfares of many different citizens. But it is not something apart from all those. How it is possible that in different men's welfares there should be an identical factor that may be called the welfare of the State is a question that cannot be answered without considering the nature of the soul; for on the understanding of this depends an understanding of what makes our welfare.

The account of the soul given in the fourth book of the *Republic* is therefore second to no other part of that work in importance. With it are connected the doctrine of the four cardinal virtues, the definition of justice, the proof offered for the contention, as against Thrasymachus, that of itself and apart from its consequences the just life is the best for a man, and the pervading parallelism between types of State and types of individual soul. A student of the *Republic* is bound to consider it very carefully, if he is to understand the argument of the book on these points. But it deserves his consideration apart from that on its own merits.

For this reason, the question how far Plato was indebted in his account to predecessors is of secondary importance. John Burnet and others have called attention in this connexion to a story told by Cicero on the authority of Heraclides Ponticus,[1] and also quoted by Diogenes Laertius from the 'Successions' of Sosicrates.[2] It is said that Pythagoras, in conversation at Phlius with Leon, the tyrant of that place, explained, as follows, what he meant by calling himself a philosopher—a word which he was the first to use.[3] The life of man, he said, may be compared to the gathering

---

[1] *Tusc. Disput.* v. § 8.　　　[2] *Vitae Phil.* viii, c. 1 § 6.
[3] Ibid. Prooem. § 8; cf. Burnet, *Early Gk. Phil.*[3], p. 278, n. 1.

at the Olympic games, whither some come in search of
gain, and some of glory, but some only to look on and see
what is done, and how; so in life, while most seek wealth or
honour, a few place before these contemplation and the
knowledge of things. Doubtless this distinction of 'three
lives' rests on such a distinction of principles within the
soul as we find in *Republic* iv; and Cicero in the *Tusculans*
expressly says that Plato's description of the soul, as containing a rational part, the principle of constancy and
tranquillity, and an irrational, whence come the disturbing
movements of anger and of appetite,[1] was first given by
Pythagoras. But how much of Socrates' argument in
support of the doctrine called that of the tripartite soul is
Plato's own, we cannot tell. In any case it is more important to consider how much is sound.

Burnet said[1] that the doctrine 'is quite inconsistent with
Plato's own view of the soul'; but the remark seems hasty,
and based upon Socrates' comparison between the relations
of the three principles to each other when a man is just
and those of a note and its fourth and octave in a 'harmony'.[2]
That the soul is a harmony of the body was a Pythagorean
doctrine rejected in the *Phaedo*,[3] and 'quite inconsistent',
as Burnet truly says, 'with the idea that the soul can exist
independently of the body'.[4] But the simile used by
Socrates in the *Republic* is no more than a simile and does
not imply the acceptance of what he rejects in the *Phaedo*.
The soul is still 'tripartite' in the *Timaeus*,[5] and the definition of it in the *Laws* as 'self-initiating motion'[6] would not
have seemed to Plato inconsistent with its being so. No
doubt the fact of its being so points to the need for a more
thoroughgoing investigation, that shall explain why it is

---

[1] *cupiditas*: see *Tusc. Disput.* iv, § 10; Burnet, *Early Gk. Phil.*[3] p. 296,
and authorities referred to, n. 2.
[2] *Rep.* iv. 443 d 5.   [3] *Phaedo* 91 c 6–95 a 2.   [4] Op. cit., p. 295.
[5] See the interesting note on *Tim.* 69 c 7, in Prof. A. E. Taylor's
Commentary.
[6] *Laws* x. 896 a 1: τὴν Δυναμένην αὐτὴν αὑτὴν κινεῖν κίνησιν.

so, than we have in the fourth book of the *Republic*.[1] There
Plato only argues regressively from the conflicts we observe in it to its constitution. No doubt also there is a real
difficulty in reconciling whether the admittedly close connexion between both spirit and appetite[2] and the body
with their continued presence in the soul after its separation from the body, or the view that soul is the principle
of life in all organisms[3] with the view that it is a tenant of
the body, a 'sojourner in the flesh'. But we are still so far
ourselves from understanding the connexion of body and
mind, that we need not be surprised to find difficulties
like these in Plato's theory. We may (it seems to me)
take the psychology of *Republic* iv as, in Plato's opinion,
true, though not the whole truth, about the soul.[4] What
then exactly was the doctrine, and what are the arguments offered in its support? When these questions are
answered we shall know better whether it has more than an
historical interest to-day, and whether we may still turn
more profitably to the *Republic* than to most modern
works on psychology, if we would understand how the
soul acts.

Socrates has described to us the organization of a State
that we should be prepared on inspection to call just.
This State is an independent or sovereign community that

---

[1] ἄλλη μακροτέρα καὶ πλείων ὅλος, iv. 435 d 3.

[2] *Rep.* vii. 518 c 9, x. 611 b 9–612 e 6.

[3] i. 353 d 3–9. So long as the 'work' of the soul is held to be living,
τὸ ζῆν, we are not justified in saying that the specific excellence, by which
it performs its work well, is justice. Similarly, if this is its work, its οἰκεῖον
κακόν is not injustice, and the argument for immortality in x. 608 d 13 *seq.*
fails (cf. *supra*, c 220). It was a sense of these weaknesses that made
Aristotle reject the immortality of the individual and transmigration,
ascribing eternity only to intelligence, νοῦς, which had no bodily organ.

[4] See an excellent paper by Prof. J. L. Stocks in *Mind*, n.s., xxiv (1915),
on 'Plato and the Tripartite Soul', where he points out (p. 220) that this
doctrine in no way conflicts with the distinction, also credited to the
Pythagoreans, between νοῦς, ἐπιστήμη, δόξα and αἴσθησις in the soul: nor
therefore, we may add, with Plato's distinction in the *Republic* between
νοῦς, διάνοια, πίστις and εἰκασία.

makes possible for its members good lives, though not the same sort of lives for all; and their lives enter into and constitute what, because of the way in which they are unified, may be called the State's life. This unification arises through community of purpose in the citizens, and is why we may call a State just, as well as a man. It is, however, not enough that the State, or its life, should be unified by community of purpose. That purpose must be directed towards maintaining a form of life that is good. To this end we need rulers with wisdom to understand what in detail this form must be, and to prescribe the activities required of individuals for its realization in the common interest. We need in their support an executive having military power which will both defend the State in its relations to others and provide that background of force which the law requires, even while it has the consent of the people; and of the citizens fulfilling this function will be demanded a courage or resoluteness, given which the State, in its corporate capacity, may be called courageous. The rest of the citizens will be doing the different jobs in whose performance the form of life conceived and prescribed by the rulers and insisted on by their executive supporters is realized. These are called Δημιουργοί, craftsmen or workers; the rulers φύλακες or guardians; and the executive their auxiliaries, ἐπίκουροι. Of the workers is required neither the wisdom shown in planning the form of life of the State, nor the courage shown in maintaining the conditions, under which they can realize it by their work. But they, as well as the other two classes, must have temperance, i.e. the disposition each to accept his place in the organization, which brings unanimity. A community thus organized, in which the different members possess these excellences as the function of the class to which they belong requires, and where every one actively discharges the work assigned to him, will appear and will be just. Hence the famous definition of Justice, τὸ τὰ αὑτοῦ πράττειν καὶ μὴ πολυπραγμονεῖν, to do one's own work and not meddle.[1]

Justice, then, in a State is an excellence which requires the presence in it of three excellences, wisdom, courage, and temperance. It is their unity. For this reason, though in his search for it Socrates first tracks down and defines the other three of the 'cardinal' virtues, and calls it residual,[2] it is a mistake to say that he seeks it by a 'method of residues'.[3] For that name has been given to a procedure by which, when the nature or cause of some part of a total subject of investigation has been ascertained, we abstract from that in our search for the nature or cause of the residue, and look for this elsewhere. But justice is not what we should find left in a State, if we abstracted from the nature or effects of its wisdom, courage, and temperance. It includes all these.

Socrates now proceeds to verify or test this result in our application of the term *just* (or *unjust*) to individuals, and this is what leads him to discuss the nature of the soul. He takes it for granted that the term is not used equivocally when we call a State, and when we call a man, just; and therefore if the State's display of justice involves or includes the display in it of wisdom, courage, and temperance, so must any man's in him. The only problem is whether, as their display in the State concerned different

---

[1] iv. 433 a 8. Cf. the words of the Catechism in 'My duty towards my neighbour'—'to learn and labour truly to get mine own living, and to do my duty in that state of life, unto which it shall please God to call me'. But in Plato's State any 'calling' is done by that 'mortal god' the Guardian, 'to which', he might have said with Hobbes (*Leviathan*, c. xvii), 'we owe under the "immortal God", our peace and defence'.

[2] iv. 427 e 13: τὸ ὑπόλοιπον; 428 a 6, 433 b 7: τὸ ὑπολειφθέν.

[3] Jowett, *The Republic of Plato translated into English*, Introd., p. lxiii. In 433 b 7 he translates 'Because I think that this is the only virtue which remains in the State, when the other virtues of temperance and courage and wisdom are abstracted'; but there is nothing about abstracting the other virtues in the Greek, which means 'what remains after the virtues which we have considered in the State, temperance and courage and wisdom'; i.e. what remains for consideration.

classes, so it is in us: there is that in us wherewith we learn, and that wherewith we are angry, and that wherewith we desire the pleasures of nutrition and procreation and such-like; or whether each of these is an activity of the whole soul.[1] The defence of the first alternative is the argument for the 'tripartite' soul.

The argument rests upon the fact of conflict or contrariety in the soul, and what this implies. Socrates lays it down that nothing can be contrarily active or affected towards the same at the same time in respect of what is the same in it,[2] and from this deduces first of all a distinction in the soul between something appetitive and something rational. For we often find ourselves rejecting or turning away from that towards which at the same time, in hunger or thirst or such-like appetites, we are drawn. If in virtue of appetite we are drawn towards it, it cannot also be in virtue of appetite that we reject or are averse to it; and if anything thus prevents us from gratifying an appetite which we nevertheless feel, it must spring of consideration, and indicate something rational in the soul.[3]

In briefly stating this argument, I have avoided using the word 'part', because Plato does not use it. He uses the word εἶδος, and that is his most usual term, when he requires a substantive; what he distinguishes is three forms (or specific forms, if various usage has blunted our sense of what 'form' may mean) in which the being of the soul is realized; and the word μέρος first occurs instead at 444 b 3, where he is describing injustice as a sort of sedition in this

---

[1] iv. 436 a 8–b 3. A discussion of the relation between this distinction of activities and that of the classes in the State belongs to a consideration of the parallel which Plato draws between the constitutions of the State and of the soul, and will be found in the next Essay.

[2] Δῆλον ὅτι ταὐτὸν τἀνάντια ποιεῖν ἢ πάσχειν κατὰ ταὐτόν γε καὶ πρὸς ταὐτὸν οὐκ ἐθελήσει ἅμα, 436 b 8. This, of course, is not the law of contradiction, as is sometimes said: e.g. Jowett, op. cit., p. 131 margin, cf. p. lxvii; R. L. Nettleship, Lectures on Plato's 'Republic', p. 155.

[3] 439 c 9–d 8.

triplicity, an insurrection of a part of the soul against the whole. It is a political metaphor, but if we are to think appropriately and not in metaphor of the soul, we shall use such terms as form or kind or mode of being, or perhaps factor,[1] rather than part.

The argument is very carefully developed, and is fundamental. If we are to appraise it, three things are necessary. We must distinguish the experience to which Plato directs our attention from another with which, as he indicates, it might be confused, to wit a mere conflict of desires. We must consider his use of the word ἐπιθυμία, which I have translated appetite, and of other words expressing what a modern psychologist might call conation. And we must ask ourselves why Plato takes for granted that what prevents us from gratifying an appetite, in situations such as he has in mind, springs of consideration, and is evidence of a λογιστικόν, of something rational, in the soul. He himself gives no reasons here for saying this.

It will probably be best to take the second of these points first. In the present context (437 b, c) there are several other words besides ἐπιθυμεῖν, which are offered as more or less equivalent; ἐφίεσθαι, προσάγεσθαι, ἐπορέγεσθαι, ἐθέλειν, βούλεσθαι. All these express affirmation, as it were, in contrast to rejection; and although the mention of τὸ ἐθέλειν καὶ τὸ βούλεσθαι is introduced by the particle αὖ which seems to contrast these words with ἐπιθυμία, yet immediately afterwards they are applied to τὴν τοῦ ἐπιθυμοῦντος ψυχήν. Aristotle, on the other hand, contrasted βούλησις with ἐπιθυμία, as rational desire with mere appetite. Nor is this really alien to Plato's thought. If a man thinks the object of his appetition good, he will wish

---

[1] At viii. 559 e 4–7 we find εἴδη ἐπιθυμιῶν in an individual spoken of as comparable to μέρη συμμαχίας in a city; at ix. 580 d 3, the soul of each of us is said to have been subjected to a threefold division ὥσπερ πόλις διῄρηται κατὰ τρία εἴδη. Plato is not pedantically rigid in his use of terms; but it may be said that, the less superficial his account at any point, the more likely he is to speak of εἴδη or γένη, and not μέρη.

for it; and we are told at ix. 577 e 1 that the τυραννουμένη ψυχή—the soul whose state is like that of a city under the oppression of a tyrant—will least of any do what it may wish, ἥκιστα ποιήσει ἃ ἂν βουληθῇ. But Plato does use the word ἐπιθυμεῖν less carefully than Aristotle, to include more than can be ascribed to the ἐπιθυμητικόν in the soul. This has led to much misunderstanding; and the matter will unfortunately require a rather long discussion.[1]

At the very outset (iv. 436 a 9) he makes Socrates ask whether we learn and are angry respectively with something different in us, and again desire with a third something the pleasures of nutrition, procreation and such-like: ἐπιθυμοῦμεν δ' αὖ τρίτῳ τινὶ τῶν περὶ τὴν τροφήν τε καὶ γέννησιν ἡδονῶν καὶ ὅσα τούτων ἀδελφά. This is not inconsistent with supposing that wherewith we learn or are angry to be responsible for our desiring not these pleasures but yet something; and so, as we learn later, it is. But Plato uses his division of the soul for two purposes, not perversely, but because the peculiar nature of the soul appears to him to point to this complexity. On the one hand, it is the *man* who acts, and therefore with his whole soul; yet its three 'forms' should (and indeed in the last resort we may say must) each make a different kind of contribution to his acting. On the other hand, each 'form' makes him capable of a different kind of particular interest or desire.

Now what makes the soul incomparable with anything else, such as a *compositum* whose parts are subject to different forces, what really justifies the definition of it as self-initiating movement, is to be found in the peculiar way in which its 'forms' co-operate, and especially in which the rational works: in the facts which justify the statement that, if anything prevents us from gratifying an appetite

---

[1] Note also the language of iv. 439 a 9–b 1 : τοῦ διψῶντος ἄρα ἡ ψυχή, καθ' ὅσον διψῇ, οὐκ ἄλλο τι βούλεται ἢ πιεῖν. Aristotle would never have written this.

which we nevertheless feel, it must 'spring of consideration'. To a scrutiny of this we must come later. What
should be noted here is that Socrates might so have spoken
of what prevents us from gratifying *any* particular desire,
not necessarily one for the pleasure of food or procreation,
one that may be called specifically an appetite, and is referred by him to what he names the ἐπιθυμητικόν in the
soul. Indeed, he himself implies this when he comes to his
proof that the spirited is something different from the
rational in the soul; for one reason given is that a man may
rebuke his anger; the considerative, τὸ ἀναλογισάμενον
περὶ τοῦ βελτίονός τε καὶ χείρονος, is there opposed to a desire
springing from his spirited nature exactly as it is here
opposed to one springing from the ἐπιθυμητικόν.[1]

But Plato makes Socrates take his example here from
such a desire as thirst because, whereas the spirited and
the rational in us, besides being responsible for particular
desires of their special kinds, have other functions in the
acting soul, the appetitive is merely responsible for its own
kind of particular desires, whereof thirst is an example.
To establish its presence and the difference from it of the
rational he must point to a man feeling an appetite, and
refraining from indulging it.

Had Plato, like Aristotle afterwards, used ἐπιθυμία only
in a specific sense, and some other word, like ὄρεξις,
generically to include both these desires referred to the
ἐπιθυμητικόν and those of which the spirited and the
rational in us make us capable, his thought would have
been much easier to follow. As it is, his use of ἐπιθυμεῖν
and its derivatives both in a specific and in a generic sense
is apt to make a hasty reader suppose that, whenever they
occur, the specifically appetitive nature of the soul is in
question; and this confounds the doctrine.

Attention must therefore be directed to two facts: (1)
that, throughout, the language in which the other principles

[1] iv. 441 b 2–c 2.

than the appetitive in the soul are described depicts them
as involving the soul in what to-day is called conation;
(2) that from time to time the word ἐπιθυμεῖν occurs in
connexion with the action of those other principles, obviously therefore in the same generic sense in which other
words so occur. Details in support of this statement are
better relegated to a note. The important conclusion is,
that each of the three εἴδη in the soul is a principle of
desire, and makes a man capable of a different kind of
interest; but the spirited and the rational have other functions as well.[1] That form of the soul's being which Plato

---

[1] In support of (1), note that at the very outset the action of what
prevents us gratifying an appetite is described by the words ἀπωθεῖν and
ἀπελαύνειν (iv. 437 c 9). But the reader will find in the following passages
divers 'conative' terms used of the action of the rational or the spirited;
and should observe that some are used alternatively to ἐπιθυμεῖν of the
action of the appetitive; the greatest variety is found in reference to the
rational. φιλεῖν, στέργειν are used generically in v. 474 c 9 seq., in respect
of each εἶδος; and in the compounds, φιλόσοφος φιλότιμος φιλοκερδής, this
generic use is manifest: ὁρμᾶσθαι, of the θυμοειδές ix. 581 a 10, and by
implication generally of all three, 582 c 5: ἐρᾶν, ἔρως, ἐραστής, of the rational,
vi. 485 b 1 (μαθήματός γε ἀεὶ ἐρῶσιν), vi. 490 b 2, vi. 501 d 2 (ἀληθείας
ἐραστὰς εἶναι τοὺς φιλοσόφους), but also ἐρᾶν, like ἐρωτικός, in its specific
sense, of the appetitive, iv. 439 d 6 et al.: ὀρέγεσθαι, of the rational, vi. 485
d 4, ix. 572 a 2: also of the rational, ἁμιλλᾶσθαι vi. 490 a 9, ὠθίς vi. 490 b 7,
Διώκειν vi. 505 d 11 (cf. ix. 586 d 7), τέταται ix. 581 b 6, ἐφίεσθαι x. 611 e 2,
προθυμεῖσθαι x. 613 a 8. In regard to (2), the following passages show that
ἐπιθυμεῖν bears also a generic sense, and it may be worth while to cite
these at more length—v. 475 b 2 ὡς ὅλως τιμῆς ἐπιθυμηταὶ ὄντες: b 4
Τοῦτο Δὴ φάθι ἢ μή· ἆρα ὃν ἄν τινος ἐπιθυμητικὸν λέγωμεν, παντὸς τοῦ
εἴδους τούτου φήσομεν ἐπιθυμεῖν, ἢ τοῦ μέν, τοῦ Δὲ οὔ; Παντός, ἔφη. Οὐκοῦν
καὶ τὸν φιλόσοφον σοφίας φήσομεν ἐπιθυμητὴν εἶναι, οὐ τῆς μέν, τῆς Δ' οὔ,
ἀλλὰ πάσης; Ἀληθῆ. Τὸν ἄρα περὶ τὰ μαθήματα Δυσχεραίνοντα, ἄλλως τε
καὶ νέον ὄντα καὶ μήπω λόγον ἔχοντα τί τε χρηστὸν καὶ μή, οὐ φήσομεν
φιλομαθῆ οὐΔὲ φιλόσοφον εἶναι, ὥσπερ τὸν περὶ τὰ σιτία Δυσχερῆ οὔτε
πεινῆν φαμεν οὔτ' ἐπιθυμεῖν σιτίων, οὐΔὲ φιλόσιτον ἀλλὰ κακόσιτον εἶναι:
vi. 485 d 6 Ἀλλὰ μὴν ὅτῳ γε εἰς ἕν τι αἱ ἐπιθυμίαι σφόΔρα ῥέπουσιν, ἴσμεν
που ὅτι εἰς τἆλλα τούτῳ ἀσθενέστεραι, ὥσπερ ῥεῦμα ἐκεῖσε ἀπωχετευμένον.
Τί μήν; Ὧι Δὴ πρὸς τὰ μαθήματα καὶ πᾶν τὸ τοιοῦτον ἐρρυήκασιν, περὶ τὴν
τῆς ψυχῆς οἶμαι ἡΔονὴν αὐτῆς καθ' αὑτὴν εἶεν ἄν, τὰς Δὲ Διὰ τοῦ σώματος
ἐκλείποιεν, εἰ μὴ πεπλασμένως ἀλλ' ἀληθῶς φιλόσοφός τις εἴη: ix. 580 d 3
ἘπειΔή, ὥσπερ πόλις, ἣν Δ' ἐγώ, Διῄρηται κατὰ τρία εἴΔη, οὕτω καὶ ψυχὴ
ἑνὸς ἑκάστου τριχῇ, [λογιστικόν] Δέξεται, ὡς ἐμοὶ Δοκεῖ, καὶ ἑτέραν ἀπόΔειξιν.

calls the appetitive or ἐπιθυμητικόν is not responsible for all the particular desires or interests which may affect the soul contrarily to how the rational in it, τὸ λογιστικόν, in the exercise of its specific function, affects it at the same time towards the same object. The desires which belong to it are those in the constitution of which our rational nature is least involved, though it may be used in their service and for their gratification. Hunger, thirst, and the sexual appetite are the clearest examples; but less animal desires also belong to it, desires, as Plato says, for the enjoyments which money will buy. We might say that its manifestations are so many forms of the impulse to get, or of the desire to have; and 'the sickness of an acquisitive society' springs from its undue influence in the life of a State.

From this, and the part it plays in the soul, Plato first of

Τίνα ταύτην; Τήνδε. τριῶν ὄντων τρ ιτταὶ καὶ ἡδοναί μοι φαίνονται, ἑνὸς ἑκάστου μία ἰδία· ἐπιθυμίαι τε ὡσαύτως καὶ ἀρχαί: ix. 587 a 13 Ἐφά-νησαν δὲ πλεῖστον ἀφεστῶσαι ⟨νόμου τε καὶ τάξεως⟩ οὐχ αἱ ἐρωτικαί τε καὶ τυραννικαὶ ἐπιθυμίαι; Πολύ γε. Ἐλάχιστον δὲ αἱ βασιλικαί τε καὶ κόσμιαι; Ναί. The passage beginning 580 d 3 continues as follows, in words that give perhaps the clearest explanation in the text, why the generic word is used also in a specific sense of one of the three 'forms' of the soul: Πῶς λέγεις; ἔφη. Τὸ μέν, φαμέν, ᾗ ᾧ μανθάνει ἄνθρωπος, τὸ δὲ ᾧ θυμοῦται, τὸ δὲ τρίτον διὰ πολυειδίαν ἑνὶ οὐκ ἔσχομεν ὀνόματι προσειπεῖν ἰδίῳ αὐτοῦ, ἀλλὰ ὃ μέγιστον καὶ ἰσχυρότατον εἶχεν ἐν αὐτῷ, τούτῳ ἐπωνομάσαμεν· ἐπιθυμητικὸν γὰρ αὐτὸ κεκλήκαμεν διὰ σφοδρότητα τῶν τε περὶ τὴν ἐδωδὴν ἐπιθυμιῶν καὶ πόσιν καὶ ἀφροδίσια καὶ ὅσα ἄλλα τούτοις ἀκόλουθα (cf. iv. 436 a 10–b 1), καὶ φιλοχρήματον δή, ὅτι διὰ χρημάτων μάλιστα ἀπο-τελοῦνται αἱ τοιαῦται ἐπιθυμίαι. Plato seems to mean that a certain sort or set of desires is to be ascribed to a specific 'form' of the soul—viz. those enumerated here and at iv. 436 a 10—from which that form might be named, as the φιλόσοφον and the φιλότιμον are from the objects of their desires; but this is difficult because of the variety of its desired objects; hence, he uses two names for it, one taken not from the names of these divers objects, but from that of the common means of attaining them, viz. φιλοχρήματον: the other, because in the desire of these various objects the generic nature of desiring is displayed (as Bacon would have said) in a glaring instance, with peculiar intensity, is the generic term itself, ἐπιθυμητικόν.

The above references, I hope, establish the contention of the text; but I do not claim that the list is exhaustive.

all distinguishes the rational, or reason, and its part, by pointing, as we have seen, to the fact that a man may abstain from gratifying some appetite which he still feels. Different principles must be involved if his soul is to be thus contrarily disposed. It is important that we should be clear what is and what is not an example of this contrariety. Appetites (and for that matter desires generally) differ from one another in what they are for; and a craving for alcohol is no more the same with a craving for tea because both are for something to drink than thirst is the same with hunger because both are for something to ingest. That a man craving alcohol should refuse tea is therefore no more a case of what is meant than that a thirsty man should refuse hay. Socrates brings this out in the passage iv. 437 d 6–439 b 2; any qualification in the desired implies a qualification in or specification of the desire, and vice versa. But the special purpose of the passage is to point out how the stipulation that the thing desired should be good is not such a qualification in the desired as this principle includes. To this we must come back later, in connexion with the other sort of conflict, which it is important we should understand not to be an example of the contrariety in question. This other sort of conflict is not expressly mentioned by Plato, and many critics have failed to see that the contrariety of which he speaks is different from it. It is the mere conflict of two different desires.

That to be similarly affected (viz. in the way of wanting, or it might be in the way of aversion) towards different objects is not the same as to be contrarily affected towards the same, should be obvious enough.[1] Yet those who say

---

[1] Contrariety in our appetitive nature alone, as opposed to competition or conflict between different appetites, would occur if we felt aversion towards that very object for which at the same time we craved; if a thirsty man shrank at the sight of water, or some food excited loathing in a man ravening for it. This, as Plato saw, does not and cannot happen. Contrary affections towards the same object may rapidly alternate; *odi et amo,* said

that a man's action is always determined by the strongest desire confuse the second of these experiences with the first.

The opinion that action must be determined by the strongest desire comes, I think, not of observation, but of the assumption that action must be explicable analogously to the explanation which physical science gives of the movement of bodies; that motives are like forces.[1] That a man acts in a certain way is therefore regarded as evidence that the motive so to act was the strongest. But that when there is a conflict of motives a man acts from that which prevails is no more than a tautology; the question is why it prevails—whether because it is the strongest. Now, so far as particular desires are concerned, strength and feebleness are characters which we recognize and are familiar with, just as we are familiar with what it is to desire, though perhaps we can no more define them than we can desire itself. We know the difference between 'wanting frightfully' to have something, and wanting it a little: between being mildly and intensely thirsty. It is perfectly possible, if a man feels some desire, that another should arise in him and determine his action because it is stronger. But if this is all, there is no contrariety. The stronger desire drives out the weaker. Lewis Carroll put the case correctly in *Alice Through the Looking-Glass*. Tweedledum and Tweedledee desired to fight; all was ready for the encounter.

> Just then came by a monstrous crow
> As black as a tar-barrel
> Which frightened both the heroes so,
> They quite forgot their quarrel.

Catullus, but it was according as he thought of this or that in Lesbia and her behaviour. Aristotle puts into a sentence what Plato argues at length, when he says, *Eth. Nic.* III. ii. 5, 1111 b 15: καὶ προαιρέσει μὲν ἐπιθυμία ἐναντιοῦται, ἐπιθυμία 2' ἐπιθυμίᾳ οὔ.

[1] Cf. Harold's words in Tennyson, *The Promise of May*, Act 2: 'Anyhow we must Move in the line of least resistance when The stronger motive rules.'

Fear, the desire to flee, drove out for a time the desire to fight. 'The most curious instance known to me', says Darwin, 'of one instinct getting the better of another, is the migratory instinct conquering the maternal instinct. The former is wonderfully strong; a confined bird will at the proper season beat her breast against the wires of her cage, until it is bare and bloody.'[1] But if we are to speak in terms of particular desires, we should speak not of her maternal instinct, but the instinct to sit on her eggs or her chicks; and if all that happens is that the migratory instinct some-times gets the better of this, the bird then ceases to feel broody. Darwin, in the chapter from which this quotation is taken, is trying to explain the origin of the moral sense.

'Whilst the mother-bird is feeding [he says a little later] or brooding over her nestlings, the maternal instinct is probably stronger than the migratory; but the instinct which is more persistent gains the victory, and at last, at a moment when her young ones are not in sight, she takes flight and deserts them. When arrived at the end of her long journey, and the migratory instinct has ceased to act, what an agony of remorse the bird would feel, if, from being en-dowed with great mental activity, she could not prevent the image constantly passing through her mind, of her young ones perishing in the north from cold and hunger.'

But why? There must be something more in the bird's soul than a capacity for particular desires and a power of imagery, if this is to occur; else the most we can suppose is that the imagination of her young ones should, like the sight of them, arouse again the broody impulse, the revival of which, indeed, might well occur without such power of imagination, after the migratory impulse had spent its force; just as Tweedledum and Tweedledee might have wanted to fight again, when their fright was over. The bird would not feel remorse unless it were capable more or less explicitly of thinking its having yielded to the migratory instinct bad, or wrong; and that, of course, may be thought

[3] *Descent of Man*, part i, ch. iv.

about yielding to any desire *while one still feels it*. But then one is contrarily disposed towards the same thing, not, like the bird while the two instincts were at issue, identically disposed towards different things. If this is all that happens, action occurs on ceasing to be thus disposed towards one of them; and that is for action to be determined merely by the strongest desire.

If, however, when desires are thus competing in the soul, a man acts according to the prompting of one because he thinks it better to act so, then it is not by its strength that this desire prevails. Nor—and this is the point that Plato makes in iv. 438 a—is it because what he rejects is not precisely what he desires. It might be objected, says Socrates, that a man, when thirsty or hungry, wants not drink or food but good drink or good food; for all men desire what is good.[1] But though Socrates holds that so far as any man is rational he desires the good, it is the nature of the ἐπιθυμητικόν in its specific sense that is here under discussion; and so far as a man is merely appetitive, when the particular appetite felt is thirst, he just wants drink. He may want strong drink, and not water; and then his appetite is not mere thirst, but thirst of a particular kind, and not for drink generally, but for drink of a particular kind. To be good, however, is not a quality of drink, as to be alcoholic or free from typhoid germs is. That the object of a man's thirst should be good drink is therefore not correlative to any such specification of the appetite as distinguishes a drunkard's craving from mere thirst; that the drink must be good is a stipulation possible only because he is rational. And that its yielding to the migratory instinct had been bad was a consideration possible to the bird only if she was in some degree rational, though necessary if she is to feel an agony of remorse. Yet Dar-

---

[1] πάντες γὰρ ἄρα τῶν ἀγαθῶν ἐπιθυμοῦσιν. The ἄρα shows (as does 439 a 4–6) that these words are put into the mouth of the objector, and are not an admission by Socrates, inserted as making the objection plausible.

win is trying to account for the moral sense from the development and play of instincts.

This has brought us to the third of the points which it was said on p. 48 must be considered, if we are to understand Plato's argument. Why does he take for granted that what prevents us from gratifying an appetite, in situations such as he has in mind, springs of consideration, and is evidence of a λογιστικόν, of something rational, in the soul?

We may answer that obviously, if a man, while able and still wanting to drink, abstains from drinking, he must have a reason; for his thirst, by itself, would make him drink. Were a stronger desire to prevent him drinking— were sleepiness, for example, to make him lie down, or fright to run away—there would be a cause for his not drinking; but there would only be a reason if he did not drink because he had thought of something else than drinking. But this is not the whole of the matter. For firstly, a man may have a reason for acting, without any contrariety being involved, as when he hails a taxi because he wants to catch a train; and secondly, he may have a reason for taking one course of action and rejecting another, without any contrariety being involved. If, for example, he desired to increase his income, and for this reason were about to invest some idle money in what he thought a safe business at 4 per cent., but then heard of another seeming equally safe which would yield 5 per cent., he would reject the first in favour of the second, but would not be contrarily disposed towards the first investment at the same time. The case is like that when one particular desire prevails over another merely because it is stronger, only that here this relation holds between objects desired as means, not on their own account; he just ceases to desire to invest his money in the first business when he learns of the second; it is not really a case of choice. If, indeed, the first business seemed safer, and the second to offer prospects of a larger income, then he would have to choose.

But so long as the question is merely by which course he can get most of some one thing, of which he desires to get as much as possible, reason has no part to play but that of investigating the means to his end.

Now distinguished writers have argued as if in fact it had never any other part; its office, according to Hume, is to serve and obey the passions, by showing us the way to the attainment of happiness and the avoidance of misery;[1] and the utilitarians generally, if they understood the implications of their own doctrines, that a man desires nothing but pleasure, and always more pleasure rather than less, and desires happiness because happiness is the largest possible quantity of pleasure, could give no other function to reason in action but what it plays in such a case as the above, when it leads a man to reject the less for the more remunerative of two equally safe investments. In fact, of course, happiness is not a sum of pleasures, as a man's income *is* the sum of what he gets from different sources. By the utilitarians' own avowal, a man shuns pain besides desiring pleasure, and the question how much pain cancels how much pleasure, which must be taken into any judgement of how to get happiness, is not one of addition and subtraction. And further, there is this to be noted. The several pleasures which are supposed to be the objects of one's several particular desires, and greater pleasures of stronger desires, are enjoyed successively; but the happiness a man wants, whatever it is, is something of which he would wish to be able to say, 'I have it'. It cannot therefore be the sum of pleasures that are for the most part past or future; not the aggregate of these, but the consciousness that they would make a handsome aggregate if they could be added, must be what makes him happy. 'Soul, thou hast much goods laid up for many years; take thine ease, eat, drink and be merry';[2] if a man is made happy now by

---

[1] *Treatise of Human Nature: Of the Passions*, Part III, Section iii.
[2] Luke xii. 19.

being able to say this, he is not less happy now because this night his soul shall be required of him; and yet those expected pleasures will in that case never be enjoyed, and his happiness cannot possibly be the sum of them.

But Plato saw that the function of reason in the soul was not merely what Hume ascribes to it, viz. the discovery of means to the attainment of what a man's passions make him desire. In two ways it goes beyond this. It makes him conceive a good that is to satisfy *him*, and not merely quench this or that particular desire; and it makes him also desire this good. Also it involves him in particular desires, which a creature not rational could not have; but so far it works as his appetitive nature works. This, too (and the spirited to boot), involves him in divers particular desires, though those in which these different forms of the soul's being respectively involve it are of different kinds. Roughly, as those of the appetitive may be called desires to have, so may those of the rational be called desires to know. But this is not what is important just now; what Plato wants us to see is that reason works differently in the soul from how *any* particular desire does, not merely by way of finding means to ends, though only as rational can a man do this either, but in the ways mentioned just above, viz. by arousing the thought and desire of good.

What is meant by speaking of that which will satisfy *me*, not some particular desire of mine?

'The felicity of this life [said Hobbes] consisteth not in the repose of a mind satisfied. For there is no such *finis ultimus*, utmost aim, nor *summum bonum*, greatest good, as is spoken of in the books of the old moral philosophers. Nor can a man any more live, whose desires are at an end, than he whose senses and imaginations are at a stand. Felicity is a continual progress of the desire, from one object to another, the attaining of the former being still but the way to the latter. The cause whereof is, that the object of a man's desire is not to enjoy once only, but to assure for ever the way of

his future desire. And therefore the voluntary actions and inclina-
tions of all men, tend not only to the procuring, but also to the
assuring of a contented life.'[1]

But supposing that I desire to assure for ever the way of
my future desires, this desire and those cannot be of the
same order. And if I had gratified this desire, I should
have the assurance that those would be gratified as they
arose. What more then could I want? Should I not be
satisfied? Should I not have attained what the old moral
philosophers meant when they spoke of a *finis ultimus* or
summum bonum, however ill the terms *ultimus* and *summum*
may express the relation of this assurance to the objects of
those other desires? About that relation Hobbes perhaps
thought no more clearly than Hume.

That a man cannot live whose desires are at an end is
true: if he no longer felt thirst or hunger, did not want to
get up or go to bed, to read or speak, to work or play, he
would be like a log. But if there were nothing in him but a
continual progress of the desire from one object to another,
though he might feel successive pleasures, he would not
enjoy felicity. For this it is required, though it does not
suffice, that he should be conscious of himself as one in the
succession of his desires. To this unity it does not matter
whether the series is long or short: that is a question of
the length of life, which is accidental to its unity. What
is not accidental is that the unity cannot itself limit the
number of its particular manifestations; and since to want
is one form of man's being, it cannot limit the number of
his particular wants. Yet these are for their several particular objects; in Butler's language, they are particular propensions, and terminate upon their objects; and if a man
had no want but these, nor any satisfaction but theirs, his
life would be, to quote Hobbes again, 'a perpetual and
restless desire', or rather succession of desires, not perhaps
'of power after power', but of one thing after another, 'that

[1] *Leviathan*, c. xi.

ceaseth only in death'. But there is that in men, because of which they are dissatisfied with this restless succession of desires, and which cannot be any one of the successive desires; it is not, for example, my present thirst which is unsatisfied because I pass from one desire to another; my present thirst is unsatisfied because I have not just drunk, and will cease as soon as I have, however many desires follow it. Nor is it any other particular desire which is unsatisfied, but I. Spinoza asked himself,[1] *an aliquid daretur, quo invento et acquisito, continua ac summa in aeternum fruerer laetitia.* That is what would satisfy me.

But my wanting this is a manifestation of my nature as a wanting creature of a different sort from thirst, and different not in the way in which my thirst is distinct from wanting to read the news to-morrow or to be elected consul, or any thing else in particular. Yet that whose acquisition would satisfy *me*, in the way Spinoza suggests, is not something to be enjoyed by a being that wanted nothing in particular. Such a *summum bonum* would be the μάταιον εἶλος, the empty form, which the αὐτοαγαθόν rejected by Aristotle in his *Nicomachean Ethics* seemed to him to be.[2] As my unity is displayed in my different and successive desires, so must what is to satisfy me be somehow displayed in the experiences which are to satisfy and extinguish these desires; though if I am to be satisfied, it is not indifferent for what my particular desires are. That is why unity of consciousness, though required if I am to enjoy felicity, does not suffice.

Such an object as would thus satisfy me is what Plato calls the good; and the thought of it belongs to me, as he held, not because I am appetitive, nor yet because I have particular propensions of another kind than appetites like hunger and thirst, but because I am rational: able to reflect on my identity in the diversity and series of my

[1] *Tractatus de Intellectus Emendatione*, init.
[2] I. vi. 10, 1096 b 20.

states and passions, and to understand that this identity, or unity, has nothing to do with how many these are, but that my good has much to do with what they are for. For when a man refrains from gratifying an appetite which he nevertheless continues to feel, the reason is that he thinks its gratification would be bad, or at least incompatible with some other which is better. The attainment, therefore, of the good which he desires depends on what particular desires he gratifies. But it could not be attained if none were gratified. It is realized in the satisfaction of particular desires, not as an alternative thereto.

But if so, it cannot be realizable only in the satisfaction of some one particular desire; that would make it as particular as the rest, and alternative to them. Now a man carrying out in a number of acts, spread perhaps over years, a purpose to the fulfilment of which they all contribute, gets in each act the satisfaction of its particular accomplishment, but also that of therein *pro tanto* fulfilling the purpose to whose execution it belongs. Plato conceived a perfectly good life as one, all whose activities were thus unified; and what unified them was to be the fact that being severally what they are, and related as they are to each other, they make the life, as one and as a whole, good. Madame de Sevigné said once that, if one is to be happy, one must desire only that the will of God should be done, and believe that whatever happens is His will. For then, in whatever happened, the one desire would be satisfied. If a man knew what form of life for him, a life how composed of what actions, would be good, and if he could so order his particular desires that he felt none but for the objects to be attained by those actions, then he would not only in each successful action satisfy a particular desire; in all he would find his good. But plainly this is only possible to a rational or intelligent being; and it is what is meant by saying of us that, as rational beings, *omnia appetimus sub specie boni.*

It will have appeared in this discussion that such action implies desire as well as conception of this good. And Plato thought that the desire, no less than the conception, belonged to man as rational. He did not of course suppose that desiring is a kind of thinking. There is no inconsistency between his psychology and the distinction dear to the moderns between cognition, conation, and feeling. When Aristotle said, with reference to Plato's doctrine, that if the soul is three, there will be desire in each (part),[1] he said nothing that Plato would have disputed; nor would the soul's being thus three be inconsistent with his own conviction, that thought alone without desire does not move to action.[2] Plato's doctrine really brings out the unity of the soul, as the moderns do when they insist that cognition, conation, and feeling are always involved together.

In the soul, then, of a man who refrains from yielding to an appetite which he still feels there must, in Plato's view, be a principle of reason, because his so refraining involves conception and desire of good.[3] There are then these two forms of the soul's being, a rational and an appetitive. But he recognized a third, which he called the spirited, τὸ θυμοειᾆές; and it is perhaps his recognition of this, more than anything else in his psychology, that has led critics to charge him with accommodating his psychology to his division of classes in the State. We must consider whether he may not have been led to it by noticing how the soul works.

'That wherewith we are angry', τὸ ᾧ θυμούμεθα, might seem at first sight of the same nature with the appetitive form; but Socrates appeals against this to the principle

---

[1] de An. iii. ix. 3, 432 b 6: εἰ ᾆὲ τρία ἡ ψυχή, ἐν ἑκάστῳ ἔσται ὄρεξις.
[2] Eth. Nic. vi. ii. 5, 1139 a 34.
[3] Kant held that reason shows itself rather in consciousness of obligation than in conceiving good; and that a man who acts from this consciousness acts without desire. I have said something about this difference of view in Some Problems of Ethics, pp. 108–12, 131–2.

already used in distinguishing appetitive from rational.
Spirit and appetite may dispose a man contrarily towards
the same course at the same time; doing what appetite
makes him want to do may make him angry; or, as we
might say, he may be angry with himself for yielding to an
appetite.[1] Spirit, therefore, must be distinguished from
appetite. On the other hand, the same principle requires
us to distinguish it from reason. For his rational or considerative nature may make him refrain from yielding to
his anger just as from yielding to an appetite; and we also
observe anger in animals, which are not rational, and in
children before they come to the use of reason.[2] This last
remark, as will appear later, is perhaps a hard saying.
Spirit, then, is distinct alike from appetite and reason; but
Socrates argues that it is more akin to reason than appetite
is, and that its function is to strengthen the soul in resisting
appetites of indulging which reason disapproves.[3] In this
connexion he observes that it is never found making common cause with the appetites, when reason decides that
they ought not to oppose it.[4] He does not, of course, mean
that a man is never unreasonably angry; but that he is
never angry with himself for abstaining from a course of
which he disapproves.

Now it might perhaps be objected to this setting up of
spirit as a third something in the soul, besides appetite
and reason, that anger is merely incident to the obstruction
of a man's effort to gratify desire; and that a man whose
better judgement has led him to refrain from gratifying a
desire is nevertheless often out of temper in consequence,
and the more so as his desire was stronger. But this perhaps
can be accounted for consistently with Plato's doctrine;
while it is hard to see why, if anger does arise as now suggested, a man who refrains from gratifying a vehement
desire is ever not angry; for we have seen that it is not by

[1] iv. 439 e 2–440 a 7.   [2] iv. 441 a 5–c 3.
[3] iv. 440 a 8–e 7.   [4] i.e. itself, reason: iv. 440 b 4–7.

greater strength that another desire in such cases over-
bears that left ungratified.

Plato thought that the assumption of a special something
in the soul, such he holds τὸ θυμοειΔές to be, will connect
together and explain not only those observed contrarieties
to which he appeals as evidence for it, but also (*a*) the
occurrence in us of certain particular desires which are not
suitably classed with those characteristic of us either as
appetitive or as intelligent, and whose relative prominence
in the soul will give rise to special types of character, those
of the combative or ambitious man, the φιλόνικος or φιλότιμος, and (*b*) the existence of a peculiar excellence called
courage, and its importance as a factor in justice, or complete virtue. For just as the function of reason is both to
engage us in particular interests or desires of a certain kind,
which we described above as desires to know, and also to
consider the relation of the indulgence of every particular
desire to the good which it makes us conceive and wish
for, so the function of spirit is both to engage us in particular interests or desires of a certain kind, which we may
describe as desires to do (or perhaps, to assert ourselves in
doing), and also to sustain us in the execution of any resolve to which reason has led us. It is this second function
which Socrates has mainly in mind in book iv; but the
first is sufficiently evidenced by passages cited in the note
to p. 51.[1]

The clue to his thought seems to lie in his conviction of
some affinity between spirit and reason. If spirit were as

---

[1] Cf. the excellent remarks of R. L. Nettleship, *Lectures on Plato's
Republic*, p. 157: 'We find that Plato's conception of "spirit" covers three
great facts which seem to him to have a common source. First, it is the
fighting element in man, which makes him resist aggression, and also makes
him aggressive. Secondly, it is something in man (not itself rational, but
seeming to have an affinity with his better self), which makes him indignant
at injustice, and again leaves him a coward when he feels himself in the
wrong. Thirdly (in Book ix), it is that which makes a man competitive
and ambitious.'

remote from reason as appetite is, there would be no
ground for treating the particular desires involving it as a
class apart from those of our appetitive nature; nor could it
well have a different function in action, relatively to reason,
from that of appetite, viz. to provide particular desires,
whose indulgence at any moment reason must consider.
But appetites like hunger and thirst arise in us, not without a cause, but without our thinking of a reason why we
should feel them, nor do we even justify to ourselves
desires excited by the thought of something to be got by
any reason why we should feel them.[1] When, on the other
hand, we feel anger, we do normally give ourselves a
reason for feeling it, and often think, with Jonah, that we
do well to be angry. Therefore Aristotle observes that
spirit in a way waits on a reason,[2] but appetite not; and
hence that not to control one's appetite is baser than not to
control one's spirit, for the latter weakness is in a way a
yielding to argument. There are, no doubt, diseased conditions in which men seem to develop anger as thought-
lessly as thirst; but we should not consider susceptibility to
such outbursts as a manifestation of spirit. And if we ask
by what in the last resort a man justifies to himself his
anger, is it not rather that he (or perhaps another) has been
wronged or slighted than merely that some desire of his has
gone unsatisfied? Only because he has some notion that
he (or another) had a right to its satisfaction does he feel
angry. Hence it seems foolish to be angry with inanimate
obstructions, and we look for personal causes.

> We for a certainty are not the first
>   Have sat in taverns while the tempest hurled
> Their hopeful plans to emptiness, and cursed
>   Whatever brute and blackguard made the world.[3]

---

[1] We may of course justify to ourselves gratifying them by a reason
why we should gratify them.

[2] ἀκολουθεῖ τῷ λόγῳ πως. See the whole passage, *Eth. Nic.* VII. vi. I,
1149 a 24–b 3.

[3] A. E. Housman, *Last Poems*, IX.

For the same reason, as Plato says, if a man thinks he is being wronged, he will go all lengths to get his way, unless his reason checks him.[1] He may have desired but little what he has been opposed in trying to get; but because the opposition is a wrong to or a slight upon himself, to get it becomes a point of honour.[2]

Now the thought that I have been wronged or slighted presupposes some degree of self-consciousness, and some sense of the distinction between myself as one, and the multiplicity of my particular desires. No doubt, as Kant said, any consciousness of a manifold depends on a synthetic unity of apperception; and a consciousness really confined to the passing moment would not be a consciousness at all.[3] But a sense of oneself in distinction from passing states and desires is something further; and the thought of a right to have one's desires satisfied is no particular desire. It does mark an advance towards intelligence or rationality, in comparison of mere appetite.

Plato then seems to be right in holding that the nature of anger points to a real difference between that in the soul of which it, and that of which any appetite, is a manifestation; and that this factor, the spirited, τὸ θυμοειδές, is more akin to reason than the appetitive. And he seems right further in thinking that there are desires (or ἐπιθυμίαι in the wider sense of that word, in which it includes more than manifestations of the ἐπιθυμητικόν) specially connected with this factor in the soul, and a special type of character dependent on their predominance in it.

We said above that these desires might be roughly distinguished from those of the rational and appetitive factors in the soul as desires to do. Wanting to do is clearly different both from wanting to know and wanting to have.

---

[1] *Rep.* iv. 440 c 7–d 3.

[2] Cook Wilson therefore used to say that τὸ θυμοειδές corresponds to a man's sense of the worth of his own personality.

[3] Cf. Plato, *Philebus*, 21 a 8–d 5.

Appetites may be satisfied for us; what we want to have may be given us; with children and domestic animals this largely happens. Doing is carrying out our purposes ourselves; it is to that extent self-assertiveness, though we call a man self-assertive in a disparaging sense when he insists too strongly on the execution of his particular purposes, merely because they are his. John Grote coined the word *acturience* to express the difference of this kind of desire from appetite. '*Acturience*, or desire of action, in one form or another, . . . is quite as much a fact of human nature as any kind of want or need.'[1] Now action is constantly against opposition, whether from within oneself, or from inanimate things and animals, or from other persons; and therefore the man in whom acturience is powerful is likely to be combative and φιλόνικος, and to love power. And if men's rationality went no further than is seen in being a man of spirit, in each conceiving himself, whatever he desired, as having a right to get his way merely because it was *his*, then only some 'common power to keep them all in awe' could check the war of all against all that would arise. Hobbes, because he thought that it went no further, believed that a State is held together by force and fear.

Yet the man who can think 'myself' thinks *eo ipso* of that in him, viz. selfhood, whereof his is but an instance. With recognition of himself grows *pari passu* recognition of other selves. This precludes solipsism; no man was ever rescued from solipsism by an argument from analogy or by any other argument, because he never needed to be rescued. He may have grown in intelligence out of a stage in which he neither thought 'myself' nor 'others', but he grew towards the thought of both together. If then he is so far advanced towards rationality as to be capable of recognizing the unity of himself in his particular desires, and is angry when a desire is thwarted because this is a wrong to himself as well as preventing the satisfaction of his desire,

---

[1] *Treatise on the Moral Ideals*, p. 301.

should not a further development towards rationality lead him to see that the rights of selfhood in him must equally attach to it in others? But to see this is to see that he cannot rightly claim either all he wants to have, because he wants it, or to get his own way, just because it is his; since others may want the same, or their way conflict with his. That, in fact, as Plato showed in the argument between Thrasymachus and Socrates, is the objection to the principle of injustice, or πλεονεξία; men may all act on it, but not rationally.

We can now see the proper function of spirit in the soul, its connexion with courage, why courage is one of the components of complete virtue or justice. Every desire, left to itself, would carry a man towards its gratification, and a man is moved by countless desires, some bestial, which it is never good to satisfy, some overmuch, so that it is not good to satisfy them in that measure which they prompt, some whose satisfaction should be surrendered because there are others which it is better to satisfy, or because of other men's rights or wants.[1] Which to satisfy and how far, which to suppress or postpone, it is the work of the rational or considerative in him to judge; a life lived according to that judgement should be a good life, and in its detail goodness should be present and expressed in the way spoken of above. But though as rational he also desires that goodness should be thus present in his life, what Butler would call the authority[2] of this desire is not the same as strength. The particular desires, whose satisfaction his judgement approves or prefers, might be themselves strong enough by their own strength to overbear any others; and this in Plato's view is the best condition of the soul.[3] But if they are not, a man needs to show that

[1] Cf. in this connexion *Rep.* viii. 558 d 8–559 c 7; ix. 571 a 7–572 b 2.
[2] Sermon 11 *Upon Human Nature*: 'Had it (conscience) strength, as it has right; had it power, as it has manifest authority; it would absolutely govern the world.'
[3] *Rep.* vi. 485 d 3–486 b 13; viii. 550 e 4–551 a 6.

resoluteness in holding by the course he judges best which the spirited man shows in getting his own way, though he may not have judged it best. Nor can we expect that the strength of his approved desires should always be such that he can dispense with the aid of such resoluteness. The hope of pleasure, present pain, the fear of pain or of the loss of pleasure, are powerful influences. To hold fast throughout, and in spite also of seductive persuasion to more attractive courses, to what he judges right, requires resolution. And this is the true excellence of one's spirited nature, the virtue of courage.[1] Herein a man in the best way asserts himself. When, in some concern, where perhaps his desire was feeble, his interest not strongly engaged, because he is opposed he goes all lengths to get his way, he is, as we saw, asserting himself, not merely moved by that particular desire or interest. He might say that to get what he wanted had become a matter of principle, but so far the principle is only to get his own way: a dangerous principle if supreme in regulating the conduct of us all, but if working in support of a right judgement concerning the way that one should take, a most valuable principle. When a man forms such a judgement, he is not on that account rid of every impulse and desire moving to action in conflict with what he has judged good or right; but these impulses and desires, though his, will be like rebels against him; if one prevails, he will say that it has got the better of him, whereas if it is overborne, he would never say that his judgement or his resolution had got the better of him, but only of this desire. For he sees *himself* in his considered judgement of what course is right or best, and in his desire for that, rather than in any particular desire that springs up apart therefrom; and to hold fast in action to that against such a particular desire is to assert himself. Hence Plato's definition of courage: 'to hold fast through everything to a right and lawful judgement of what is and is not to be

[1] *Rep.* iii. 412 e 5–414 a 7; iv. 429 e 7–430 c 2.

feared.'[1] For in truth nothing is to be feared except evil; but *knowledge* of good and evil comes to very few. Most of us, in Plato's view, must act upon judgements or opinions induced in us by good laws and sound education and the authority of those who know.

The courage then which Plato sees as an ingredient in justice and in every just act is nearer to what we now call moral than to physical courage. It is not freedom from susceptibility to the passion of fear; for if a man never feels fear nor the impulses it prompts, there is so far nothing for him to hold out against. But it is only in the proper sense excellent or a virtue when acting, as he puts it, in alliance with reason. Otherwise, we might indeed call it an excellence of a part of the soul, but hardly of the soul. Plato perhaps came to realize this more clearly in later years. In the *Laws* he repeats one of the reasons given in the *Republic* for treating courage and wisdom as separate virtues. Courage is concerned with fear which beasts also display, and quite young children; and a soul may grow up courageous naturally, without reason; but without reason no soul ever has grown or will grow up wise and intelligent, for reason is something other.[2] But he also distinguishes sharply the sort of courage which makes merely a good fighter from that which makes a good citizen. Many mercenaries show the first; and they, all but a few, are rash, insolent, unjust, and stupid men; fine as their courage is, yet standing alone it must rank lowest of our four virtues. But the courage of a man steadfast and sound in the battle of life[3] is impossible without complete virtue, and might be called perfect justice. Indeed, no one 'part' of the soul can reach perfection, nor therefore show fully the particu-

---

[1] σωτηρία διὰ παντὸς δόξης ὀρθῆς τε καὶ νομίμου δεινῶν τε πέρι καὶ μή, *Rep.* iv. 430 b 2.

[2] *Scil.* from what displays courage, the spirited in the soul: *Laws*, xii. 963 e 1–9.

[3] So we may render ἐν πολέμῳ χαλεπωτέρῳ, *Laws*, i. 630 a 7; see the whole passage, 629 b 8–630 d 1.

lar excellence of which it is capable, without the rest; and so not without perfection of the soul's rational nature, i.e. wisdom. This is Plato's answer to the question whether virtue is knowledge; no other virtue is perfect without knowledge; and it is his answer also to the question whether the virtues are one or many.

The last twelve stanzas of Browning's poem, *The Statue and the Bust*, show well the character and function of what Plato called τὸ θυμοειδές.

> Let a man contend to the uttermost
> For his life's set prize, be it what it will!
>
> The counter our lovers staked was lost
> As surely as if it were lawful coin:
> And the sin I impute to each frustrate ghost
>
> Is—the unlit lamp and the ungirt loin,
> Though the end in sight was a vice, I say.
> You of the virtue (we issue join)
> How strive you? *De te, fabula!*

And perhaps Plato would have agreed that the lovers were not better for lacking courage. But would Browning have agreed that 'since their end was a crime', their courage, had they shown courage in pursuing it, would have been less of a virtue?

That issue is really connected with the question in what sense reason, spirit, and appetite are *parts* of the soul. Is not the unity of the soul such that no one of them is un-affected by changes in the others? That is why the term 'analysis', as applied to our attempts to understand the soul, is so unsatisfactory. The most vulnerable of Plato's statements about spirit is surely that it is found in irrational animals. Not that the beasts do not possess it; but what after all is its affinity to reason if it can be present in what is quite irrational? If it is true that anger is not on a level with an appetite because it implies some setting of oneself over against the particular appetites, does it not imply a germ of rationality? Appetite, spirit, reason, seem to be on an ascending scale of rationality. One might imagine that an oyster is not unconscious, but lives in an alternation of discomfortable craving while the tide ebbs, and comfortable repletion as it flows, but without memory or expectation. Even those alternating experiences would involve some power of holding the flow of feeling into one. In us, feelings as they come and go, and particular cravings, are different from what they could be in an oyster because thought, through which we are conscious of the unity and order of our states, is so much more developed. But in a spirited horse or dog that advance must have begun. The difference between a dog that will fight for his bone if you try to take it away and some mean-spirited cur that will merely sulk and whine is not simply that the first has a stronger appetite. It is that he has something more than appetite; and it is difficult to describe that something more except in language that would seem to ascribe to him more power of thought than perhaps he possesses. In a man the development of this power has gone so much further that not only is his appetition infected (if any one likes to put it so) by his rational nature, so that he may be said *appetere sub specie boni*; his anger is in reflection recognized by him to be according to the principle of self-assertion. But as his power of thought develops yet further, he can see the irrationality of mere self-assertion. This irrationality, however, is not complete non-rationality, such as might be alleged of a mere craving. It is like the irrationality of Mrs. Nickleby's conversation; even this could not have gone on in a completely non-rational creature. Mere self-assertion is not fully rational, because the principle which inspires it makes of what it inspires a scene of irreconcilable conflict, unless the purpose which a man demands to assert himself in pursuing is one which others, claiming on the same principle to assert themselves, can pursue with him. Spirit, or self-assertiveness, is therefore a factor or 'moment' in the action of the soul; but modified and working differently according as the rationality incipient in it is developed beyond it or not; and anger because another has been slighted belongs to a more advanced stage than one need have reached for anger to be roused by a slight upon oneself.

The sort of unity which, on this view, belongs to a soul is very unlike what we seem to find in the compounds that any science studies, and a stumbling block to those psychologists whose modes of interpretation are drawn from the sciences. Especially when they essay a 'comparative psychology' do they feel the difficulty of bringing into harmony their accounts of 'soul' in animals and in man. There are in principle two ways of dealing with this difficulty. One is to start with the beast, and give such an account of the working of its 'soul' as is consistent with its assumed irrationality and as what may be called a mechanistic psychology allows. Its behaviour is then explained, not necessarily as if it were unconscious, though the Behaviourists have gone as far as this, and such great thinkers as Descartes and Spinoza believed it possible; but in terms of distinct feelings, images, impulses, and desires, interacting with each other according to supposed psychic laws, without the supposition of any self or personality that is more than the aggregate, or whose action is more than the resultant, of these various psychic 'states'. This method then proceeds (but here Descartes and Spinoza are no longer with the Behaviourists) to assimilate the experience or action of a man to the account given of a beast's, with due allowances for a greater degree of complexity but without admitting a real difference of kind. The other way is to start with man, and to give such an account of his soul and its working as the facts seem to require, which after all are accessible to us as what passes in a beast's 'soul' is not; and then to fit to this, as best we can, the account to be given of the beast's 'soul'. This is the only method that deserves the name of genetic psychology; for the transition from less to more complexity is not becoming. But it suffers from a drawback common to every treatment of development. Mechanical principles of explanation may perhaps not be so intelligible as we are apt to suppose; but at any rate they are not less intelligible because applied to a more complex subject. But what exists at different levels of development is never as intelligible at the lower as at the higher level. The undeveloped is the undisplayed. If we ask *what* is undisplayed, we must describe what the thing has not yet come to be. To describe without reference to this a thing imperfectly developed is to treat it as complete, and so we are in danger of falling back into mechanical ways of interpretation; for the less complex is as complete as the more.

The notion of comparative psychology was not strange to the thought of Plato and still less to that of Aristotle, though of course their investigations in the field were slight. Of the two ways of dealing with the difficulty that it presents which has just been mentioned, Plato inclined rather to the second. But in what he says about the display of spirit by irrational creatures he seems to show insufficient appreciation of the difficulty.

We may now try to bring together the chief points in the above attempt to elucidate Plato's account of the soul. If its lines are correct, Plato conceived the soul as a unity of three factors, an appetitive, a spirited, and a rational, whose functions are partly alike, and partly different, and are so related that, while the factors may co-operate, they may also conflict; and again the co-operation will take different forms, according as they exercise their functions more or less rightly, better or worse. For, like Bishop Butler, Plato conceived of human nature as a constitution whose parts were intended to work together in a certain way; though, if we had been asked by whom, he would more readily have said by nature than by God.[1] The functions of these three factors are alike, so far as each is the source of various particular desires. By calling them particular is here meant that they could be discriminated by stating what they were severally for; in this differing from the desire to be happy, or to do one's duty, or to attain for oneself the good, about each of which it has still to be asked, by gratifying what particular desires or doing what particular actions is this desire to be fulfilled. But though all in this sense particular, they differ immensely in comprehensiveness or scope; and this difference is connected partly with the functions which are not alike in all three factors, partly with the interplay of these functions. Plato did not sufficiently consider these differences in comprehensiveness. When he argues, in book ix, that as men decline from justice, so their happiness is less, he overlooks the extent to which the particular desires connected with our appetitive or spirited nature may acquire a comprehensiveness otherwise foreign to them from an interplay of the three factors, in respect of their distinct functions, which can be much the same, from whichever factors the desires to whose satisfaction a man devotes himself may spring.[2]

The least comprehensive of particular desires are the recurrent appetites, whose satisfaction is necessary to the continuance of life but also for the time brings them to an end. A creature purely appetitive would live in alternations of craving and satisfaction, perhaps with memory and anticipation, but without thought of itself as subject

---

[1] Cf. what is said *Rep.* i. 353 d 3 about the soul's ἔργον with Butler's remarks in the *Preface* to the *Sermons*: 'Every work, both of Nature and of art, is a system; and as every particular thing, both natural and artificial, is for some use or purpose out of and beyond itself, one may add to what has already been brought into the idea of a system, its conduciveness to this one or more ends.' But the idea of a system cannot take the place of an immediate recognition of the difference between better and worse, and the duty to realize the better.

[2] Cf. *infra*, pp. 80–1, 107, 140–1, 153–4.

to recurrent cravings, or provision of what was desired not for its own sake but for satisfying them as they arose. Plainly more than appetite is required for this provision. With these cravings Plato classes as grounded in our appetitive nature all other desires to have, though the things for whose possession we crave may be such as, if we were not also intelligent, we should not appreciate or desire.[1]

He classes separately from these, as we have seen, desires to assert oneself either in opposition to others or in action that does not involve such opposition. These, too, may differ in comprehensiveness, and some impulses to activity are on a level in this respect with appetites; but they differ in that they cannot be satisfied for but only by us. Massage is not taking exercise, though it be sometimes as good for the health. But the special function of spirit is to give to any particular desire a new character as one whose satisfaction is pursued, not merely because and in proportion as its object is desired, but because the desire to get one's way is for the moment made precise and determinate in it. This character is independent of the comprehensiveness of the particular desire invested with it. It may invest a mere appetite, or some far-reaching scheme for amassing wealth. It may also invest a desire springing

---

[1] It may be objected that to desire knowledge is also a desire to have; for it is to desire that one may himself know, not merely that knowledge may 'grow from more to more', no matter who has it. But the desires of the φιλοκερδής are to have what, at the moment at least, because he has it, another will lack. No doubt X's knowledge is not Y's knowledge, any more than X's sheep are Y's sheep; and if X acquires a flock desired by Y, another flock may be raised for Y. The notion that there is a fixed stock of material goods, of which if X has more there must always be so much less to go round among others, is no more accurate than the theory of the wage-fund. Nevertheless, at any moment the stock is fixed; it contains many things that cannot be duplicated; and by its nature there is a limit to its increase. Of knowledge, on the other hand, as distinct from the wealth which gives command over opportunities to acquire it, this is not true. On this ground my desire to know, though it is a desire that I should know, is not to be classed with the desires to have.

from our rational nature, as in Browning's Grammarian,
who 'decided not to Live but Know'.

> Back to his studies, fresher than at first,
>   Fierce as a dragon,
> He (soul-hydroptic with a sacred thirst)
>   Sucked at the flagon.

And it may invest any particular desire of the spirited part
itself; and when, as by the 'ambitious man', power is
sought for its own sake, the desire to get one's way, instead
of becoming determinate in a particular desire, becomes
determinate in the desire of that which is to make possible
the satisfaction of any particular desire in which it may
become determinate. Thus the rational nature of the soul
functions in making possible a life of ambition in the same
way as at a lower level it functions in making possible a
life of acquisition.

A third class of particular desires springs directly from
our rational nature; these are desires to know. Here, too,
there are degrees of comprehensiveness, from transitory
manifestations of curiosity to the passion to master some field
of knowledge found more inexhaustible as one proceeds.

In spite, however, of their differences in comprehensiveness, desires of all these three kinds are particular; not only
may they conflict, and the satisfaction of one interfere with
that of another; none of them is such that its fulfilment
would by itself satisfy the soul. But the soul's rational
nature has the special function of making it conceive
and desire a good which would satisfy it completely. This
good can only become determinate in a system whose
constituents might be objects of particular desires; and the
desire of it must invest such particular desires with its own
nature, as we have seen that the desire to assert oneself
may, so that in them we seek not now our own way but the
good. Particular desires not so invested may conflict with
the desire of the good, as they may with one another; but
the desire of it is itself no particular desire; for the good is

what would by itself satisfy the soul.[1] To know of what
constituents, which particular desires might set us seeking,
that in which the good would be seen to be adequately
embodied must be composed, is also the function of the
soul's rational nature. It is the μέγιστον μάθημα: the hardest
thing to know, and most worth knowing.[2]

If then we consider the three factors in that respect in
which their functions are alike, viz. as giving rise in the
soul to divers particular desires, the appetitive may deserve
to be called a many-headed growth.[3] To it belong the
desires to whose satisfaction, or to providing means for
it, most men devote most of their time; and since each
recurrent appetite is a separate desire, the desires of this
'part', though it is hard to say what is *one* desire, may
perhaps be accounted the most numerous. But if we consider the factors in that respect in which their functions are
different, though co-operating in any and every action, the
least simple is, in a way, the rational, in spite of what Plato
says.[4] For the appetitive only engages us in particular
desires; the spirited does this, and makes us capable of
distinguishing from any one of these and its satisfaction
the self whose it is, so giving rise to what is none of those
particular desires, the desire to have one's way, the assertion of the self's claim to satisfy any particular desire; the
rational (1) does what both the others do, viz. it gives rise
to particular desires; it also (2) takes us beyond the stage
which is all that a purely appetitive soul could reach to, at
which we should be merely at the mercy of each desire as
it occurred, and enables us to consider how the possibility
of satisfying the particular desires, from whichever of the
three they spring, may be secured; but besides, (3) it makes
us conceive and desire a good in the attainment of which

---

[1] Therefore Aristotle said of εὐδαιμονία, which he identified, as Plato
did not, with the ἀνθρώπινον ἀγαθόν, that it was πάντων αἱρετωτάτη
μὴ συναριθμουμένη—*Eth. Nic.* i. vii. 8, 1097 b 16.

[2] *Rep.* vi. 504 c 9–506 b 1.   [3] Ibid. ix. 589 b 1.

[4] Ibid. x. 612 a 3–5.

the self would be completely satisfied; and leads us to fill
in the blank conception of this good with detail from the
objects of particular desires. In the second of these functions it may work in the service of either of the other
factors; and this Plato describes as a usurpation of its
function by them. But of course our appetitive or spirited
nature cannot give rise to desires for knowledge, or form
the conception of good, or desire it, or judge what are the
particular desires whose objects, if combined, would furnish
an adequate detail for the conception of good, or how to
secure that these desires may be satisfied as they arise.
Therefore Plato says that without false opinion no one
would do wrong. Opinion, however, is likely to be falsified
under the influence of particular desires, or not to be held
fast; and self-assertion may easily take some other direction
than that of holding against opposition to our better judgement. It is when these things happen, that what is lower
in the soul may be said to usurp the function of the
rational to rule. The constitution of the soul is as it should
be, when each factor engages it in particular desires, such
as are for what the rational includes in its conception of the
good; when the spirited besides exercises its function of
self-assertion on behalf of those desires whose fulfilment
would satisfy the self against any others that may arise; and
when the rational besides exercises the various functions,
peculiar to it, which have just been enumerated. When
this is secured, the 'forms' of the soul are doing each its
proper work, and the man is just. This is the meaning
of Plato's definition of justice in the soul, that it is for
each of them τὰ αὐτοῦ πράττειν καὶ μὴ πολυπραγμονεῖν.[1]

But though in such a case the three factors would work

---

[1] It is sometimes objected that justice, Δικαιοσύνη, is insufficiently distinguished from temperance, σωφροσύνη. But temperance is excellence
of the soul in respect only of its desiderative or orectic nature. We must
not, because of ὁμολοξῶσι in *Rep*. iv. 442 d 1, suppose that Plato thought
each εἶδος of the soul could think. But the definition of temperance there
has to cover it both in πόλις and in Ἰδιώτης.

harmoniously together as they should, they may also work harmoniously together in prosecution of some organized plan of life which a right judgement would not pronounce good. If a man at times became vaguely conscious of a discrepancy between his notion of good, and the detail he was treating as adequate to it; or if particular desires, whencesoever arising, whose satisfaction was not included in his plan, induced a more definite sense of this discrepancy; or if he lacked resolution, in the face of such desires, to hold by his plan, then no doubt the harmony of his soul would be disturbed. But without these things occurring a man may live a life that satisfies a wide range of acquisitive desires, gives play to his love of self-assertion, and exercises his intelligence in planning what objects to pursue, and how to secure their attainment, and in the pursuit of divers forms of knowledge; and yet in living this life he need not always have proper regard to the rights of others. Such a man will not be at the mercy of his lusts, like the tyrannic man, nor of the chance succession of particular desires, better and worse, whose unregulated influence in determining a planless life characterizes those called by Plato democratic men. He need not be the mere seeker after wealth whom Plato calls oligarchic, nor so lacking in interest for the things of the mind as those called timocratic. The right interplay of the functions of the different forms of the soul's being will be preserved, though not in the service of a perfectly just life; and this man (at any rate in a State not so perfectly just that he will be promptly called to account) may practise much injustice and still be happy.[1] If this seems to follow from Plato's account of the soul, and also to accord with experience, as his contention that men are always more unhappy as they are less just does not accord, we may be the more disposed to think he based his account of the soul on contemplation of the facts, and did not accommodate it to other parts of his argument.

[1] Cf. *infra*, p. 154.

M

IV

PLATO'S *REPUBLIC*: THE COMPARISON BETWEEN
THE SOUL AND THE STATE

No thought recurs more constantly in the *Republic* than that of a similarity of some sort between a State and the human soul. It is found already in the first book;[1] it is made the ground of Socrates' proposal to look at justice and injustice first in States, if we are to discover what they are in men and which is truly profitable;[2] it is defended at length in the fourth book, when Socrates comes to discuss the nature of the soul;[3] it is elaborated in arguing that the outstanding types of better and worse States and soul are the same in kind and number;[4] it underlies the first of the arguments by which Socrates endeavours to prove that, as a man's life declines from virtue, so it does from happiness;[5] as well as being implied elsewhere by the way. It is, therefore, clearly very important, if we would understand Plato's thought in the dialogue, not to misapprehend his meaning in using this comparison.

Writers often speak of his analogy between the State and soul; and he is credited, or charged, with arguing from the first to the nature of the second. An attempt has been made in the preceding Essay to show that his account of the soul's nature was based on a direct consideration of the soul itself; and in any case the term 'analogy' is ill chosen. For what he held was that State and soul were systems whose constitution was in certain respects identical. It would be better to speak of the identity of constitution in State and soul.

It is sometimes supposed that his view may be expressed by saying that he held the State, or society, to be an organism; and Herbert Spencer, in an early Essay on *The Social Organism*, afterwards for the most part incorporated

---

[1] i. 352 a 5. [2] ii. 368 d 1. [3] iv. 434 d 2 seq.
[4] v. 449 a 1–5; viii–ix. 576 c 9. [5] ix. 576 c 10–580 c 8.

in *The Principles of Sociology*,[1] fancied that he was doing in a more scientific manner what Plato had very imperfectly attempted. But by an organism is meant a living body; and Plato, whatever exactly he meant by a State, was comparing it not with a living body but with a soul. It is true that the points of Herbert Spencer's comparison show that he did not know what *he* was comparing it with, whether with a soul or with a living body, any more than he knew what he meant by the other term of his comparison, a State, whose parts are sometimes counties, roads, houses, railways and telegraph wires, sometimes men, industries, cattle, and vegetation, sometimes the monarch, his ministers, and the general body of citizens. We need not pursue these vagaries. But we may spend a little time considering whether it is a useful description of Plato's view to say that he regarded the State as an organism.

The description is plainly only useful if we know what we mean by an organism. Now we know what we call by that name, viz. animals and plants; but what we wish to ascribe to them all in common by calling them organisms is harder to say. It has been said that the features characteristic of an organism are spontaneity, irritability, assimilation, and reproduction; but in the sense in which these terms are intended by a biologist, they cannot be predicated of a State. Kant defined an organism as a whole of which the parts are reciprocally ends and means, and McTaggart as a whole which is the end of its parts. But both these definitions really imply an attempt to explain what happens in living bodies after the fashion of what we find in the purposive activity of men, individually or in communities such as States, and therefore it is absurd to suppose that the notion of an organism as thus defined can be used to throw light on the nature of a State. For so long as we do not think of what happens in organisms in terms of purpose, we have no right to speak of means and ends, but

[1] Vol. i, pt. ii, ch. 3.

only of conditions and consequences; and if we do think of
what happens in them in terms of purpose, we shall have
to look beyond bodies and their parts. Consider some
vertebrate. If its parts are limbs, head, and trunk, in what
sense are they reciprocally ends and means? Blowing up a
bridge is a means to preventing the passage of an army,
because if the bridge is destroyed the army cannot pass; and
its destruction is brought about with that purpose, though
not by the bridge; there is a taker of the means. Now it may
be true that if the limbs do not grow healthily neither will
the head or trunk, and vice versa (though some otherwise
healthy animals may have a limb faulty from birth); but
there is no such time relation between their respective
growths as between means and end, nor do the parts
reciprocally bring about their own growths with the purpose of producing the other parts. McTaggart's definition,
if pressed, turns out equally unsatisfactory, so long as the
whole in question is the corporeal whole. When, in
Ezekiel's vision,[1] the dry bones came together, bone to his
bone, and then flesh came up upon them, the parts of each
man were not means to the aggregate they constituted, any
more than 5s. and 7s. are means to 12s.; at best their coming
together was a means to the institution of a certain form
or organization in the aggregate they made. It is not the
whole and the parts, but the form of the whole and the
processes in the parts, to which this language of end and
means is applicable, if we are to use it at all; and not only,
therefore, are we thinking, when we use it, in terms of
purpose, but we are looking beyond the organism as a
corporeal whole to some form of organization, εἶδος, to be
realized in it. And if the parts are limbs, trunk, and head,
or sensory organs, it is their forms, too, whose realization
can be called each an end relatively to processes in the
other parts; though, if Dr. J. S. Haldane is right, we cannot
treat any one such part as merely a structure provided for

---

[1] Cap. 37, vv. 1–14.

the sake of the functioning of others, like the fixed parts of a machine in relation to the functions of its moving parts, because the metabolism of the body involves that too, and the maintenance of its form depends on the due functioning of the others.[1] The fact is that those who talk about the organic nature of society or of the State are primarily concerned to indicate that it cannot be explained like a machine, but they would generally be hard put to it to say in what respects it is to be explained like an organism, or how an organism is to be explained. Even the famous analogy used by Menenius Agrippa and by St. Paul—'Shall the eye say to the foot, I have no need of thee?' and 'If one member suffer, all the members suffer with it'—which Plato also uses,[2] is really vitiated by the fact that it is not the eye which needs the foot, or suffers when the foot is hurt; it is the man, with whose whole body is somehow connected his one consciousness, that suffers, whatever part is hurt, and needs them all; and to this fact there is nothing analogous in a State. Herbert Spencer explained this by there being no social sensorium—i.e. no part of the State corresponding to the brain in a human body; the 'discreteness of parts prevents it': as if you could make a brain for the State out of a number of citizens, if only you could bring them into some close physical union.[3] But the real difference is that citizens are conscious and the State not, whereas the parts of a man's body are not and a man is. It is no doubt true both that what happens to some parts of the body may affect the health of other parts and that in a State what happens to some citizens may affect the welfare of others; but it is also said that, when European women gave up using hair-nets, the population of a whole region of China was ruined, though European women do not belong to the same State as those Chinese.

---

[1] See e.g. *Organism and Environment as illustrated by the Physiology of Breathing*, c. iv. [2] *Rep.* v. 462 c 10.

[3] *Principles of Sociology*, vol. i, pt. ii, ch. ii, § 222.

It may be questioned whether the analogy between the
State and an organism has any but a literary and rhetorical
value. Nothing can be inferred about a State from the
study of an organism, and what is supposed to be so inferred is really based either on an independent study of
States or on general considerations from which those who
have studied States and those who have studied organisms
can draw inferences independently about either.

But this is not the comparison on which Plato builds.
Where he uses it, as in the passage just referred to, it is
irrelevant to the underlying thought of his comparison.
He knew that sometimes illustrations from things sensible
and familiar may be helpful towards understanding things
not sensible; but also that 'what is incorporeal, being
noblest and greatest, can be clearly shown only by discourse, and not otherwise'.[1] Elsewhere he warns us of the
danger of similes: a safe man should above all things ever
be on his guard against them, so slippery they are.[2] Now
a State, really, is incorporeal. It is not an aggregate of
human organisms, more or less densely dispersed over a
territory; it has no weight, though these have an aggregate
weight expressible in thousands of tons. It cannot, then,
be profitably compared to an organism, and Plato does not
so compare it; he compares it to a soul, which is incorporeal too.

There are those who believe that what are called the
feelings, thoughts, and actions of a soul are really no
more than events in or referable to a living body; but
Plato did not. And whatever the difficulties about the
relation of what we call soul and body, we are at any rate
familiar with the distinction, and with at least plausible
grounds for drawing it. We are less accustomed to recog-

---

[1] *Politicus*, 286 a 5–7: τὰ γὰρ ἀσώματα, κάλλιστα ὄντα καὶ μέγιστα,
λόγῳ μόνον ἄλλῳ δὲ οὐδενὶ σαφῶς δείκνυται.

[2] *Sophistes*, 231 a 6: τὸν δὲ ἀσφαλῆ δεῖ πάντων μάλιστα περὶ τὰς
ὁμοιότητας ἀεὶ ποιεῖσθαι τὴν φυλακήν· ὀλισθηρότατον γὰρ τὸ γένος.

nize that there are somewhat similar grounds for distinguishing a State from the 'body of citizens'. 'The State (or
constitution)', said Aristotle, 'is a kind of life a city leads.'[1]
Life here is not meant in the sense in which a biologist
uses the word; the proper Greek for that is ζωή, not βίος.
The life meant is something that goes on in consciousness.
But Aristotle was not saying that a city lived a conscious
life distinct from those of the citizens, as one citizen lives
a conscious life distinct from those of others. There is a
kind of unity into which the lives of the citizens enter, in
virtue of their living together with common purposes.
That is also what Plato thought; it is true that as things
are this unity is sadly to seek; existing States are each
many, and not one; at the very least each is two, one of
rich and one of poor.[2] But this is the great evil for which
he would find a remedy; the greatest good that could befall a city is that it should be united and made one; and to
this end nothing can so much contribute as that, so far as
possible, the same events, falling out well or ill, should
bring joy and sorrow to all citizens alike.[3] The unity of a
State, then, in Plato's view, depends on community of
feeling among its citizens; but that in turn requires community of interest and purpose. That a common purpose
makes men one, not as organisms, but in the lives they
live, is sufficiently familiar on a small scale. Consider, for
example, a conspiracy; it is constituted by unity of purpose.
If the customers of a bank, by mere unhappy coincidence,
were all to go and withdraw their deposits on the same
morning, the bank might be broken, but there would have
been no conspiracy. For this it is required that they should
have agreed together to do it in order to break the bank.

Of course such concerted action is impossible unless
there are men to take it; and these men are not disembodied
souls. The life a city leads requires the bodies of its

[1] *Pol.* VI (IV). xi. 1295 a 40: ἡ γὰρ πολιτεία βίος τίς ἐστι πόλεως.
[2] *Rep.* iv. 422 e 7–423 b 2.   [3] Ibid. v. 462 a 9–c 6.

citizens, just as the life a man leads, not in the biological sense of the physical growth, maturity and decay of the organism, with its constant metabolism, but in the sense in which it can be ascribed to a soul, requires nevertheless the body of the man. But we do not commonly reflect on the fact that the 'body of citizens' who are said (or which is said) to have and execute purposes is from one point of view the bodies of the citizens, and yet that these no more are the State than a man's body is his soul.

That there is a State so long, and only so long, as there is this concerted action of its citizens may be seen if we consider thus. It has been at times supposed that all the movements of men are effects merely of what happens to and in their bodies, and that their thoughts and feelings are by-products of the same causes, having no influence on their movements, otiose and 'epiphenomenal'. Let us then suppose further that these were not produced, but still the same movements occurred as now. At once it follows that there would be no States, any more than there are States in 'the sea-blooms and the oozy woods which wear The sapless foliage of the ocean'. And that Plato realized this is borne out not only by his holding that what unifies a State is community of interest, so that its members rejoice and grieve together, but by what he says its virtues are. Its wisdom is that shown in the care of its members' common concerns, in rightly understanding how best they may consort with one another and it with foreign States; its courage that shown in defending against danger from the purposes of foreigners or dissentient citizens the form of life whose maintenance is the chief common concern of its members; its temperance the acquiescence of all in the parts respectively assigned to each, their willingness to live their proper lives; so that when these three excellences are all displayed together, the State in its 'corporate' life will be just.[1]

[1] *Rep.* iv. 428 a 11–434 d 1.

What makes a State just, then, is the maintenance of the right relations not between classes of citizens but between those actions of these classes in and through which the kind of life they can best live together is to be realized.[1] If we bear this in mind, we shall be better prepared to understand what Plato meant by saying that justice or injustice was the same thing in a State and in an individual soul. For in a soul it is the maintenance of the right relations between the actions or activities of its different 'forms' or factors or 'parts'. And/if it be said that the activity of one of these is not an act of the man, and that the relations among acts of men and among activities of the soul involved in any one act are not the same, the answer is that what the acts of a man are depends on the relations among these activities of his soul, and the relations among the acts of men are grounded in what these acts are; so that in the last analysis it is the relations among the activities in the souls of men that determine the justice or injustice alike of men and States. But if this is so, and is really Plato's doctrine, it is not to the identity of constitution in soul and State that we must look for arguments to defend the permanent assignment to different and non-intermarrying classes of citizens of government and defence on the one hand, and of the various 'economic' callings on the other. Nor in fact is it by appealing to this identity that Plato defends it; but having argued for it on other grounds, he mistakenly treats it as a feature of the identity which he believes in.

There is a way to understand this identity, different from that which Plato follows, but in some respects better. We may start not, as he does, by contemplating in description the growth of a city from its first germ as a group of men mutually supplying each other with the simplest necessaries of life more adequately than any one man could supply himself with them alone;[2] but by so contemplating the

---

[1] ὄντινα τρόπον αὐτή . . . πρὸς αὑτὴν . . . ἄριστα ὁμιλοῖ, Rep. iv. 428 d 1.
[2] Rep. ii. 369 a 5 seq.

growth, in a community already established, of some large undertaking that gives occupation to a multitude of men and women, from its first germ as a work undertaken by one. Many examples might be given: the creation of the Polytechnic movement by Quintin Hogg, of the Salvation Army by General Booth, of his great system of Homes for orphans by Dr. Barnardo; or, on a larger scale, of great world religions by their founders, or of political revolutions by leaders like Hitler or Mussolini. For the sake of giving definiteness to the picture, we may imagine how the Salvation Army grew up; historical accuracy of detail is not required in order that the principle should be clear.

As a young man William Booth was distressed by the misery and crime which he saw around him in the poorest parts of London, and resolved to do what he could to help. That brought into his life new tasks, which in one way were to take precedence of all others, yet in another, so long as he was single-handed, must be postponed to those, without discharging which what Plato calls the necessary appetites, for food and drink, sleep, shelter, and clothing, could not be satisfied; for the satisfaction of these appetites was necessary to maintaining the health and strength required if the work he put first was to be carried on. What, then, was the problem constantly presented to him? First he must think out his plan of life. In doing this he must take into account as facts his passionate desire to help his unfortunate neighbours, his physical needs, the demands upon his time of the work by which he earned means whether to meet those needs or relieve the wants of others. Nor need we suppose he had no other desires and interests, for the satisfaction and pursuit of which he must ask whether any place in his scheme of life could be found. And we must remember that it was not possible to think out this scheme unless at the same time he gave precision and detail to his conception of helping others, settling with himself what in particular that meant that he should do. All this, if he was to succeed, required what Plato calls wisdom; the task belonged to his reason or intelligence, τὸ λογιστικόν.

But it is only to be expected that he should have felt many desires, whose indulgence would interfere with his salvationist work. In fact, for example, he fell in love, married, and had a family. It happened that his wife shared his evangelistic zeal, and he was spared the pain of conflicting loyalties to her and to the cause he had at heart; but even so, his family must have made rightful demands upon his time, and he may well have been sometimes tempted for their sakes to neglect that cause. Weariness again must be fought; and in particular the work frequently exposed him to ridicule or even danger of bodily harm. To go through with it, in the face at once of opposition from others and of that proceeding from his own competing interests and desires, required resolution, or courage: to be shown, Plato would say, by the spirited nature of his soul, τὸ θυμοειΔές.

Thirdly, we must not forget that all the time there were the various interests and desires, for which, or some of them, his wisdom found a place in the scheme of his life. These included the dominant interest in helping the unfortunate; and though he would no doubt at times have judged it well, or that he ought, to do what for itself he was not inclined to, yet for the most part in what he did he would have been satisfying particular desires that prompted him to do certain things before or independently of his judging that he ought, or that it was well, to do them. And those desires concerning whose satisfaction he judged contrariwise must obviously have been felt before and independently of that judgement. For the execution of the scheme of life he had adopted as the best, it was plainly important that these last desires (which a man can hardly help feeling) should, as it were, die away upon his judgement against indulging them; and that his desire should so far as possible be towards whatever he judged it incumbent on him to do. This is true in respect of all particular desires, not only of those springing from one's appetitive nature; and the excellence required in one's desires, which Plato calls σωφροσύνη, or temperance, is therefore an excellence of the whole soul, as rational, as spirited, and as appetitive, since it belongs to the first two of these, as well as to the third, to engage him in particular desires.

So far we have merely expounded with some detail, in a not wholly imaginary example, Plato's view of how in an individual soul its three 'forms' should work together, and in displaying their different appropriate excellences make the whole soul, or its whole life, just. We must next notice in particular that William Booth's salvationist work, though taking precedence in his life, was not and could not be his whole life. It and the rest therefore had to be adjusted together in his life. Nevertheless it, considered by itself, is a sort of whole, whose component activities must be adjusted to one another in the plan of the work. And we saw that wisdom was needed not less to settle what in particular he should include in that plan than what, besides its execution, he should include in his life. We may add that courage was required of him in carrying it out, as well as in those parts of his life that fell outside it; and in fact that, within it, as a partial whole, the same excellences were required which were required in the whole life of which it was a part, and must co-operate in the same way.

All this is on the assumption that he was working single-handed; but in fact he soon attracted others to help him, so that there came to be what is known as the Salvation Army. And without others' help he obviously could have done little. Still, there are a few (like Napoleon) who are able in a day to do the work of several ordinary men. Let us make for a moment the extravagant supposition that General Booth had powers far beyond Napoleon's, of preaching in many places at once, providing funds by working at one place while preaching at another, devoting the same time also to correspondence, and so forth. What has already been said of the need for him to show wisdom in planning his life, courage in holding to his plan in action, and temperance, would still apply if this supposition could be fact; and it would still be true as well that the work which, if he had not these miraculous powers, would require an army, would not be his whole life, but only a whole within that, and that these excellences would need to be shown co-operating in the same way in his Salvationist work as in his whole life.

Now this is not less true because in fact the work could not all be done by him, but required an army. When a man calls others in to help him in carrying out a work that has expanded beyond his unaided powers, what they do in its execution is related to the rest of what the execution of the work requires precisely as if it were done by him. Take, for instance, the appointment of a secretary. A man may engage a secretary to do the correspondence which his work requires either in order to be free to do other things required by it, or in order to have time for occupations lying outside it; but either way the letters required by it are much the same, whether he or the secretary writes them; and he will probably at first dictate the letters, and may long continue to dictate, or at least to inspect before dispatch, the most important. And there are many other parts of a man's work, as it grows, that may be similarly delegated; but however many they are, their place in the work is the same as if the one man did them all; and what exactly they should be has to be determined by the same kind of planning, requiring the same wisdom on the part of him who plans the work, however many persons are to be concerned in its execution. And it may well be that the originator of such a movement as the Salvation Army may, as the work grows, have no time for anything except planning, and directing others, and later not even for all of that; so that, while retaining the general direction, he must leave to others to work out the detail; and this working out of the detail holds the same place in the work of the organization, as one organization, which it would have held had he still been able to develop his general directions into detail himself.

On the other hand, whereas, if all the work could have been done by one man, only he would have been called upon to fit it into the whole scheme of his life, now that it is shared out among many members of one organization, each of them must fit his own share of it into the whole scheme of his own life. Hence, even if all the planning and direction of the work is still concentrated in one man, and the wisdom required for that is demanded only of him, the wisdom required for planning one's life so as to make room for executing the tasks comprised in the work is demanded of every one to whom any of these tasks is assigned. Equally there is demanded of every one courage or resolution not to fail in his particular task, just as originally this was demanded of the one and only man concerned in carrying on the work. And what was said about the need in him for temperance, in the sense explained, may now be extended to all members of the organization.

So what specially requires wisdom for its right performance has thus come to be divided; the planning and direction of the work remains with one or a few at the head of the organization; whose life or lives must also be planned so as to make room for carrying out the first-mentioned planning; but this second-mentioned planning is equally called for from every one concerned in carrying out any part of the work. From all, whether director or subordinate, wisdom is called for to order his own life, but only from the director to order the work in which they are engaged together. And it may well happen that what specially requires courage or resolution may similarly be divided. At first the man who started alone but has brought in others to help may, by his own energy and spirit and determination, inspire them with the same resolution which he shows himself. But the larger the organization grows, the more difficult this is; and he may then assign to others not tasks comprised in the execution of the work planned, but that of inspiring those on whom these tasks devolve with the resolution to carry them out. In the army this is expected of non-commissioned officers, in an industry of foremen or overseers. It is plain that the duty can only be suitably assigned to men possessed of more grit or courage or resolution than those whom they are to keep up to the mark. Yet just as the director cannot undertake to order the private lives of all members of the organization, but having told them what are their tasks in it must leave them to arrange their lives accordingly, so these overseers or auxiliaries (to use Plato's word) cannot stimulate the executant members—the Δημιουργοί—in all they do, but only in what they do that belongs to the work of the organization. Some tasks indeed requiring courage they can take over altogether. If it is a matter of defending the executant members from attacks by outsiders, this may be done altogether by a specialized set of members—the army in a State, the police in a strike, and so forth. But so far as the executant members' work is in jeopardy from their own sloth or negligence or love of pleasure or from interests, however praiseworthy otherwise, in competing directions, though an overseer may help them, stimulating resolution in them when by, yet they will need resolution in the whole conduct of their lives, as well as in what belongs to the work of the organization, and must in some measure provide it for themselves.

The work of the organization, therefore, falls into parts of three sorts. There is the planning and directing; there is the carrying out of the various jobs included in the plan; and there is defence of those who carry these out from outside interference, and keeping them up to the mark. If there were no outside interference, and every member could be trusted to let nothing divert his energies from the job assigned to him, the persons entrusted with this last contribution could be dispensed with. But in a large organization not every one can be thus trusted; and if the organization is a State, instead of being one defended from outside interference by the forces of a State within which it works, then it must itself defend its workers. These three sorts of work in the whole work of the organization will fall to different members, and yet be mutually adjusted and co-operate in it. Together they will make the life of the organization. And in respect of this life of the organization, if all are loyal, it is enough that those who direct should have the wisdom to plan it, and certain others the courage or resolution to defend and sustain those who execute the plan.

But every piece of work comprised in the life of the organization is done by some individual member. Therefore it has a place not only along with pieces done by other members in the life of the organization, but also along with all else done by that individual in his own life. And here it belongs to the plan of his life, as there to the plan of the life of the organization. These plans must be adjusted together; and that is true for all the members, so that in the last resort the plan of no one individual life can rightly be settled without regard to the plans of the rest, since none can rightly be settled without regard to that of the work of the organization which they co-operate in carrying on.

In any small organization evoking the enthusiasm of all its members, this mutual regard may be observed. Where the organization is one in whose purposes its members are little interested on its own account, and from which they can easily withdraw, withdrawal is an alternative to adjusting one's life to those of other members in the way required. From the State a citizen can with difficulty or, it may be, noway withdraw. Here therefore it is very necessary that there should be such a scheme of common life as will offer to the citizens tasks suitable to their capacities, complementary to and not clashing with one another, so far as any general direction of the life of the State is attempted; and some general direction, some plan of life together and division of occupations, there surely must be.

The difficulty is to know how far it should go. Most people would agree now that the once fashionable distinction between self-regarding and other-regarding actions, by reference to which it was hoped that the proper limits of State interference with individual lives could be fixed, breaks down. No action of a man who lives in society is wholly irrelevant to his life as a citizen; at least it affects his capacity or his readiness to do the other-regarding actions required of him. Yet much must be left to the decision of the individual, not only because, if he did not in any way order his own life, he could show little virtue, but also because the task of working out into the ultimate detail of all particular actions a scheme of common life is impossible. With a limited purpose, like that of the Salvation Army, or of a business or a farm, it may more nearly be done. But theirs are purposes within the whole community, which certain members choose to pursue together and which the State permits but need not prescribe to them. Of some purposes, however, it may be the business of Government to secure the pursuit—e.g. the conveyance of mails. And there are others, which if any members of the community chose to pursue they would be stopped by the Government as doing what was 'contrary to public policy'. There is need of some supreme authority to decide what these two sorts are. So far as the community is organized to provide this authority, it is organized as a State. Those invested with the authority are the rulers of the State. Their task is to determine what sorts of particular purposes shall be included in the life of the State and what forbidden: some of them perhaps such as individuals can carry out, many requiring organizations or associations of individuals. This is really a much harder task than the direction of a particular association like the Salvation Army; for in the latter a more or less definite conception of what has to be provided for is given at the outset; but in this the problem is for what to provide. 'If what occupations were how distributed among the members of this community would their life together be the best of which they are capable?' is plainly a harder question than is the question, 'If what tasks were how distributed among those who can be drawn into this business, who are employed upon this farm, who may be enrolled in the Salvation Army, will the business or the farm prosper best, will men be saved in the largest numbers from misery and vice and crime?' And the wisdom required to answer it is more like that required of each of us in ordering his own life than like that required in directing an organization with limited purpose. When I have some limited and definite purpose, my knowledge of means and ends will help me to determine what its fulfilment requires, and even if the detail of what I would achieve needs filling in, I shall be helped here by having an outline or general notion already in my mind. But when I deliberate what purposes to find place for in my life, there is no such help; all I can do is to pronounce upon different schemes of life that suggest themselves, which is better and which worse. Both tasks require wisdom; but the rarer and harder wisdom is that which finds the best answer to the second problem. And that on a large scale is the wisdom required of a statesman and ruler; for the other he can go to experts, if he has not himself the special knowledge required. Experts may know and tell him what means are required for the achievement in the life of the community of some particular ends, which he would like included in the general plan, and what consequences its achievement is likely to produce; and this knowledge is most important. Thus the Limited

Liability Acts made possible a great increase of large-scale enterprise, and such enterprise was a valuable element in the life of the country; but they did much to destroy friendly personal relations between employers and employed; the right sort of economic or psychological expert might perhaps have foreseen this. But if it had been foreseen, the question would have still remained, are the benefits of so much enterprise worth purchasing at that cost? No technical or expert knowledge can answer that, and therefore to fill the highest posts in government with men of science is no solution for the troubles of States. They have knowledge which is needed. They may have the wisdom required of rulers as well. But just as likely they may not.

In illustrating Plato's doctrine that in the life of the State the functions of his three classes are related together like those of the three 'forms' of the soul in the life of an individual, we took an illustration from the growth of a great organization like the Salvation Army, because there two things could be seen: (1) when jobs belonging to and constituting the work of the Army were done, some by one man and some by others, they were related together precisely as while the same man did them all; and as then different jobs had made demand on different 'forms' of his soul, so now they made those demands on those same factors in the souls of others; (2) as, while one man did the work single-handed, the virtues of the several 'forms' of the soul were required, and might be displayed, both in it and in the ordering of his whole life in which it was included, so afterwards these virtues were required both in it, and in each man's ordering of his whole life, in which life not now it, but the particular job in it on which he was engaged was included. When we turn from a comparison between the individual lives of the members of such an organization and the life of the organization, to consider Plato's comparison between the individual lives of citizens and the life of the State whose citizens they are, *mutatis mutandis* these two statements still hold good. What are the *mutanda*, the qualifications required? The first strengthens the comparability. The wisdom required of a statesman is more like that required of each man in the general direction of his life than is the wisdom required of him or those directing an organization with a given and limited purpose. On the other hand, just because it is much easier to see what different jobs there are to provide for in the carrying out of a given and limited purpose than to see by including what limited purposes in the State the citizens of the State will live best, the unifying function of the wisdom of the rulers in a State is less manifest, and unfortunately often less present, than is that of the directors of a lesser and limited association. Further, when, as often happens, men enter into such an association voluntarily, it may be presumed that their particular desires chime in with its purpose; and so that 'temperance' which consists in a man's various particular desires having severally such degrees of strength as makes easy his following the plan of life which he approves, and wherein scope is given to some at the expense of others, is more likely to pervade the work of the association. Unhappily, to industrial undertakings, which nowadays fill so large a part of men's lives, many belong more of necessity, because otherwise they cannot earn enough to satisfy their 'necessary appetites', than because their natural interest is towards doing work of the sort required of them there; hence in an undertaking of this kind a man's capacity for desire is less likely to be drawn off from other directions into the service which it requires of him. The same is true in the all-embracing association of the State, which we do not enter voluntarily, and where the scheme of associated life, to which we should all contribute, is commonly imperfectly worked out, and so far as operative is difficult for most of us to apprehend. Indeed, the doctrine that what best profits the community profits each member best, i.e. that there is a possible ordering of the community through which all the citizens will live better than any could by living otherwise than as it prescribes, is a hard doctrine. Plato tries to maintain it; and if a man *lives best* who does what duty requires of him, it may be true. But *happiness*, which Plato vindicates in greatest measure for the best or most just life, is another matter. Unless a man's concern for the common weal is so deep that successfully to make his contribution towards that will compensate him for all disappointments elsewhere, he might surely be happier, in certain conditions, if he did the duties of his station less scrupulously; and such deep concern for the common weal implies a 'temperance' of the particular desires hardly as a rule to be expected. All the more necessary, in Plato's view, is the work of the Auxiliaries, in whom courage to serve the State, 'though it were to their own injury', is strong enough spontaneously for them to be able to exact the necessary service from weaker natures. But he allows that the common purposes of the State may be sufficiently attained, even though there is considerable failure among the commonalty or δημιουργοί to do their proper work.[1] So long as its order and institutions are preserved, its laws and education sound, its defence secured, its economic needs supplied, luxury with its attendant evils avoided, and its numbers regulated, we may hope for the best. And for this we must rely, in his opinion, on a select body controlling the whole State, a few of the best and wisest among whom direct and the remainder police the State, and defend it and hold the various subordinate executive positions.

Now many might be disposed to say that, while there is some real correspondence between, on the one hand, what the wisdom of the directing 'Guardians' and the courage of the 'Auxiliaries' do for the common interests and con-

[1] *Rep.* iv. 434 a 3–8.

cerns of the State and, on the other, what an individual's
wisdom and courage do for the general conduct of his own
life, Plato's analogy breaks down when he goes on to compare the function of the commonalty[1] in the State with that
of the appetitive principle in the soul, and indeed that this
comparison is libellous, for the virtues of the commonalty
have often sustained the State against the vices of the
ruling class. Plato, indeed, thought that, when a people
saw their rulers setting chief store by military power, or
wealth, or freedom to follow each desire as it arose, or
sensual pleasure, they were likely to do the same themselves. He may have been justified within the range of the
experience of his day; and a virtuous peasantry under
vicious rulers is perhaps less probable where slavery prevails; but anyhow, it would not be inconsistent with the
fundamental thought underlying Plato's comparison of
State and soul. For that is, that how what concerns the
whole community is carried on depends on the character of
its members; that it is human nature which is seen in and
controls politics; and if there is a virtuous peasantry, its
virtues will be displayed in the maintenance at least of that
part of the order of the State which depends on what
they do.

The difficulty felt by some about this part of Plato's
comparison is partly connected with his ambiguous use of
the word ἐπιθυμία, sometimes for those appetites which he
rates lowest in the soul, sometimes for every particular
desire, lower or higher, whether springing from its appetitive, or spirited, or rational nature; partly it is due to
forgetting that the comparison by no means implies that
the Δημιουργοί have nothing in their souls but appetite, nor
even but particular desires. It cannot be too carefully

---

[1] The term 'commonalty' is suggested by *Laws*, iii. 689 b 1: τὸ γὰρ
λυπούμενον καὶ ἡδόμενον αὐτῆς ὅπερ Δῆμός τε καὶ πλῆθος πόλεώς ἐστιν.
There is no very suitable English equivalent for the word Δημιουργοί used
in the *Republic*.

remembered that reason and spirit belong also to the soul of every man, and that if he is 'just', or lives aright, they function in the same way, displaying the same *sort* of special excellence, though not to the same *degree*, in the comparatively narrow field of his life, as they are required to do in the wide field of all those activities, drawn from the lives of all the citizens, which together make up the carrying out of the common or public purposes of the State, or purposes whose carrying out is their common interest. In this wider field it is the wisdom of the Guardians and the courage of the Auxiliaries that count. But again it must be remembered that in their souls, too, there are all three 'forms' present; and that neither does it suffice if the reason of the Guardians is used in directing, nor if the spirit of the Auxiliaries is used in defending and maintaining, that in the citizens' lives which concerns their common interest. A Guardian must use his wisdom also to plan his own life (which some great statesmen have failed to do), and an Auxiliary his courage to go through not only with his tasks for the State but with what else he sets himself or has set to him. This appeared in working out our illustration from the growth of an organization with limited purpose; for we saw that every act contributory to its execution belongs to two wholes, one that of all acts thus contributory, and one that of all acts making up the life of the member doing it; and that each of these wholes depends for being ordered aright on the exercise of wisdom, courage, and temperance. These are exercised in the second whole, the individual's life, all by one man, the man contributing that action to the first whole; but in the first, the wisdom chiefly by those who direct and the courage by those who defend and maintain it, and the temperance by all. If we bear this in mind, we shall not lapse into supposing that Plato thought the Δημιουργοί lived only by appetite.[1]

What he did think was that most of them lived lives

---

[1] See the *Note* at the end of this Essay.

chiefly devoted to providing for their material needs,
either by their own production or by purchase with what
they could get for the surplus they produced. But they had
(unlike the smaller and superior classes in the State) their
private families and the interests these bring; they had
their friendships; nor need we suppose that they would be
debarred from presence at religious festivals and games and
incapable of caring about worship and beauty; though the
spectacle of tragedy was denied. Their particular interests
then were not wholly those of the acquisitive life; but the
pursuit of these interests would occupy most of their time;
nevertheless, if they were good men or women, these
interests would not be allowed to encroach on others which
they judged it right to pursue, nor be neglected in favour
of others, so far as they understood that the welfare of the
State required them to devote themselves to their work of
production. The doctrine of the economic interpretation
of history ought to make us more ready to do justice to
Plato in this matter. According to that, different methods
of production are favourable to different distributions of
political power, but power is sought for the sake of the
control it gives over the distribution of what is produced,
and economic motives (which have their root in the appetitive nature of the soul) have the chief influence in men's
lives. Plato was anxious that in the lives of those who controlled the State they should have as little influence as
possible; but he did think that in most men's lives they
have great influence, and must particularly in the producers' lives. And the fact of their influence there does for
the provision of the material things needed to support the
community what their influence in any one man's life does
for satisfaction of those 'necessary appetites', without
whose satisfaction life and all its other interests must come
to an end.

But even among our 'desires to have', which Plato refers
to our appetitive or acquisitive nature, many would be

judged worthier than the necessary appetites. The soul is
one, and its higher infects or colours its lower nature. At
the old French Court, said Burke, 'vice lost half its evil in
losing all its grossness'; at any rate to care for graciously
appointed meals with bright conversation is better than
gluttony and bibulosity, even if such pleasures belong to
the βίος φιλοκερδής. The occupations which make provision for such entertainment are δημιουργίαι; if such entertainment is to have a place in men's lives in our State, to
the δημιουργοί belongs the provision for it; and to the
appetitive nature of the soul belongs the desire of it.

And Pheidias was a δημιουργός; perhaps even a poet
training his chorus would belong (if admitted) to this class
in the State. Greek cities were less complex than nation
States to-day, and the crafts carried on in them fewer and
less differentiated. And presumably every occupation not
reserved for the Guardians and Auxiliaries would fall
among δημιουργίαι. They were carried on indeed for a living, though the two higher classes were maintained by the
labours of others, in return for their special services to the
State; and Plato would not have admitted any 'idle rich'.
But the inspiration of those who carried them on need not
have been merely desire for wealth; indeed, in the best
State it would not have been, since there in all service, by
whatever other motives impelled, the desire to serve the
community would play a part; and this would reflect (or
be) the fact that in the workman's soul acquisitive desires
were indulged under the condition that he believed their
indulgence to be wise or right. Moreover, we need not
suppose that love of good craftsmanship and interest in his
work for its own sake would play no part in a δημιουργός;
for to work for gain is not incompatible with these.

Certain occupations, however, would be carried on in
any State that Plato would approve, which could not be
included among δημιουργίαι (as the practice of the arts
could), and yet are part of what the wisdom and courage

shown by the ruling classes in the direction and control
of the State would provide for, not part of the exercise
of that wisdom and courage. This fact corresponds to
the fact that in his individual life a man's wisdom may lead
him to find place for, and his resolution sustain him in
following, interests that spring from his rational or spirited
nature, interests in knowing or doing rather than in getting
and having. Two of these occupations Plato dwells on at
length, viz. science and philosophy. Science, indeed, will
be studied partly as a training to fit the mind for philosophy,
and this by the Auxiliaries, the best of whom will be promoted to the higher and harder study; but we cannot
suppose that Plato did not value it also on its own account.
Philosophy he so valued that he thought that the government of the State would be accounted in comparison a
necessary service rather than a thing to covet.[1] These
activities should plainly have a place in the State, even if
per impossibile all citizens spontaneously turned to the
callings to which a wise ruler would assign them, and
needed no spur or support in order not to neglect them, and
if absence of enemies outside made an armed force unnecessary. That is why they belong to what the wisdom
and courage of the higher classes must provide for, not
to their providing. What other occupations are there of
which this must be said, that would not fall to δημιουργοί?
The question is not considered by Plato. We may wonder
whether he would have included war; both in ancient and
modern times it has been thought by some an activity
worth engaging in for itself, and not merely necessary.
But there is no evidence that Plato would have regretted,
though there is evidence that he did not expect,[2] perpetual peace. Exercises, however, that train the body for
war he would have held to be part of a good life though
no war impended; and probably he would have thought

---

[1] *Rep.* vii. 540 b 2–6; cf. i. 347 b 5–d 8.
[2] iv. 422 a 4–423 b 3, v. 452 a 4–5, 470 a 1–c 3, &c.

that the life of the community as a whole would be the richer for there being some who showed specially prowess in hunting or in the games, as well as for there being some who were philosophers. The work of education again he might have said was noble as well as useful. Nevertheless, it must be allowed that he was not mindful enough of what should correspond in the State to the facts that in the individual there are particular desires springing from each 'form' of the soul, and that the satisfaction of some, at any rate, of them is to be provided for: viz. that there should be occupations carried on, for which men are fitted by special gifts of intelligence or spirit that would be wasted in the ordinary routine of cultivation or petty industry. Creative literature, historical investigation, exploration, would be recognized as falling among these to-day; and there are many kinds of post in the designing and carrying out of great works of engineering, or the conduct of great businesses, that demand higher qualities than Plato ascribed to the Δημιουργοί. And because of this unmindfulness Plato overlooked another fact. Men who do not show their courage and wisdom in the work done for the State by Auxiliaries and Guardians may yet show as much, and with almost the same indifference to acquisition, in callings that are like Δημιουργίαι in this respect, that they are no part of governing the State, but of the ordered life of the community governed. And these men's lives will give scope as fully to the powers of one in whose soul the rational and spirited natures are highly developed, as will the life of Auxiliary or Guardian; and therefore may be for him as happy.

It may be asked, why then should they not be allowed to exchange their occupations for the work of ruler or soldier, as the Guardians turn to ruling from the pursuit of philosophy, and the Auxiliaries, when war comes, to fighting from what occupies their time in peace? There is in fact no reason, so far as the facts that underlie Plato's comparison of State and soul are concerned, viz. the facts of how activities involving the different 'forms' of the soul are related in the life of an individual and in those parts of many individuals' lives which, lived in the furtherance of purposes that concern the whole community, under the direction of its government, constitute the life of the State. The positive reasons for the segregation of classes given by Plato are two. One is the value of specialization, the other that men differ by nature in their fitness for different sorts of work.

As to the first, he would so far as possible, on this ground, have workmen once trained for any calling stick to the calling for which they were trained;[1] though a breach of this rule among them is not fatal. But the business of war and government is much more difficult, and it is of much greater moment to the State that it should be well done; the training must be longer, and the exclusion of those not trained rigid.[2] As to the second reason, not only did Plato think, at least when he wrote the *Republic*, that by nature the differentiation of men in their capacities went very far;[3] he thought also that for the most part these differentiated capacities were inherited. This is implied in the 'Phoenician tale' of the earth-born men in whose bodies different metals were mixed;[4] and he noticed how certain human races seemed specially to love learning, and others fighting, and others the pursuit of wealth.[5] There were exceptions to the prevailing heritability; and if a child was better fitted for the work of another class than that to which it was born, it should be transferred thereto.[6] It is implied in the

---

[1] ii. 374 b 6–d 7; iii. 394 e 2–6, 397 e 4, 5.

[2] ii. 374 b 6–e 2; iii. 397 d 10–398 b 4; vii. 535 a 3–540 c 2, where the distribution of the parts of the required training over the first fifty years of life is described.

[3] ii. 370 a 8–b 2, 374 e 4; iii. 395 b 3–6; *Laws*, iii. 689 c 6–e 2, implies some change of opinion.

[4] iii. 414 b 8–415 d 5.   [5] iv. 435 e 1–436 a 3.

[6] iii. 415 b 3–c 6; iv. 423 c 6–d 6; *Tim.* 19 a 1–5.

summary of the early part of the *Republic* given in the *Timaeus* that this would occur at various ages; and in the *Republic*, degradation to the ranks of agriculture or industry is prescribed as a penalty for cowardice in war.[1] But upon the whole, if care were exercised in the supervision of mating, the stocks were expected to breed true. Between the Guardians and the Auxiliaries, indeed, the dividing line is less sharp than between these together and the Δημιουργοί. They were to share the same education and employments up to the age of fifty; every Guardian would have been a soldier. They were to live together and form one group so far as the selection of men and women from time to time for raising children is concerned; for no children were to be reared who were born among them of parents who had reached the age at which the selection of Guardians was first to be made. But the Δημιουργοί had a very different education, and between them and those above them there was no *jus conubi*. There was, however, apparently no caste system among them; it is not suggested that a boy must follow his father's trade.

If these assumptions concerning the differentiation of men's natures, the hereditary character of the differentiation, and the kind of training and apprenticeship needed for the tasks of war and government were true, Plato's proposal of a sharp separation between a governing class and a class engaged in economic activities might be defensible. That it has anything really to do with the comparison of soul and State is an illusion. What that shows to be important is that men with the requisite gifts of wisdom and of courage should undertake those larger tasks in the life of the State for which each of us in ordering his own life needs wisdom and courage. Whether these men are only to be found in certain human stocks, which should, therefore, be kept apart and not interbreed with the remainder of the population, has nothing to do with that. If

[1] v. 468 a 5–7.

it is not so, it will remain none the less urgent to find and promote such men to the work they are fitted for; perhaps it will also be more difficult, but that cannot be helped. And as to the argument from the long training required, it is a question of fact how long it takes to make an efficient soldier and administrator, but one which has nothing to do with the part he plays, and the qualities of soul in virtue of which he plays it, when made. The experience of the late war suggests that both military men and artizans are apt to underestimate the rapidity with which new-comers can acquire their skill. If indeed there were, as Plato believed, a science of statesmanship, for which a training could be found, but one of necessity as long and as elaborate as he described, then it would be foolish to call Cincinnatus from his plough and make him Dictator. But if, as we found reason to think, the task set to a statesman is not that of learning or thinking out what is required for the achievement of a definite and limited purpose, then the wisdom he needs is not like the knowledge of a scientific expert, and Plato may have deceived himself in believing that it could be taught, as that can, though only by a longer and more difficult course of instruction. We must remember that to raise up such a genuine statesman would, by his own confession, be a new thing in the world; in comparison even of the best who have hitherto governed states, he would be 'like Teiresias among the shades'.[1] If we must do the best we can with the help of statesmen who are wise by the grace of God, without that demonstrative understanding of what is good for a State and how it is to be realized[2] which is the true science of kingship,[3] we may also expect to find men fit for government springing from very divers parentage. But whencesoever they spring, and however they approach or fall short of the wisdom which Plato hoped for, as we

---

[1] *Meno*, 100 a 2–5.   [2] Cf. *Meno*, 99 e 6.
[3] Xenophon, *Comment.* IV. ii. 11: τέχνη βασιλική.

too might, in those who were to govern States, the wisdom which they exercise in governing will still stand related in the same way to the courage others show in supporting them, and the 'temperance' of all in accepting the functions assigned to them, whether in directing, supporting, or carrying out the common purposes and concerns of the State.

And what is true of their comparability when these common affairs of the State and the life of an individual are both of them justly or rightly ordered is true when they are not. The same perversion or defect in the action of the directing intelligence that should plan and prescribe wisely, of the courageous spirit that should be shown in insisting on the execution of what is wisely planned, of the desires, whether for bodily comfort and pleasure, or of other kinds, which should not be clamorous beyond the measure of indulgence allowed them in the plan, may be shown in the conduct of State affairs and of private life. That is why Plato holds that there must be as many kinds of human character as of character in States; for it is the dispositions of the men and women in a city which turn the scale, and drawing other things after them determine of what sort the State shall be.[1] He is interested in the outstanding or conspicuous types that may arise, in pure cultures, as it were, of certain sorts of principle or lack of principle in living one's life.[2] If we counted all varieties that a mixture of several principles may generate, the list would be much longer than his five. Again, he is interested, so far as States are concerned, in the way their public affairs are conducted, as that depends on what those who conduct them count most worth achieving; and though political institutions will in some measure reflect these different estimates of what it is best to live for, and will in turn help to determine how far the better or worse elements among the

---

[1] *Rep.* viii. 544 d 6–e 2.
[2] *Rep.* viii. 544 c 8: ἥτις καὶ ἐν εἴδει διαφανεῖ τινι κεῖται.

citizens will make their weight felt in the conduct of public affairs, Plato is not primarily interested in constitutional forms. Nor, of course, because in his account of the four outstanding types of less and more corruption in the lives of individuals, he describes the degradation as proceeding from father to son, does he mean that the passage from best to worse will be complete in four generations. That belongs merely to the literary presentation.

Aristotle's strictures on this part of the *Republic*,[1] in the fifth book of his *Politics*,[2] show little appreciation of what Plato was trying to do. He thinks in terms of constitutional forms, and points out truly enough that the order of change from one type to another is not in fact always that of progressive deterioration; that revolutions need not involve a change of constitutional form; and that the same constitutional form may go with very different ideals of government. He makes a difficulty also of the fact that Plato has not told us what is to follow tyranny. But what he points out is only what on Plato's principles is to be expected. If the spirit in which the affairs of the State are conducted depends on what those who conduct them value most highly in life, it is natural that not autocratic power but the uses it is put to will determine to which of Plato's types a constitution is to be referred. The Platonic tyranny only exists when the ruler is ἀνὴρ τυραννικός. No doubt his experience at Syracuse tended to make him think chiefly of such cases. And when Aristotle says that a tyrant pays no regard to the general interest, except as his private advantage requires, and lives for pleasure, whereas a king lives for what is noble,[3] he says what agrees with the conception for which Plato reserves that name; his account also of the arts by which such men preserve their power is as black as Plato's, from which indeed it borrows much.[4] But of other

---

[1] Scil. vii–ix. 576 b 9.   [2] viii (v). xii. 1316 a 17–b 27.
[3] *Pol.* viii (v). x. 1311 a 2–5.
[4] Ibid. xi. 1313 a 18–1314 a 29.

tyrants whose methods he contrasts with these[1] it is not
fair to say that they lived entirely for pleasure and had no
regard to the general interest except for purely selfish
reasons. To the question what is to succeed a tyranny
Plato would presumably have replied, that it depends on
what degree of reformation can be effected in the ideals of
a sufficient number of citizens. If none, it can only be
another tyranny, as seems to have happened too often in
some of what are called the South American Republics.
The influences that change the hearts of men for better or
for worse are many and divers, and the wind bloweth where
it listeth. There is no necessary order in the forms of
decay, nor yet of recovery. But, according as those in
power esteem most highly in life valour and success in
war, or getting rich, or freedom to follow every impulse as
it comes, or the gratification of bodily lusts, so will they
judge any proposed law or institution or measure of policy,
and these will be moulded to the fashion of men's souls.
It is not difficult to illustrate this from history. The feudal
nobility showed many of the characteristics of timocratic
men, and the States of their time many of those of timo-
cracy. What Plato calls an oligarchy we might better call
a plutocracy, and the latter days of the Roman Republic,
when the constitution had become plutocratic, produced
just such a class of 'drones', through the ruin of rich young
men, as Plato describes; Catiline, had he succeeded, might
well have set up a tyranny. It is because such intelligence
as the rulers have, in these corrupt States, is used to promote not a form of life in them that their rational nature
has conceived and approved, but one their interest in
which is prompted by their combative or appetitive nature,
that Plato speaks of the proper relations between these
factors in the soul being upset in them; and when men of
such inferior type are in the seat of government, then the
proper relations between the classes are upset also. It is

---

[1] Ibid. xi. 1314 a 30–1315 b 10.

Plato's political philosophy that order and disorder alike in States are the outward and visible sign of order and disorder in the souls of men.

NOTE

This book was written and sent to press before the appearance of Mr. M. B. Foster's *Political Theories of Plato and Hegel*. In that book Mr. Foster accepts the Hegelian criticism that Plato did not sufficiently recognize the 'element of subjectivity'. I fully agree that Plato has not justified, as a necessary condition for a State to be (in Aristotle's phrase) κατ' εὐχὴν ἀρίστη, a rigid separation of classes, with the largest or producing class taking no part in government. But Mr. Foster connects Plato's insistence on this condition with a supposed doctrine about the soul which, if Plato had held it, would, as I think, make nonsense of the comparison drawn between its constitution and the State's. I have argued that this comparison, and the doctrine of the soul underlying it, have much truth, but that their truth does not support the separation of classes. The doctrine of the soul imputed by Mr. Foster to Plato has no truth, though he thinks it would, if true, support the political doctrine. It involves ascribing to members of the three classes souls of radically different kinds. The Δημιουργοί have only an appetitive soul, the φύλακες only a rational or intelligent, the ἐπίκουροι (but about this, I think, he supposes that Plato was less definite) only a spirited. Plato, he seems to hold, does not consistently teach this; but he does teach it, and it is this teaching which connects with his political theory. I do not believe that it ever entered his mind.

The following quotations show what the doctrine is which Mr. Foster thinks Plato held:

'Hegel's conception of ethical freedom', he says (p. 128), 'involves the union in the same individual of the two faculties of To Logistikon and To Thumoeides which Plato had conceived in separation as residing the one in the ruler as tutor, the other in the auxiliary as pupil'; so that no faculty is left for the Δημιουργοί but the ἐπιθυμητικόν. And earlier, on p. 59, 'One further consequence of the tripartite organization must not be ignored. It results, as we have seen, in the exclusive attribution of two essential human excellences, Sophia and Andreia, to the guardian classes and hence

in a necessary inequality between guardians and producers. But
the inequality is not wholly one-sided. If the ruling and fighting
classes are the exclusive bearers each of one essential element of the
soul, so also is the producing class. In it alone the element of desire,
the third element of the soul, receives its proper and natural satisfaction, namely in the activity of money-making' (χρηματιστική).
Mr. Foster actually seems to suppose that Plato denied desire
altogether to the guardians. 'The guardians are maimed men also.
In lacking desire they lack the capacity either to enjoy or to produce' (p. 61). 'The activity of the subject in Sophia is directed upon
a form or universal and is wholly determined by it, whereas desire
is directed upon a particular object. It is therefore quite incompatible
with that self-surrender to direction by the universal which is the
essence of just rule for Plato. It is clear that Plato must exclude such
an element from the souls of his rulers, just as he excludes all economic differentiation, which is the machinery of Chrematistike,
from the organization of their class' (p. 76). And again, 'Σωφροσύνη
can find no place in the souls of the rulers, because it is produced by
the education of the sensuous element of the soul, whereas the
function of ruling demands the subjection or even the eradication
of this element, rather than its education. It can find no place in the
souls of the ruled, because it must be assumed that the satisfaction
of his appetitions in χρηματιστική is immediate and natural, neither
requiring nor admitting an education, but at most availing itself of a
technical training. Σωφροσύνη implies, in a word, that the sensuous
element of the soul is educable, while the distinction of classes implies that it is not. . . . Σωφροσύνη is possible for a man only so long as
his position is not determined either as ruler or ruled' (pp. 99–101).

Mr. Foster seems to think that only 'as the distinction between
the classes became increasingly explicit' did Plato realize its implications for his theory of the soul (p. 100). As I have said, it appears
to me, for reasons which these Essays sufficiently show, that the
distinction of classes has no such implication as Mr. Foster sees in it;
and that Plato ever thought it had I find incredible. To justify
this expression of dissent I have put together in this *Note* some
considerations against Mr. Foster's interpretation of Plato's thought.

A. So far as the teaching of the *Republic* is concerned, there is
a superfluity of evidence.

1. Plato compares the threefold constitution of a State with the threefold constitution of a soul. Mr. Foster imputes to him the doctrine that souls are of three alternative kinds, and that no soul has a threefold constitution. What becomes of the comparison?

2. That the θυμοειᾶἐς εἶᾶος, the φιλομαθές and the φιλοχρήματον, which are more conspicuously active among some peoples than among others, must be sought in individual souls is asserted as obvious, 435 e 1–436 a 4. And the question is then asked whether we—that is, men generally—learn, are angry, and desire the pleasures of food, drink and sexual intercourse, with the whole soul, or do each with something different in it (436 a 5–b 3). The second is the position taken by Socrates, and it is meant that men generally do all three, but not with the whole soul.

3. At ix. 591 d 1–3, a wise man is said to establish ἁρμονία in his body for the sake of συμφωνία in his soul. But how could there be συμφωνία in a soul that did not contain more εἴᾶη than one?

4. τὸ θυμοειᾶές is ascribed to beasts (441 b 2, 3). It is ranked higher than τὸ ἐπιθυμητικόν as the timocratic man is than the oligarchic. Are we to believe that Plato ever thought the bulk of the population of the most perfect city that could be were inferior to the beasts?

5. In the same context (441 a, b) it is said that children may be noticed to be full of spirit from their birth, though some of them seem never or only late in life to acquire any power of consideration (λογισμοῦ μεταλαμβάνειν). Socrates has just said (440 e 8–441 a 3) that the spirited is a τρίτον εἶᾶος in the soul, to be identified neither with the appetitive nor with the rational, and his remark about its presence in children and beasts is evidence of this. All this is inconsistent with supposing that souls are of three sorts, characterized respectively by one of the three εἴᾶη.

6. Could a merely appetitive man receive a 'technical training'? Shoemakers are said to be 'educated in shoe-making', τῇ σκυτικῇ παιᾶευθῆναι, 456 d 10. Is this possible without intelligence? If carpenters had only appetite, could there be any τῶν τεκτόνων ἐπιστήμη (428 b 12)?

7. There is a difference between σκυτική and χρηματιστική: to be interested in making shoes is not to be interested in making money. A man to whom the satisfaction of his appetites seems the most important thing may be called a χρηματιστής. In a just State, the producers would not think it so. But that any one should implies the

presence of τὸ λογιστικόν in his soul, not its absence; it implies the absence only of σοφία, the virtue of that element. Incidentally, it may be mentioned that Mr. Foster seems to make no distinction between the μισθωτική or μισθαρνητικὴ τέχνη of i. 345 b 7–347 d 8 and χρηματιστική. But it is plain from that passage that an over-ruling regard for μισθός need not be one for money.

8. In i. 343 e 7–344 c 8 Thrasymachus bids us, if we would see how much more profitable it is to be unjust, to consider tyrants, who can practise injustice on a great scale, and not temple-robbers, kidnappers, burglars, swindlers, and thieves. In *Rep.* ix it is precisely tyrants whose misery, if we look into their souls, is alleged to prove the contrary of Thrasymachus' contention. But a tyrant, as there conceived, is a man of tyrannic soul invested with despotic power. And the argument for his misery assumes throughout that the better elements in his soul, the rational and spirited, are enslaved to the worst, some great lust of the appetitive. The tyrannic soul clearly contains all three elements. The principle is the same for temple-robbers and other lesser criminals, whom surely Plato would have expected to find among the Δημιουργοί, if not exclusively, at least as well as in the other classes.

9. In the figurative description of man (ix. 588 b 6–590 d 6) as containing within his human semblance man and lion and many-headed beast, there is no suggestion that the citizens of the ideal State were not of this kind, but according to their class contained only one of these three beneath their skins. On the contrary, the description is quite plainly meant to indicate what Plato takes to be the truth about men generally (see especially παντί, πάντες, in 590 d 3–5).

10. That the λογιστικόν and the θυμοειΔές reside in separation respectively 'the one in the ruler as tutor, the other in the auxiliary as pupil' contradicts Plato's teaching that the rulers are to be those who have best acquitted themselves as auxiliaries. No doubt the function of training the young requires of the rulers the exercise of their intelligence. But it seems as if Mr. Foster thought that Plato could not have distinguished the functions specially assigned at any time to the members of each different class in the corporate life of the State without denying to them any element of soul required for exercising any other function in their private lives, or in some other period of their public lives.

11. In the account of the genesis of the oligarchic type of soul by degeneration from the timocratic (viii. 553 d 1–9) we read that such a man reduces and subdues the λογιστικόν and θυμοειδές in him beneath the ἐπιθυμητικόν. If they were not all three in his soul, how could he? And is not the man of oligarchic soul such as Mr. Foster thinks the δημιουργοί to be, i.e. bent on χρημάτων κτῆσις?

12. The same is implied in the account of further degeneration to the democratic type. Consider the words at 561 b 7, καὶ λόγον γε, ἦν δ' ἐγώ, ἀληθῆ οὐ προσδεχόμενος οὐδὲ παριεὶς εἰς τὸ φρούριον. There *is* a citadel of reason, but the man judges falsely.

13. The statement that 'in lacking desire' the guardians 'lack the capacity either to enjoy or to produce' is irreconcilable with the account of the necessary appetites at 558 d 11–e 3 (for by desire presumably Mr. Foster means appetite; he would hardly deny to the guardians love of knowledge, or desire of good). The necessary appetites, Plato says, it is impossible to get rid of, and their satisfaction benefits us. Indeed it seems absurd to suppose that Plato ever imagined that his guardians would eat without being hungry and drink without being thirsty, or that when he proposed (v. 460 b 1–5) as a reward to youths who distinguished themselves on campaign or elsewhere that they should be allowed more frequently to sleep with women, he thought they would lack desire. Why else than because they did not was there to be an astute arrangement of lots determining intercourse (460 a 8–10) or permission for the sexes to cohabit after the prescribed ages of child-getting and bearing were passed, provided no offspring were born, or at any rate none reared (461 b 9–c 7)?

14. The same statement is equally irreconcilable with what is said at ix. 582 a 8–b 3, that the philosopher must from childhood upwards have had experience of the pleasures characteristic of the concupiscent life, the βίος φιλοκερδής. And as to the capacity for enjoyment, we are told at 586 e 4–587 a 1 that in the philosophic soul *each part* enjoys the best and truest pleasures of which it is capable.

15. Lastly, not because this is the last passage that could be adduced, but because what has been adduced already may seem sufficient, what can be meant by the contrast (x. 611 b 9–612 a 6) between the soul in its purity and as it is under the stress of its partnership with the body, if not that there is in it something akin, as Socrates says, to the divine and immortal and eternal, and some-

thing animal and different? And Socrates is speaking of all men's souls, for it is not only the souls of guardians that are immortal, as the Vision of Er plainly indicates. I can think of no passage in the *Republic* countenancing the view that Plato ever thought there are men in whose souls there is only the rational, only the spirited, or only the appetitive kind. Nor do I think there are any views expressed which require in consistency that he should have thought this. I would suggest that any interpretation that really requires this ought on that account to be rejected.

B. If we turn from the *Republic* to other dialogues, there is the same consensus of evidence in favour of the doctrine that every human soul contains the three εἴδη, and none that I know of for the view that Plato ever supposed there were men in whose souls is only one.

1. The famous myth in the *Phaedrus* (246 a 2–d 5) likens the soul to a charioteer driving two winged horses; the charioteer seems to be the rational, the horses the spirited and appetitive parts of the soul. This image not only covers all human souls, but the souls of gods also; but for them horses and driver are of good stock and themselves good.

2. According to the teaching of the *Timaeus*, the divine or rational part of the soul is lodged in the head (44 d 3–8), that which participates in courage and in spirit is lodged in the breast above the midriff (69 e 3–70 a 7), and that which desires food and drink and suchlike below (70 d 7–e 3). Here again the account is quite general; every human soul is in question; and it seems to me as plausible to suggest that Plato thought some men only had heads, some only chests, some only bellies, as that he thought some men's souls only had a rational, some only a spirited, some only an appetitive nature.

3. Though there is nothing in the *Gorgias* as explicit as these passages, the account given, 493 a 1–c 7, of those men's views who think the body is the tomb of the soul ascribes to every soul an appetitive part, τῆς ψυχῆς τοῦτο ἐν ᾧ ἐπιθυμίαι εἰσί, which in foolish men is like a sieve, leaky and never satisfied. And the doctrine that all men wish for the good, though they may be mistaken as to what is good (467 c 5–468 e 5), ascribes to every soul a rational part. This doctrine, of course, appears in a number of other dialogues.

4. In the *Phaedo*, 67 d 7–10, Socrates ascribes to those who

follow wisdom aright the 'practice of death', the effort to break even in life as much as possible with all dependence on the body. There is nothing in the *Republic* so ascetic in doctrine as this passage. But even here (64 c 10–67 d 10) it is not suggested that the philosopher can purify himself altogether in this life of the body and its desires.

5. It is perhaps not unfair to cite from the *Definitiones* (411 d 8–e 1) two definitions of justice which must at least have been thought Platonic: Δικαιοσύνη ὁμόνοια τῆς ψυχῆς πρὸς αὑτήν, καὶ εὐταξία τῶν τῆς ψυχῆς μερῶν πρὸς ἄλληλά τε καὶ περὶ ἄλληλα. In a soul that had not more parts than one, how could these things be?

C. If Aristotle had supposed that Plato in the *Republic* or elsewhere taught that there were men in whose souls only one εἶδος was present, we might expect that he would have noticed it. But he nowhere suggests such a thing. No statement of his that seems to refer to Plato's doctrine of the soul betrays the least suspicion that Plato thought the souls of some men were different from those of others in the way that Mr. Foster suggests. *Eth. Nic.* I. xiii. 9, 1102 a 26 may well be a reference to Academic teaching: λέγεται δὲ περὶ αὐτῆς (scil. τῆς ψυχῆς) καὶ ἐν τοῖς ἐξωτερικοῖς λόγοις ἀρκούντως ἔνια, καὶ χρηστέον αὐτοῖς· οἷον τὸ μὲν ἄλογον αὐτῆς εἶναι, τὸ δὲ λόγον ἔχον. It is no objection to supposing such a reference, that the ἄλογον is not here distinguished into appetitive and spirited; later, III. x. 1, 1117 b 23, we read that temperance and courage seem to be the virtues of the irrational parts, and the *Magna Moralia*, I. i. 1182 a 24, expressly ascribes to Plato the division of the soul into τὸ λόγον ἔχον and τὸ ἄλογον. But all men's souls are included. (That the *Magna Moralia* may not be Aristotle's does not affect the value of its testimony for the present purpose.) The passage in *de An.* III. ix. 3, 432 b 6, εἰ δὲ τρία ἡ ψυχή, ἐν ἑκάστῳ ἔσται ὄρεξις (quoted above, p. 63), must refer to Plato, and betrays no suspicion that he did not think every soul threefold. The *de Virtutibus et Vitiis* cannot be cited as Aristotle's, but it also may be taken as early evidence of what Plato was supposed to have taught, when it says, 1249 a 30, τριμεροῦς δὲ τῆς ψυχῆς λαμβανομένης κατὰ Πλάτωνα, τοῦ μὲν λογιστικοῦ ἀρετή ἐστιν ἡ φρόνησις, τοῦ δὲ θυμοειδοῦς ἥ τε πραότης καὶ ἡ ἀνδρεία, τοῦ δὲ ἐπιθυμητικοῦ ἥ τε σωφροσύνη καὶ ἡ ἐγκράτεια, ὅλης δὲ τῆς ψυχῆς ἥ τε δικαιοσύνη καὶ ἡ ἐλευθεριότης καὶ ἡ μεγαλοψυχία.

I agree with Mr. Foster that there are features in Plato's political philosophy not warranted by the doctrine of the tripartite soul. I have tried to indicate what they are and how I think Plato arrived at them. But Mr. Foster tries to account for them by ascribing to him, not apparently as his consistent and only doctrine, but as one to which he was led 'as the distinction between the classes became increasingly explicit', a doctrine of the soul which I can see no evidence that he ever held, and which it is hard to see how a reasonable man could hold.

CHAPTER V

PLATO'S *REPUBLIC*: THE PROOF THAT THE MOST JUST MAN IS THE HAPPIEST

AFTER Socrates has shown, by help of his investigation of
the soul's triform nature, what justice and injustice are in
a man, he observes that it remains for them to consider
whether it profits a man to do justly and act nobly and be
just, be this known of him or not to other men, or rather to
do unjustly and be unjust, provided he is unpunished and
unreformed.[1] Glaucon thinks that, now that justice and
injustice have been revealed for what they are, the question
is become ridiculous; the unjust life is not worth living.
And Socrates agrees; nevertheless before deciding he proposes, as he has expounded by what constitution of the
soul a man is just, so to set forth the main types of its
perversion, whereby a man may lapse farther and farther
from being so. From this undertaking he is diverted by
the discussions which fill Books v–vii, and in the course of
which Plato would lead us to a fuller understanding of
what the soul is, more particularly in its intelligent nature,
of how this form of its being may be best developed, and
of the institutions and order in a State that are required
both to secure for all citizens the well-being of which they
are capable and to bring to perfection the powers of the
best endowed few. But at the beginning of Book viii
Socrates professes in so many words to undertake the task
proposed before this long digression,[2] and proceeds to
describe, in order (as he holds) of progressive deterioration,
the four outstanding types of corrupt constitution in a
State and corruption in a soul, which he was about to
mention before.[3] The political constitutions he calls timo-
cracy, oligarchy, democracy, and tyranny; and there may

[1] iv. 444 e 7.   [2] 543 c 4.
[3] v. 449 a 2–b 1: ἐν τέτταρσι πονηρίας εἴδεσιν οὔσας.

be individuals of timocratic, oligarchic, democratic, or tyrannic character. The thing most fatal for himself and the community over which he tyrannizes is that a man of tyrannic character should be a tyrant.

Of this description something has been said in the preceding Essay,[1] and we are not concerned with it now. But when it is completed, and the man of tyrannic soul ruling as a despot has plainly appeared to be wickedest or worst,[2] Socrates asks whether the worst is also the most wretched. In three successive arguments he and Glaucon agree that it is so, contrarily to what Glaucon had said at the outset that men believe; they believe (he had said) that so far as it profits a man to live justly rather than unjustly, this is only because of rewards meted out to a man when he acts justly, whether by men or gods, and penalties imposed when he acts unjustly. That intrinsically a just life is better for a man than an unjust, that by what it is and irrespective of consequences it profits him more, this they do not believe. This is what he, and Adeimantus with him, challenged Socrates to show; and this is what Plato thinks that he is making Socrates show at last.

The ensuing arguments, therefore, must have been regarded by Plato as important. They are the considered answer, or reason for his answer, to the contention of Thrasymachus, that injustice is more profitable than justice, λυσιτελέστερον ἀδικία δικαιοσύνης,[3] as well as to the question of Adeimantus, what it is that each of itself effects in the soul of him that has it, whereby justice and injustice, whether gods or men take notice of them or not, are good and evil.[4] What indeed each is in the soul of him that has it has been shown already; but that by being such the one is good and the other evil, this, it would seem, is to be shown now.

Yet there are grave difficulties both in the statement of

---

[1] pp. 111–14.
[2] πονηρότατος, ix. 576 b 11.
[3] i. 348 b 9, 354 b 7.
[4] ii. 367 e 3–5.

the problem, and in the present arguments to solve it. In regard to the statement of the problem, it will be remembered how the position of Thrasymachus that complete injustice is more profitable than complete justice[1] was taken to include three contentions: (i) that injustice is excellence, ἀρετή, and justice the contrary;[2] (ii) that it makes a man stronger and more capable in action than if he were just;[3] (iii) that the unjust live better and are happier.[4] The question, therefore, whether a life is just is treated as in some way distinguishable from the question whether it is excellent, and this again from the question of its happiness. But what its being good is, if neither its being just nor yet its being happy, might seem puzzling. Yet the language Plato uses seems natural enough. That its being just is not the same as its being good is very clearly intimated in Book vi. There[5] we are told that men are often ready to accept for themselves in their actions what seems just, though it is not really so, but that no one is content with what only seems good; all seek what is so really. Every soul pursues what is really good, divining that there is something really good, and for its sake acting always, but at a loss to know what it is, and having no sure conviction of it; for lack of this men fail to get what else may be of service to them; but those to whom everything in the State is to be entrusted must not remain in darkness about this good; for they are guardians of what is just and noble, and he who does not know how and wherein these are good will be of little worth as guardian of them. But the knowledge of the good which this guardianship requires is the climax of the education to be given to the rulers of the State. The disproof that living as the unjust man would live is living well and wisely is not drawn from this knowledge. What then is this goodness, excellence, or

---

[1] i. 348 b 9.   [2] Ibid. 348 c 2–10.
[3] Ibid. 351 a 2, 352 b 7.   [4] Ibid. 352 d 2.
[5] 505 d 5–506 a 7.

ἀρετή which Thrasymachus claims for the unjust life, and
Socrates vindicates for the just? May it be that there are
goodnesses of different kinds, that the excellence claimed
by Thrasymachus for the mode of life called unjust is not
that which, because we recognize it in a just life, makes it
paradoxical for him to say that injustice is ἀρετή, and again
not that which Socrates says that every soul pursues, and
will not knowingly accept a counterfeit? The excellence
we have in mind when we say that a just man or a just life
is good is moral excellence; this consists in acting from a
sense of duty, or from benevolence or gratitude, or some
other of certain motives. It is in this sense that Socrates
expects Thrasymachus to agree that justice is excellence,
injustice evil.[1] The excellence Thrasymachus claims for
an unjust man is that of the intelligence, by which to
succeed in the aim, by him ascribed to us all, of aggrandiz-
ing oneself at the expense of one's neighbours. It is in this
sense that he says that those who are in a position to be
thorough in their injustice are wise and good.[2] The good
which every soul pursues is what would make a man's
existence excellently suited to bring satisfaction of his
desires. It is in this sense that Socrates speaks of the just
as 'living better and being happier' than the unjust—
ἄμεινον ζῶσιν καὶ εὐΔαιμονέστεροί εἰσιν.[3]

It must be admitted that different subjects of which men
say that they are good differ in their goodness; but it is not
an accident that they are all called good. We have not to
deal with a mere equivocation, with calling by the same
name various subjects to which we intend to ascribe nothing
the same in so calling them, as different streets are called
King Street, or water and bread in different languages are
both called *pane*. No doubt to say that the establishment of

---

[1] i. 348 c 5: οὐκοῦν τὴν μὲν Δικαιοσύνην ἀρετήν, τὴν Δὲ ἀΔικίαν κακίαν
⟨καλεῖς⟩;

[2] i. 348 d 3: φρόνιμοί καὶ ἀγαθοί.

[3] i. 352 d 2.

socialism in England would be good is not the same as to say that it would be good for the rich; and we may be tempted to explain that 'good for the rich' merely means what the rich would like or what would bring them pleasure. But this seems inadequate. Do I really mean, when I say that something is good for me, merely that I get pleasure from it? Can I not ask intelligibly whether pleasure is good for me, as well as whether pleasure is good?' Does not to say that something would be good for me, e.g. an increase of wages and so of command over 'material goods', mean that my life, not as a biological process, but as my experienced doing and suffering, would be better for the modification in this experienced doing and suffering that this greater command would bring about? Whether its betterment would include moral improvement is not the question, if there are other differences between one life and another, in respect of which one life is better than another, than differences in their moral excellences, in the virtue of those living these lives. And if moral action is not the only thing that can be good, why should there not be?

Certainly Plato did not think moral action the only thing that can be good. Had he so thought, he could not have said that a man who had discovered what it is to be just, i.e. to act morally well, might still be unable to state the nature of the good which he divined to be. Even Kant, who thought that there could be no good without it, did not think it the only good thing. Only a good will was good unconditionally, *ohne Bedingung*; but happiness was conditionally good, good provided that the happy man was virtuous. There are, however, difficulties in the notion of being conditionally good which Kant did not discuss. He is not saying that a man can only be happy if he is virtuous, as one can only be healthy if one takes a sufficiency of food and exercise, but that his happiness can only be good if he is virtuous. Would it not be absurd to say that a man's

health can only be good if he takes a sufficiency of food
and exercise? What produces health is an interesting and
important question; but health is a certain condition of the
organism, and if a thing is good because of what it is, that
condition of the organism will be good however produced;
its goodness is conditional on nothing but its own nature.
That is Kant's opinion in regard to moral virtue; nothing
makes it good but its being what it is, the manifestation
of a will determined by respect for the law. Happiness is
not this; let us suppose that it is the pleasurable consciousness of attaining whatever one desires. If that is good,
should it not be so just because it is this consciousness?
How can the fact that a man thus pleasurably conscious
does, or does not, determine his actions from respect for
the law affect the goodness of this pleasurable consciousness, supposing it to be good?

We seem forced to admit that what makes happiness
good is not its being what it is, but the whole life of the
man who has it being what it is. And the goodness of that
life is not constituted by the coming together of the goodnesses of those factors which together constitute his life.
Their goodnesses somehow come through its goodness,
not vice versa. This is one reason why the current popu-
larity of the word 'value' in these discussions is to be
deprecated. Not only, in the ordinary use of that word, is
the value of anything measured by the amount of something else which it will obtain for us, so that value is not
intrinsic, as goodness is. Besides this, the value of a man's
estate is the sum of the values of the parts of it. No doubt
there are exceptions. When we say that a piece of land has
a high accommodation value, we may mean that for the
whole site which would be formed by the addition of this
piece a man would be prepared to give more than the sum
of what he would give for the rest without it and for it
without the rest. But why should he be prepared to give
anything for either? If it were a business question, the

answer would be, because the amount of money to be made by possessing this piece was very much greater for a man already in possession of the rest than for any one else. And where money is concerned, the whole is the sum of its parts, and the value of the whole the sum of their values. But if the question were one of amenity, or of the strategic importance of the piece of land in question, or of its serviceableness to the comfort of the lives of old people whom the purchaser was supporting on the rest of the site, the considerations by which he must be guided in determining what price to pay are not a matter for arithmetical calculation. Judgements of better and worse, not of more and less of the same valuable, are involved; and the alternatives between which a man wishes to decide which is better must be the whole states of affairs wherein his being or not being in possession of the piece of land, and his parting or not parting with such and such a sum in exchange for it, are only factors. Whether it is good to buy it at this price is not a question that can be settled without looking beyond the individual transaction, and considering the whole alternative states of affairs, one or other of which will exist according as he does or does not buy it.

The apparent exception to the principle here illustrated is where moral issues are involved. We are inclined to think that there are situations in which we know that we ought to do some act, without any necessity to look beyond it to the whole context of life in which our decision falls to be taken and to ask whether this whole would be better if we did it or if we forbore. It is not denied that to act from a sense of duty is to bring into being new good. It is denied that the question whether we ought to do this act requires for its decision any consideration of better or worse. The knowledge that to act from a sense of duty is good cannot inform me what I ought to do; to know what I ought to do, therefore, I need not consider the goodness of acting from a sense of duty; and, as we are often inclined to think, there are occasions when we know what we ought to do without regard to the goodness of anything else than acting from a sense of duty, and so without regard to the goodness of anything at all; of course not without regard to the specific character of what we know we ought to do, but without regard to any goodness in its being of that specific character. *Fiat justitia, ruat caelum* is a classical expression of this conviction. And the official doctrine of the Roman Church is that the knowledge of no amount of suffering however great which an action may entail would justify a man in abstaining from it, if the most venial moral fault were otherwise committed in abstaining.

This isolation of our judgements of obligation from other judgements in which words like ἀγαθόν or ἀρετή, good or excellence, occur is not made by Plato. He tries to justify the divers uses of the words without sacrificing the consistency of their use. But does he succeed? That thing in any kind is good which best fulfils its own function, ἔργον. But what is the function of anything? What only it, or it more completely than anything else, is capable of. And of what is only the soul capable? Living. Therefore the good soul is that which lives well. But only a soul is capable of living viciously; why then is not the good soul that which best lives viciously, τελέως ἀδικεῖ? Because we ought to live virtuously. Does not this bring us back to isolated judgements of obligation? For this reason it has been urged that Plato should have made Socrates refuse the challenge to show that justice profits the man who practises it, of itself and without regard to its consequences. What does it matter, he should have made him say, whether justice profits the man or not? A man knows he ought to do justice, and that is the end of it. To ask to be shown that it profits is to ask something irrelevant; and if he is not prepared to do justice unless he is shown it, he may then do just acts, but he will not be a just man.[1] Plato thought

[1] Cf. Prof. H. A. Prichard, *Duty and Interest*, pp. 9–10.

8

the challenge was a proper one. It seemed to him better to be just than unjust, but also better for the man who was so. That it was better for him meant that he made the good his own, so far as goodness can be realized or embodied in a man's life. Goodness can take other forms than that of a rightly lived or ordered individual life. A community of lives, the life of a State, is not a mere aggregate of individual lives, and it may be well or rightly ordered; and Plato would have agreed with Aristotle that this is κάλλιον καὶ θειότερον, nobler and more godlike, than an individual's life.[1] But this too is less than, and no more than a factor in, the one all-embracing world or κόσμος, whose goodness requires that its parts should be good; the goodness of the parts, however, requires that they should severally be not all alike but perfect of their kind; and the goodness of the whole, that it should be what it is made by its parts being diversely perfect, not that it should be what they are, any more than each of them must be what the rest are.

Now if Plato had been content to maintain that justice advantages a man because to live justly is the greatest good that can befall a man, or rather that he can secure for himself, and that if he is enlightened he will understand this, perhaps we should not need to dissent. We might admit that so a man satisfies himself: not indeed that he satisfies every particular desire of which the soul is capable, nor that he ceases to want; he may even feel cravings which are not indulged. But if so, they are not indulged because he regards them as occurring in him, but not belonging to the form of life which all the time he desires and is resolved should be the form of his life; in Green's language, he does not identify himself with them. He lives upon a principle which secures that, though he has particular desires which do belong to this form of life, and they are continually changing, yet they are all manifestations of his desire for a life ordered on this principle; and the satisfaction of this

[1] *Eth. Nic.* I. ii. 8, 1094 b 10; cf. *Rep.* vi. 497 a 3–5.

desire is abidingly his. Somewhat so, in a different sense
of 'satisfaction', the law of acceleration for a body falling
to the earth, which is that its velocity should increase at the
rate of 32 feet per second, is always satisfied, though at
every moment its velocity is different. Green said that a
man desires self-satisfaction; it would be better to say that
he desires what will satisfy himself. This means that he
desires that which, so far as he achieves it, does not leave
him desiring something else as well or instead, not that
what he desires is the pleasure incident to satisfying his
primary desires. It may be asked whether to live justly is
good because a man is satisfied in so living. If that means
because of the pleasure incident to carrying out his desire
to live justly, the answer is no. Yet in Plato's view a man,
being what the nature of the soul makes him, cannot be
satisfied unless he lives justly. Otherwise that in him
which is most truly himself will be always wanting what
it is never achieving; but in living justly this will be
always achieving what it wants. We may say that a man
is good because thus to live satisfies him, and equally that
thus to live is good because it is what a good man wants.
And if happiness is not the satisfaction attendant on so
living, then Plato *should* have said that whether or not justice
makes a man happy was irrelevant. But it would not be
irrelevant to a being who desired to do right that a certain
way of living would leave that desire unsatisfied. Now, as
Plato thought, there is in us a desire of the good, and the
good is something we can only make our own by living in
a certain way, and we approve the life that is ordered by this
desire of the good, and think that to satisfy it is to satisfy
not any chance craving but ourselves. If this be so, we
must, when we reflect, desire to satisfy ourselves.

But when he comes to offer proof of his contention that
it profits a man to be just, Plato is not content with developing the above considerations. He wants to prove that
by its very nature the just must be the happy life, the

unjust the miserable, and by happiness he does mean something other than the satisfaction attendant on living justly. It is difficult to say what he means, or indeed what any of us means, by happiness. Notoriously the utilitarians have tried to define it in terms of pleasure, and so provoked Carlyle to ask what right a man has to be happy. And Plato, as he proceeds, does the same, and shifts from asking what life is happiest to asking which is pleasantest.[1] He still maintains that the best or justest life, judged by this test, stands first. But he does not succeed in proving this, and it may be questioned whether it can be proved. Moreover, even if the best life is on this count preferable to the worst, the life of the true philosopher ruling a well-ordered State to that of a man of tyrannic soul in the position of despot, that is not all that Socrates undertook to prove. He undertook to prove that for any man in any station to live justly is more profitable than to live unjustly; and if that means, brings more happiness, he must show that no man can ever be more happy because of his injustice. On any ordinary interpretation of the word happiness, this is not true; at any rate, Plato's arguments fail to prove it.

The arguments are three, drawn the first from what has been maintained about the identity of constitution in a soul and in a State; the second from the distinction between the several lives, in which a man lives for what the desires proper to the rational or the spirited or the appetitive nature of the soul respectively set him on seeking; the third from what has been taught in the central books about the difference between the genuinely and fully real and what seems to be but partly is not real.

The first of these arguments[2] makes a use of the doctrine, that we find writ large in the State what is to be found also in an individual soul, which the truth in this doctrine does not justify. In a State under the heel of a tyrant what is best is dishonoured and enslaved; only the tyrant is free;

---

[1] *Rep.* ix. 581 c 9.   [2] *Ibid.* 577 c 1–580 c 8.

the State as a whole is least of any able to do as it wishes; it is needy and unsatisfied. So when some lust tyrannizes over the soul, the man goes unsatisfied, so far as most of his capacities are concerned; what he really wishes for, what would satisfy *him*, he does not get; all that is best in him is kept under, starved of what it craves for, while the ruling lust is insatiable, so that he lives full of fear and torment and discontent. The full development of the thesis that a man of the character which Plato calls tyrannic, in the position of a despot, must needs live wretchedly, is convincing enough. Because he had no regard for the welfare of his subjects but used them only as instruments to the gratification of his own appetites, they would be his enemies, and he would go in perpetual fear of them. But all this is independent of any similarity between State and soul. What is that similarity, when the tyrannic man and the State under a tyrant's heel are concerned? It is that on the one hand in the State there is no single purpose, in the pursuit of which its members, rulers and ruled alike, co-operate; that what the subjects do at the tyrant's behest they do unwillingly from fear of punishment, not because it helps to achieve a result in the achievement of which they find their own good; on the other hand, the man has no one settled purpose in the pursuit of which all his powers are harmoniously enlisted and interests and desires of which his rational, his spirited, and his merely appetitive nature severally make him capable are alike engaged and satisfied. The nature of the tyrant is such that he can only get his way at the expense of his subjects, who are forced to live otherwise than as would content them; the nature of the lust that drives the tyrannic man is such that it can only get indulgence at the expense of other desires, interests, hopes, aspirations in him being ignored, thwarted, unsatisfied. Now for this reason a tyrannic man is wretched, and wretcheder when a tyrant than if he were not tyrant; and the subjects of a tyrant, who need not be such men, are also wretched or at least not happy. But just because there is no unifying purpose in whose execution the citizens cooperate, there is nothing which it can be said that the State wishes. If it be true that a State enslaved and tyrannized does least of any what it wishes, that is not because there is in it a common wish which it cannot carry out, but because there is no such wish. And if there were, it would be the citizens' wish, and the State's only in the sense that each of them knew that the others shared it and that they knew he shared it. There is no happiness or misery that is the State's but not its citizens', as there may be happiness or misery that is one citizen's and not another's; no wish or purpose that is the State's except as it is a wish or purpose in which the citizens, or at least those who act in their name, concur. What we call the justice or injustice, the happiness or misery of the State has its being in its members' lives, according as these are more or less unified both each within itself, and by men's sympathy and mutual understanding one with another. It is through understanding what an individual soul is and how it works that we can understand what is meant by the justice or injustice of the State; in the same way it is because through understanding the soul we can see how a man of tyrannic character must be miserable, and how happiness is connected with the disposition of the soul as well as and more than with fortune, that we can understand why the citizens are unhappy when a tyrant rules, as well as the tyrant himself. We cannot therefore use what we judge true about such a State, a τυραννευομένη πόλις, to prove the same true about the bad man, the τυραννικὸς ἀνήρ. For if we did not see that it must be true about him, we should not know, except as a matter of empirical fact, that it was true about the State; and to know it merely as a matter of empirical fact would not be to know that similarity of State and man on which the argument is supposed to rest.

To this we must add that Socrates' conclusion, though

it refutes Thrasymachus, does not go as far as Glaucon and Adeimantus required. Thrasymachus indeed had taken tyranny as a test case for the truth of his thesis, that to live justly is to benefit others but not yourself, to live unjustly is to benefit yourself, though not others. The tyrant is in a position both by trickery and by force to rob alike from private and public, secular and religious funds, and make slaves of whom he will; he carries injustice to extremity, and his is the supreme happiness.[1] Socrates may have shown that on the contrary his wretchedness is the most profound. But does it follow that every man, no matter what his station, so far as in any way or measure he acts unjustly, is *pro tanto* less happy than he would otherwise have been, and so far as in any way or measure he acts justly, is *pro tanto* happier? That is really what was to be shown if our profit is in being happy: what it is in justice, if it is of itself good and not only has good results, in respect whereof barely of itself it benefits him that has it, and injustice injures.[2] How far Socrates' present arguments are from showing this we shall see more fully as we proceed.

The second of them,[3] like the first, and indeed the third also, rests on the analysis of the soul, but it makes no useless appeal to the correspondence there may be between a soul and a State, through the presence in each of the same form of order or disorder. The εἴδη of the soul, its rational, its spirited and its appetitive natures, are considered now not primarily as having heterogeneous but co-operant functions in the detailed determination of a man's life, but as each alike a source of particular desires, a spring of action, a condition for the enjoyment of pleasure; and from this point onwards Plato speaks more of the relative pleasantness than of the relative happiness of different ways of living. The rational in the soul is that whereby it is capable of learning and is set on the pursuit of knowledge; the spirited is that whereby it contends and is set on gain-

[1] i. 344 a 3–c 8.   [2] ii. 367 d 2.   [3] ix. 580 c 9–583 a 11.

ing the mastery of others, on victory and reputation; the appetitive is that whereby it craves food and drink and sexual activity and is set on these and what serves them. Plato calls the three forms of the soul's being respectively φιλόσοφον, φιλόνικον, and φιλοκερ∆ές or φιλοχρήματον; the implication of desire with each of the three εἴ∆η of the soul comes out glaringly in these names. According as the interests proper to one or other are dominant, three types of life result; and since to the satisfaction of each sort of interest is attached its own peculiar pleasure, we may ask which type of life is pleasantest.[1] The men who follow these different ways of life would each say that his own is pleasantest: the philosopher that other pleasures are negligible in comparison of those of discovering truth, the ambitious man, in comparison of those of fame and honour, the concupiscent man, in comparison of those of gain; and Plato expressly distinguishes from the question which life is nobler or ignobler, better or worse, the question which is most pleasant and most free of pain. In face of these discrepant answers, how are we to decide? Experience, wisdom, argument are needed in order to make a decision[2]; who is qualified in these respects? Plato argues that only the philosopher is so qualified, and therefore his verdict must be accepted.

For in respect of experience, whereas those who seek gain or honour do not know what the pleasure is of discovering truth, the philosopher, besides experiencing how sweet is knowledge, must equally with the others have

---

[1] *Rep.* ix. 581 c 9. They are recognized by Aristotle as three outstanding types of life, each claimed by some as the happiest, under the names of βίος θεωρητικός, βίος φιλότιμος, and βίος ἀπολαυστικός. He objects to the term χρηματιστικός, because it is not money but the pleasures money can buy, of which the pursuit dominates the kind of life intended, and money can be used in the prosecution of other purposes than the pursuit of pleasure. Cecil Rhodes, for example, sought money in the service of very different ends; and many scientific pursuits are very costly. See *Eth. Nic.* I. v. 1095 b 14 sq.

[2] *Rep.* ix. 582 a 5: ἐμπειρίᾳ τε καὶ φρονήσει καὶ λόγῳ.

tasted sensual pleasure and the pleasure that comes from other men's respect; the rich, the courageous and the learned all have their admirers. And so far as wisdom and the power of argument are concerned, if wealth or honour, which others seek, gave these, they might by their pursuits be equipped with the means of judgement; but it is rather the philosopher who acquires them, and whose instrument they are.

What are we to say of this argumentation? It is true that no man is wholly a stranger to the pleasures of sense or those of being praised; but it is equally true that no man is wholly a stranger to the pleasures of learning. The concupiscent or ambitious man may not have practised his intelligence in study of the problems which interest the philosopher; but neither need the philosopher have sought the pleasures of bodily indulgence or of honour from those sources to which the devotees of other ways of life resort. Nor is it clear that the philosophers' verdict is unanimous. For some who have known the pleasure of intellectual pursuits have deserted them for a life of bodily indulgence or money-making or ambition.[1]

J. S. Mill, indeed, in his *Utilitarianism* argues very similarly to Plato. Like Plato he thinks that the pleasures incident to different kinds of activity differ in kind, and is therefore driven to ask how one who aims at getting as much pleasure in life as possible is to choose between them; and 'it is', he says,' an unquestionable fact, that those who are equally acquainted with, and equally capable of appreciating and enjoying, both, do give a most marked preference to the manner of existence which employs their higher faculties'.[2]

---

[1] No doubt Plato held that no man does evil without a false opinion that what he does is good; and the genuine philosopher, who knows good and evil, will not give a wrong verdict about them. But the most that Plato could say is that no genuine philosopher prefers one of the lives here said to be rejected, not that his preferring the philosophic life is evidence that he finds it pleasantest. Yet this is what the argument requires.

[2] p. 12.

He does not say that these are only the philosophers; and therein he is wiser than Plato. But whether they are or not, is the statement true? Not unless the fact that a man gives the preference to a manner of existence which employs his lower faculties is taken as evidence that he is not equally acquainted with, and equally capable of appreciating and enjoying, the other. And this Mill takes it to be. He admits that it is common for men to begin life with aspirations after everything noble, and to sink later into indolence and selfishness; but he holds that, before they devote themselves to the lower, they have become incapable of the higher pleasures.

Now supposing this to be true, what follows? Only that for them the kind of life to which they turn is pleasantest. To seek pleasure is not like collecting pictures with a view to selling them. A man who becomes incapable of recognizing the more valuable pictures will acquire the less valuable, and herein he will make a mistake; for the more valuable are so, from whosoever hands they come to market. But the man who has become incapable of the pleasures of learning or of the service of others will make no mistake in taking to other occupations, if pleasure is what he wants; what he wants is not something for which he can sell his activities in a market where those employing his higher faculties would always fetch more. It may even be true that the philosopher gets more pleasure out of life than either the concupiscent or the ambitious man does, without its following that they would get more if they tried to be philosophers. No one should pursue philosophy, Plato has said,[1] unless he learns easily, for he will not love what he does with pain and little success. We cannot therefore allow either that only a philosopher has had the requisite experience of all three kinds of pursuit, or that his verdict should be taken by others as equally sound for themselves. If, indeed, a man has not tried

[1] *Rep.* vi. 486 c 3–5.

exercising his intellectual powers he may be well advised to try, and see whether it does not give him more pleasure than his present mode of life. But should he on trying report that it does not, it is useless for another to say that his experience is different; we are not all made so as to get most pleasure out of the same occupations.

It may be retorted that Plato is only maintaining that the philosophic life is the pleasantest; but if so, that is not all that he has to prove. He has to prove that it profits any man rather to be just than unjust, and profiting is now taken to consist in being pleasantest. Now though he thinks the philosophic to be the highest life, he thinks that in every station a man may live more and less justly. That the philosopher's is the pleasantest as well as the highest may be an interesting fact and important to any one among the few who are capable of it, if he is tempted to diverge into other activities, as Plato thinks he is almost sure to be.[1] But it does not follow that, whatever station a man holds, he will find more pleasure in life if he lives justly.

Bernard Bosanquet, in his *Companion to Plato's Republic*,[2] observes that what in this argument Plato indicates is that 'the life of the "lover of wisdom" includes the lives of the other two, while theirs does not include his, and therefore the comparison is by implication not one of part against part, but one of whole against part. . . . It is only in as far as the intelligent life implies a more adequate object for the whole man, a larger and more harmonious being, that it claims ethical priority. Plato's argument, like Mill's, suggests, but does not arrive at, this conclusion.' This is certainly Plato's doctrine, though the question here is of hedonistic, not ethical, priority. And it may be said to be a conviction underlying the whole of his present discussion. In the first of his three arguments, that the soul of the tyrannic man is needy and unsatisfied, that is because such a life affords gratification only to clamorous and recurrent

---

[1] *Rep.* vi. 490 e 2–495 b 7.   [2] § 96, p. 350.

lusts, leaving the man still capable of other kinds of desire which are never gratified. A man's reason approves a form of life in which none of the three forms of the soul is unexercised, but they work together, the rational in planning out what interests and appetites shall be allowed play, and each how far, the spirited in holding him to the execution of this plan, however the strength of any interest or appetite may threaten to upset it, the appetitive and the other two as well in submitting particular desires originating from any of them to the limitations judged necessary, if the one life into which they all enter is to be good. This is Plato's fundamental doctrine; such order in a man's life is its justice. A man's wisdom or insight, φρόνησις, may apprehend such a life to be good; argument, λόγος, may convince him that other modes of life, in which the factors of the triform soul do not work together according to such a scheme, not only are bad but, so far as they involve him in unsatisfied cravings and longings, will bring suffering. Plato has argued in the *Republic*, and perhaps convincingly, very much as Butler does in his *Sermons*, that the happiness, if not the greatest pleasurableness, of life depends upon an adjusted development of a very complex system of divers capacities, interests, and desires in the soul; that a life which refuses play and satisfaction to some large element in his nature will involve a man in restlessness and discontent, and his pleasure be mixed up with pain; and that some appetites (as is argued more at length in the next section) cannot be indulged far without their pleasures, by the very conditions of their being, alternating with very notable pains to counterbalance them. That is why the philosophic type of life is happier, and perhaps pleasanter, than the tyrannic. But what Plato has not shown, either in this section or the preceding, is that the philosopher's is the only systematized life. Where the voluptuary fails, the efficient man of business may succeed; where the man of unregulated ambition fails, another may succeed who seeks

the first place in the State in preference to seeking knowledge. The reasoning that shows the happiness of life to
depend on its being organized so as to give play to the soul's
various powers does not show that it can only be organized
in one way so as to do this. The management of a great
business, the conduct of public affairs or of a campaign,
call for intelligence, though not for the use of intelligence
in the discovery of speculative truth. A life devoted to the
disinterested pursuit of knowledge may or may not be
higher; it need not offer a more adequate object to the
whole man than these. So too there are opportunities for
fighting courageously in lives that are not devoted to the
defence of what is best. When Plato compares the philosophic with the ambitious and the concupiscent lives, are
the latter such as no good or just man would live, or are
they the lives of his auxiliaries and craftsmen? If we say
the former, then besides the philosophic life and those with
which he compares it there are the lives which auxiliaries
and craftsmen ought to live, and how do they stand in
respect of pleasure? If we say the latter, then, granted
that the philosophic life is pleasantest, it remains a question whether these others are necessarily pleasanter if lived
justly; for in every station a man may be just or unjust.

It may indeed well be asked what is meant by saying of
one life that it is pleasanter than another. I may compare
in this way more or less isolated experiences. A mountain
expedition may be delightful at the start, while the air is
fresh and I am full of vigour; later on, if a storm has blown
up, and I am battling against wind and snow, with hands
half-frozen, hungry, and uncertain of my way, I can intelligibly say that this is by no means pleasant; and if the
storm passes, and I come out upon the summit, with a
magnificent view, sitting for half an hour in a glow of
sunshine and restored circulation and taking long-needed
refreshment, I can say that this is one of the pleasantest
half-hours I have ever spent. But what am I to say of the

expedition as a whole? That I have enjoyed it does not mean that I enjoyed it all the time; but I may enjoy the recollection of it all and be very glad that I undertook it. So I may look upon a longer stretch of life and judge it good. But this will not be because all of it was pleasant, nor yet because it contained a balance of pleasure over pain. For it is not sufficiently noticed that the metaphor involved in speaking of a balance of pleasure over pain is altogether inappropriate. In the scales of a balance we place things homogeneous in the respect in which we compare them: two masses, each of which is attracted towards the earth, not one whose natural motion is towards the centre, and another whose natural motion is from it, as Aristotle conceived the natural motions of earth and fire to be in contrary directions. Pleasure and pain are regarded, by those who would discover what form of life is pleasantest, as contraries, in the sense that one makes us inclined and the other averse to the activities which bring or are characterized by them. But if the same activity brings or is characterized by both of them, what is to settle whether I shall be inclined to it or averse? To measure the pleasures and the pains, if that were possible, would not settle it, because I should measure them in different units, and have no rule by which to determine how many units of the one cancel how many of the other. It is true that I can decide for or against the activity, and in some sense may be considering my profit when I do so. But I do not proceed like a man of business deciding by consideration of profit for or against a proposed enterprise. For the pros and cons in his survey are respectively pounds gained and pounds forgone or spent; the number of each can be estimated, and according as the number of pounds to be gained appears greater or less than the number of those to be forgone or spent, the enterprise promises a profit or a loss. No doubt the prospective profit may be small; and it may appear that much extra work will be involved, and perhaps the welfare of others will suffer and the ill will of friends be incurred. These matters may be taken into account, and the enterprise, in spite of the pecuniary profit to be expected, may be rejected. But in taking account of these, and 'weighing' them against the pecuniary profit, so as to determine whether on the whole the enterprise is 'worth while', a wholly different procedure is employed. The pros and cons are both incurred; or, if the ill will of friends be regarded as loss of their friendship, it is not loss of something homogeneous with pounds to be gained, so that one may compute whether what is to be gained or what is to be lost is greater. And even if it be held that a man has regard to the loss of friends only because of the pain he suffers from it, to the gain of money only because of the pleasure its use or possession brings him, and so with any other of the items which he takes into consideration, the case is the same. The pros and cons are both incurred; they are not homogeneous either respectively among themselves or with one another; they cannot be expressed as amounts whose magnitudes are independent of the importance we attach to them, like the items which make up a pecuniary profit that is in prospect, equally whether or not a man thinks it worth the labour and ill will involved for him in getting it and the injury to others' welfare. The question which of two ways of living is more profitable pecuniarily may be hard to decide in advance, but its meaning is clear. But it is very hard to say what we mean by asking which is pleasantest. Plato's third argument[1] for the supremacy of the philosophic life might be regarded as in part an attempt to explain this. It is to be noted that Socrates regards it as inflicting on his opponent the most crushing defeat of the three.[2]

In it he urges that only the wise man's pleasure is genuine and pure. Pleasure and pain are contraries; between them is a quiet of the soul, ἡσυχία, a state in which

---

[1] ix. 583 b 1–587 b 10.   [2] 583 b 6.

neither is felt.   But we observe that men who pass into this
from pain or pleasure take it each for the contrary of the
state out of which they pass.   That one should recover his
health, that some agony should cease, are not the contrary
states to pain; the cessation of some delight is not the
contrary state to delight.   Yet the last will be painful, the
first most pleasant.   Now this middle state of quiet which
is neither pain nor pleasure cannot be both.   We must say
therefore that it appears what really it is not, and puts a
trick on us.[1]   Not all pleasure is mere cessation of pain, nor
pain of pleasure.   Even among the pleasures which arise in
the soul through the body, those of scent, great and sudden
as they are, depend on no previous pain.   Yet the most and
greatest of this class are really reliefs from pain,[2] not
genuine pleasures, any more than the pain of anticipating
future suffering is genuine pain.   Socrates offers a comparison which he thinks illustrates these facts.   In nature
—i.e. in the physical world—we distinguish an upper
region, a lower, and a middle.   A man carried from below
to the middle region, standing there and viewing whence
he has come, will think he is in the upper region, falsely,
because he has never been thither to learn what it is like; but
if again carried down, he will think truly that he has been
borne to the nether region.   It may be surmised that Plato
has in mind here the same myth which he introduces at
the end of the *Phaedo*.   There it is supposed that the
Mediterranean Sea lies in a deep trough, and is fed by
rivers coming up from Tartarus.   If we could climb out of
this trough on to the upper surface of the earth, above the
mists that collect in it and obscure our vision, we should
know for the first time the real glory and beauty of the
heavens.   As it is, though we are borne up from the nether
regions, few of us ascend beyond this middle place, and
learn what the upper world is really like.   Thus it is with
men, according to the argument of the *Republic*, in regard

[1] γοητεία τις, 584 a 10.   [2] λυπῶν τινες ἀπαλλαγαί, 584 c 6.

to pleasure and pain. Of the middle state we all have experience, and when we pass from this to what is painful, our pain is genuine, our judgement of our condition true. But when we pass from pain to the middle state, we are convinced that this is pleasure, because we have had no experience of a state beyond it, like men who in comparing grey with black mistake it for the white which they have never seen. Genuine pleasure is not that which reaches us through the body and is conditioned by preceding states of the body such as hunger and thirst. These we may call depletions of the body, κενώσεις, as ignorance and un-wisdom are an emptiness of the soul.[1] We get pleasure in filling the body with food and drink, the soul with know-ledge and true opinion. To be filled with what is by its nature suitable (to soul or body) is pleasant. But soul and body are not equally real, neither are what respectively fill or complete them, and satisfy their needs. The soul is akin to what is unchanging and immortal and to truth; the body to what never abides in one state, and perishes; the same holds of that on which they feed. The truest and most genuine pleasure then must surely be what arises when that in us which most truly is is most truly filled with what most truly is. Then our pleasure is pure and abiding; but most of us have no experience of such pleasure. We offer to that part of our nature which is less real and will not hold it what is itself less real. Our pleasures are mixed up with pains, and get a false colour from their contrast one with the other. And this is most seen in those attendant on lustful and tyrannical desires.

---

[1] Plato speaks of κενώσεις τῆς περὶ τὸ σῶμα ἕξεως, but of κενότης τῆς περὶ ψυχὴν ἕξεως, 585 b 1, b 3. The difference can hardly be insignificant. The reason would seem to be this. When I have eaten and drunk, I cannot renew the pleasure given me till there has been a wastage of the substance which eating and drinking increased; till then I shall not be hungry and thirsty again. But when I have learnt something, and had the pleasure of learning, I need not lose the knowledge I have gained in order that I may desire to learn again and may renew that pleasure.

That pleasures and pains admit of being distinguished
as true or false is argued at greater length again by Plato
in the *Philebus*,[1] and since Protarchus is there made at first
to object altogether to the notion of false pain or false
pleasure, we may perhaps suppose that some criticism of
it had been made by others, or arisen in Plato's own mind,
after the appearance of the *Republic*. There is little new in
the *Philebus* so far as the facts on which Plato builds his
case are concerned. The distinction between pleasures and
pains that do and those that do not involve the body recurs.[2]
We are told again how misleading may be hopes and
imaginations, especially in evil men,[3] and this character is
alleged to attach equally to the pains and pleasures they
involve.[4] These are said to seem greater or less than they
really are by contrast and comparison one with the other.[5]
Again they are both contrasted with a middle state, and
men are said to mistake for pleasure the absence of pain,
though we hear now of students of nature who, out of
mistrust of pleasure and because of these illusions, deny
that there really is a pleasure which is not relief from pain;[6]
but if we would discover their error we must look not to the
most intense pleasures but to the purest, among which
those of scent are once more mentioned as well as those of
colour and visible form;[7] and the pure and unadulterated
are declared to have more truth than the vehement and
great, and not only to be truer and nobler, but pleasanter
as well.[8] The metaphor of filling and emptying is re-
peated,[9] and it is added that the loss of learning acquired
is not painful, as bodily wastage is, because it is a forgetting
or not noticing.[10] We may feel pain in considering our loss,
but that is not the process of losing. There is indeed one
fresh consideration adduced: in dreams or when out of

---

[1] 36 c 6 seq.   [2] 39 d 1–3.   [3] 38 b 6–41 b 6.
[4] 40 d 4.   [5] 42 b 8.
[6] 44 b 6–d 6: λυπῶν ταύτας εἶναι πάσας ἀποφυγάς, c 1.
[7] 51 a 2–52 d 2.   [8] 52 d 6, 53 b 8.
[9] 35 b 4.   [10] 52 a 5–b 5.

their mind men may seem to feel pleasure or pain,[1] without (in Socrates' opinion) really doing so. This example is not without importance in judging why Plato applied the distinction of true and false to pleasure and pain; but the arguments whether of the *Republic* or of the *Philebus* do not seem to justify it.

Perhaps his case rests chiefly on the supposition of a state of quiet that may be alternately mistaken for pleasure or pain according as we pass into it from either contrary; and about this it must be said that his illustration from a middle region between the nether and the upper world will not bear investigation, and that his use of the notion is not throughout consistent. If we examine the illustration, we may admit that men borne upward to Mediterranean lands might think they had reached the upper surface of the world, until they had risen out of this great trough to the real summits. But were they so to rise and to return to the middle region, they would not mistake it for Tartarus, nor if they redescended thither and came up to Mediterranean lands again would they repeat the mistake of supposing they were on the topmost surface. But each time that men pass out of agony or sickness they find their state pleasant; each time that a state of positive delight comes to an end, they feel pain in the neutral state succeeding it. Plato may be right in supposing that there are bodily and psychical processes of filling and emptying, building up and breaking down, restoration and decay,[2] which are respectively pleasant and painful; and that between these there is a state of rest, or only slight change,[3] which normally gives rise neither to pain nor pleasure, like ordinary good health; and he may be right in thinking—though there are difficulties in working out the hypothesis, because it is hard to see what the heightened physical state is, from which there is a passage to normal good health, that can be called decay or breaking down—that in it we are at most times conscious

[1] *Phil.* 36 e 5–8.   [2] Ibid. 42 c 9–d 7.   [3] Ibid. 43 c 4–6.

of neither pleasure nor pain, but do notably feel one or the other when we pass into it from states involving the contrary. But this would not show that the pain or pleasure felt on such occasions is less real than when felt at other times under conditions to which it is constantly attached. Plato confuses the physical or psychical conditions with the feelings attached to them. We may think when we have passed into the middle state that we have passed into one that will continue pleasant or painful, and find ourselves disillusioned. But it does not follow that we are mistaken in thinking we are feeling pleasure or pain.

As he proceeds, however, he shifts his ground. When the notion of a middle state is first introduced, he speaks as if it and those between which it lies were stages on one continuous process through which we might pass in either direction, as lower, middle, and upper regions lie on one journey, that may be travelled either way. Men in pain, we are told, extol rest from pain, and not delight—τὸ χαίρειν—as what is pleasant; but when delight ceases, rest from pleasure seems painful.[1] The delight, one would suppose, lies on the same scale with the pain. But it turns out later that this is not so. The most and greatest pleasures that arise through the body are mere cessations of pain;[2] while the cessation of those which are not so, like the pleasures of smell, is not said and could not be said to be painful; nor is the cessation of the pleasure of learning said to be so. The real gravamen therefore of the charge against the pleasures of the voluptuary and of the concupiscent life is not their falsity or unreality but their impurity. They are often mixed with pain themselves; the condition of having them is that we alternate between them and the pains of the state to which the cessation of their enjoyment reduces us, or through which we must pass before we can have them again.

And there is another thought in Plato's mind, connected

---

[1] *Rep.* ix. 583 d 6–e 2.   [2] 584 c 4–7.

with his condemnation of them on this account. The man
who lives for these pleasures has possession of no permanent source even of pleasure. He is at the mercy of
circumstance. The real condition, not indeed of the
moment's pleasure, but of a happy life is to be deeply
interested in something that abides; to make as it were
some object yours which grows under your hands and en-
larges your being. By object is meant, of course, object of
interest, not a thing in space. Now what the voluptuary
cares for is not of this kind. It slips from him as fast as he
attains it. It is like Penelope's web; there is no more to his
life one day than the day before. That is why Socrates
compares such men to those who pour water into a sieve—
οὐδὲ τὸ στέγον ἑαυτῶν πιμπλάντες,[1] and as consummated in
becoming—ἐν ταῖς γενέσεσιν ἀποτελούμενοι.[2] What makes
life worth having must be that we make our own something
that can abidingly satisfy us, and for this it must be itself
abiding, not as material goods last, though their possession
may for that contribute more to our happiness, but as a
purpose abides and its achievement is present in a long
succession of particular activities. Knowledge is of this
kind, more particularly in its increase, when all we learn is
but fresh mastery of the same system of reality. We do not
lose what we have gained before we can gain more. In
devotion to a great cause, a man finds that all his great or
small achievements bring him the gain of promoting the
same purpose. Madame de Sévigné's remark may be re-
peated here,[3] that the secret of happiness is to desire only
that the will of God be done and believe that whatever
happens is His will. Nor was Spinoza's notion of felicity
very different. If one could reach to it, then in all one did
he would hold himself to be attaining the only thing that he
desired, and be really independent of fortune. At any rate,
if one is to be happy, there must, as Bosanquet said, be 'an
adequate object for the whole man', and none is adequate

---

[1] *Rep.* ix. 586 b 3.   [2] *Phil.* 54 e 1.   [3] Cf. *supra*, p. 62.

which does not either give him all he wants or else at least
increasingly approximate to being such. A life in which
he makes his body a vehicle of pleasures which when they
have passed leave it as poor and empty as it was before
furnishes no such object.

All this is true and important, and perhaps Plato is the
first man to have pointed it out. But to ask what life comes
nearest this ideal is not to ask which is pleasantest. So long
as we distinguish its pleasure from the goodness and even
also from the happiness of life, and concentrate on pleasure,
we are considering that in life which does not abide, and
cannot be present as one in its different parts, but must be
taken for what it is felt to be as it passes. And it cannot be
the pleasure of the moment, μονόχρονος ἡδονή, which makes
the practice of justice profit a man, nor is it that really
which even the hedonist prizes, however he may deceive
himself. Neither is it the aggregate of such passing
pleasures; for that is never felt as a pleasure. This is part
of what Plato, who noticed so much, means in the *Philebus*,
when he says that to live all one's life feeling the greatest
pleasures cannot by itself and without any knowledge be
one's real good. For if a man can neither remember that
he did enjoy, nor take note that he is enjoying, nor reckon
that he will enjoy pleasure, his life is no better than some
mollusc's.[1] The man who pulled down his barns and built
greater[2] was happy, if at all, in enjoying not the sum of the
pleasures for which he had made provision, but the consciousness how great a sum it was. And herein lies the
point of Socrates' reference in the *Philebus* to what men
seem to feel when dreaming or out of their mind.[3] For
such pains or pleasures stand isolated; we cannot in feeling
them take into account with them those of sane or waking
life as contributing to the happiness of life as a whole. It
has often been said that there is no sure mark by which

[1] 20 e 4–21 d 5.   [2] St. Luke xii. 18.
[3] 36 e 5; cf. *supra*, pp. 146–7.

what we seem to apprehend in dreams can be rejected as unreal in comparison of what we say we apprehend in our waking hours. For the first may be as internally coherent as the second; there may be a continuity of dreaming from one night to another; and dream-objects are not less vivid than any others. But this surely is true, that we never in sleep remember and condemn our waking consciousness and take it into the account of our life, as, when awake, we so treat our dreams. For this reason dream-pleasures may perhaps be called unreal, in comparison of those enjoyed awake, even though any one would rather have pleasant than painful dreams, and the first are really pleasant.

The only defence then that can be offered for Plato's distinction of true and false pleasures and pains is that he was not really resting just on these the superiority of one life to another, though he professed to be doing so.[1] He has shifted from the question what form of life is best or most excellent to the question which is happiest, and thence again to the question which is pleasantest, and claims to answer them all as different questions in favour of the philosophic life, and to do this, so far as the last is concerned, by showing the falsity of the pleasures attaching to inferior lives. But what is really shown to be false is that such pleasures can make life happy. That he is not really judging the competing lives in respect merely of their pleasantness appears when we compare the language of 585 d 11 with that of 586 e 2. In the first passage we are told that for anything in the soul to be filled with what is by its nature appropriate to it is pleasant—εἰ ἄρα τὸ πληροῦσθαι τῶν φύσει προσηκόντων ἡδύ ἐστιν—and to the inferior parts of the soul it is suggested that whatever gives them pleasure is appropriate; there would really be no test of appropriateness but the pleasure received. But

---

[1] This perhaps is what Professor H. H. Joachim's defence amounts to, in the *Philosophical Review*, vol. xx, pp. 471–97, Sept. 1911. But he does not put it so.

in the second we read that the appetites that arise in the soul so far as it is concupiscent or contentious—φιλοκερδές or φιλόνικον—will receive the pleasures that belong to them, if guided by wisdom; for that most belongs to anything which is best for it—εἴπερ τὸ βέλτιστον ἑκάστῳ, τοῦτο καὶ οἰκειότατον. This is to interpret the test of what is by its nature appropriate in a way that makes not the immediate pleasure, but the character of the life with which its enjoyment is connected, the test; and only those enjoyments are any longer to be rightly accounted pleasures, which it is good that we should enjoy. That is not a hedonistic ranking of different lives.

The passage in which these last quoted words occur[1] is important on another ground. It was observed above that to prove the superiority in happiness of the philosophic to the tyrannic life is not to prove that in any station a man's life will be happier if he is just than if he is unjust; and for the most part Plato's arguments are directed only to the former conclusion, whereas the latter is what, if to profit is to bring happiness, Socrates was challenged to prove. But here he brings the argument to bear upon the latter issue.

'"Well then", said I, "may we confidently say of the desires in which the concupiscent or contentious ⟨in us⟩ is concerned, that those which follow knowledge and reason, and in their company pursue and obtain such pleasures as attend on wisdom, will obtain the pleasures which both are truest, so far as it is possible for them to be true, inasmuch as the desires are following truth, and belong to them, if ⟨as we must admit⟩ what is best for anything most belongs to it?" "It is this", he said, "which most belongs to it." "When the whole soul then follows the philosophic ⟨in it⟩ and is not rebellious, each part succeeds not only in doing its own ⟨work⟩ and being just, but in enjoying each the pleasures that are its own and best and to the measure of its capacity are truest." "Certainly so." "But when one of the other ⟨parts⟩ rules, it will not succeed in finding its own pleasure, and will constrain the rest to pursue a pleasure not their own nor true." "So it is", he said.'

[1] *Rep.* ix. 586 d 4–587 a 6.

Here, when the philosophic part of the soul is spoken of, Socrates is not thinking only of philosophers, but of the rational or λογιστικόν in every man, whence springs in those capable of it that passion to know reality as it is which he calls philosophy, but in all of us the notion and desire of good. Only the philosopher has knowledge of the good, and can regulate all his life by that; and his of all men's may be the truest pleasure, and he happier than victors at Olympia.[1] But in any station a man may have true belief or false concerning the good, so far as it can be realized in his own life; if he acts by true belief he will be following the guidance of what is philosophic in him, and will, as Socrates argues here, have the truest pleasure of which he is capable.

Yet has this been proved? Are the happiness or misery which in their several degrees are held to characterize men's lives not as a result of others' action, but necessarily in respect of how far their lives are justly or unjustly lived, really such direct functions of justice and injustice as Plato tries to show? When his three arguments are finished he offers a fanciful computation of the interval which separates in pleasure the life of the philosopher-king from that of the tyrant; the first is 729 times pleasanter than the second.[2] We need not take this mode of expression too seriously; but we cannot ignore the statement that follows: if the just and good man wins by so much in pleasure, in grace and beauty and excellence of life—εὐσχημοσύνῃ τε βίου καὶ κάλλει καὶ ἀρετῇ—his superiority will be immeasurable.[3] Why so, if pleasure is a direct function of excellence? But if it is not, must the order be the same, by whichever difference lives are ordered? Do we find it in experience to be so, as far as we can judge? We may admit to the full that a man cannot be happy unless he has so much system in his life as will furnish him with abiding interests, and provide 'an adequate object for the whole man'. But very

[1] v. 465 d 3.   [2] ix. 587 b 11–e 4.   [3] ix. 588 a 7–10.

diverse kinds of life, business, administration, conquest, exploration, farming, engineering, and what not, can provide a constantly growing and abiding subject of interest and activity to those pursuing them; and is it clear that, as men ordinarily count happiness, no man pursuing any of them is ever the happier, or even ever not the less happy, for not being too scrupulously just? When Peary would not allow the only white companion of his journey to the North Pole left with him at latitude 87° 48', the highest then ever reached, to advance with him on the final stage, in order that the glory and satisfaction of first reaching it might be his alone among white men, was that what Plato would have called just, or we can approve? But what evidence is there that his happiness was not the greater for it? And if we look to pleasures, as something we get and enjoy in separate 'parcels', is there any proof that a just man is more secure of a succession of these than an unjust? In a perfect society a bad man might find his efforts so repressed and thwarted that he would be less happy than his better neighbours, and perhaps get less pleasure in life. But we do not live in a perfect society; in the world as it is, much may enlarge the life of one man (to borrow Plato's metaphor) by depleting the lives of others. There have been many great business concerns whose founders, if report speaks truly, were not over-scrupulous to respect the rights of their rivals; but is it certain they were less happy than honester men whose businesses they ruined?

A man indeed may be so good that he would be unhappy in the enjoyment of anything that came to him through any action of his which he disapproved. He then would be less happy if he acted unjustly than if justly. But it does not follow that acting justly he is happier than any other man who, being of less heroic mould, is ready to advance the attainment of some life-filling object of desire by an action which he knows to be unjust.

If, when Aristotle said that most men are agreed about the name of the highest good and call it happiness,[1] he meant that this was a sort of proper name, signifying nothing till we learnt to what it was applied, he would be making it a mere tautology to say that the best life is the happiest. But he did not mean this; for he considers later the characters required in what is best, and says that happiness appears especially to possess them.[2] And in fact the word 'happiness' bears a meaning in common speech which makes it possible to dispute whether the best life is the happiest. It may be true that happiness depends largely on character, and on features of character which are found in a just man. But they may be present in a way sufficient for happiness without being altogether sufficient for justice. In any ordinary sense of the word 'happiness', the degrees of it and of justice do not run *pari passu*, and Plato has not proved that they do. Yet it does not follow that he has not shown that justice profits a man, and what it is that justice and injustice each makes of the soul so as respectively to be good and evil.

[1] *Eth. Nic.* i. iv. 2, 1095 a 17–20.
[2] Ibid. i. vii. 3–6, 1097 a 25–b 8.

VI

ARISTOTLE'S DEFINITION OF MORAL VIRTUE, AND PLATO'S ACCOUNT OF JUSTICE IN THE SOUL

NICOLAI HARTMANN, in an interesting discussion of Aristotle's account of moral virtue,[1] has called attention to the difference between the contrariety of opposed vices and the contrast of certain virtues. The ἄκρα or extremes, somewhere between which Aristotle thought that any morally virtuous disposition (with the possible exception of justice) must lie, are not conciliable. The same man cannot combine or reconcile, in the same action, cowardice and bravery, intemperance and insensibility, stinginess and thriftlessness, passion and lack of spirit. These are pairs of contraries, between which a virtue lies; but the virtue is not a synthesis of the extremes in a pair. It is true that on one interpretation of the doctrine of the mean, the mean is a synthesis of contraries, but not of contrary vices. According to this interpretation, which Burnet adopted, there are contrary tendencies or impulses, e.g. fear and delight in danger, and the virtuous disposition combines these in right proportion; but the vicious dispositions also combine them, in other and wrong proportions, the contrariety of these dispositions arising from the fact that either impulse may be unduly preponderant over the other. In support of this interpretation Burnet appealed to the theory of bodily health accepted by Aristotle in the *Physics*.[2] 'Bodily excellences', we read, 'such as health and a good state *of body* we regard as consisting in a blending of hot and cold *elements within the body* in due proportion, in relation either to one another or to the surrounding atmosphere';[3] and a

---

[1] *Ethik*, c. 61, 'Gegensatzverhältnis und Wertsynthese'.

[2] *The Ethics of Aristotle*, pp. 69–73.

[3] *Phys.* VII. iii. 246 b 4–6, Oxford translation by R. P. Hardie and R. K. Gaye. I have italicized the words not in the Greek, as the A.V. of the Bible does.

few lines later we are told that, though the acquisition or loss of states is not itself an alteration, they are acquired or lost through the alteration of the hot and the cold, the dry and the moist *elements*, or of whatever the primary *things* be on which the states depend.[1] The excellences and defects of the soul seem from what follows to be included in this general statement, though of course they do not depend on a due blending of the primaries *hot*, *cold*, *dry*, and *moist*; these, as we learn elsewhere, are the primary differences and contrarieties to which all other contrasted qualities of body that are perceived by touch can be reduced;[2] but the alterations of the sensitive part of the soul on which its excellences and defects depend are (or are such as produce) pleasures and pains.[3] Many objections, both speculative and empirical, might be brought against this theory of health, but they do not concern us here;[4] though it is well to note in passing that the word *element*, used of the hots and the colds, the dries and the moists, which Aristotle in places[5] calls στοιχεῖα, does not mean what it means in chemistry to-day. What a chemist to-day calls elements are bodies of determinate kinds; but these primary contraries are somethings whose blendings yield the determinate forms into which and a common matter or ὕλη the elementary kinds of body recognized by Aristotle, earth, air, fire, and water, are analysable in thought. Whatever view, however, we take of his theory of health, it is doubtful whether the definition of moral virtue in the *Nicomachean Ethics* is to be interpreted in the light of it. For in the passage of the *Physics* the contraries mentioned are

---

[1] Ibid. 246 b 13–17.

[2] *de Gen. et Corr.* II. ii. 329 b 16: αὐτῶν Δὴ πρῶτον τῶν ἁπτῶν Διαιρετέον ποῖαι πρῶται Διαφοραὶ καὶ ἐναντιώσεις. 330 a 24: Δῆλον τοίνυν ὅτι πᾶσαι αἱ ἄλλαι Διαφοραὶ ἀνάγονται εἰς τὰς πρώτας τέτταρας, αὗται Δὲ οὐκέτι εἰς ἐλάττους.

[3] *Phys.* VII. iii. 246 b 20–247 a 18.

[4] For some criticisms of it see *infra*, note on pp. 170–1.

[5] e.g. *de Gen. et Corr.* II. iii. 330 a 30, and note *ad loc.* in H. H. Joachim's edition.

pleasures and pains; but in the *Nicomachean Ethics* there
is no suggestion that pleasures and pains are the primary
contraries, which, or whose conditions in the sensitive
soul, must be blended in due proportion in order that we
may acquire and possess virtuous dispositions or states.
Moral virtue is indeed said to be concerned with pleasures
and pains,[1] but it is acts and affections, πράξεις καὶ πάθη,
which according as we are or are not virtuous are said to
exhibit a mean or not,[2] and the virtues are distinguished
from one another by differences in the acts and affections
concerned. Courage is said to be a mean in respect of
fear and confidence; temperance in respect of certain
pleasures and pains; generosity in respect of giving and
taking money,[3] and so forth. This does not agree with the
language of the *Physics*. It is moreover to be noted that
the theory that the mean involved in moral virtue is a
synthesis of contraries in due proportion is inapplicable
to the only illustration offered by Aristotle to show how
the mean of which he is here speaking is relative to the
individual; the right quantity of meat for one man is not
the right quantity for another, though it is always a mean
between too much and too little. I have only mentioned
the theory here in order to point out that, even if it were
accepted, the synthesis of contraries which, according to
it, is involved in a virtuous disposition is not that of contrary bad dispositions, the Aristotelian ἄκρα. These cannot
be combined in an action, neither do we think that they
ought to be; they ought both to be avoided.

[1] *Eth. Nic.* II. iii. 1, 1104 b 8: περὶ ἡδονὰς γὰρ καὶ λύπας ἐστὶν ἡ
ἠθικὴ ἀρετή· Διὰ μὲν γὰρ τὴν ἡδονὴν τὰ φαῦλα πράττομεν, Διὰ Δὲ τὴν
λύπην τῶν καλῶν ἀπεχόμεθα.

[2] Ibid. II. vi. 18, 1107 a 8: οὐ πᾶσα Δ' ἐπιΔέχεται πρᾶξις οὐΔὲ πᾶν
πάθος τὴν μεσότητα.

[3] Ibid. II. vii. 2–4, 1107 a 33: περὶ μὲν οὖν φόβους καὶ θάρρη ἀνΔρεία
μεσότης. b 4: περὶ ἡδονὰς Δὲ καὶ λύπας—οὐ πάσας, ἧττον Δὲ †καὶ† περὶ
τὰς λύπας—μεσότης μὲν σωφροσύνη, ὑπερβολὴ Δὲ ἀκολασία. b 8: περὶ
Δὲ Δόσιν χρημάτων καὶ λῆψιν μεσότης μὲν ἐλευθεριότης, ὑπερβολὴ Δὲ καὶ
ἔλλειψις ἀσωτία καὶ ἀνελευθερία.

But there are contrasted dispositions that we approve, from which, however difficult it may seem to combine them, issue actions both of which may seem to be required of us. A familiar instance is afforded by the respective claims of justice and forgiveness. Hartmann does not mention this, but he mentions justice and love of one's neighbour (*Gerechtigkeit* and *Nächstenliebe*). These stand contrasted; and the action to which a man with a strong sense of justice might be prompted in a given situation may be one from which neighbourly love by itself would hold him back. It is quite possible for a man to have this neighbourly love in strength, with very little regard to the observance of justice, or to have a strong sense of justice and be lacking in love of his neighbour. But both are good dispositions; and virtue would not be shown, in a particular situation, by an action displaying neither, as it would be shown by one displaying neither of the related and contrary vices, the ἄκρα to the μεσότης. Rather we think that we ought somehow to satisfy the claims of both. The case, therefore, is different with antithetic *Werte*, 'values', and with antithetic *Unwerte*, 'disvalues'. Other examples of such antithetic 'values' are purity (*Reinheit*) and fullness of life (*Fülle*); or love of one's neighbour (*Nächstenliebe*) and love of those remote (*Fernstenliebe*).

This antithetic of values is neither so frequently recurrent as the antithetic of disvalues, nor do the two correspond; i.e. the opposed virtues are not respectively contrary to the opposed vices, to both of which, as Aristotle said, in spite of their contrariety to each other, the one virtue which is in a mean between them is, in another way, contrary. Courage is in this way contrary both to cowardice and foolhardiness. On the other hand, the ideally courageous man should display both stout-hearted endurance (*beherztes Ausharren*) and thoughtful foresight, cool presence of mind (*bedachtsame Vorsicht, kaltblütige Geistesgegenwart*); and it is the former which is specially lacking in the coward, the latter in the foolhardy. So again self-control (*Beherrschtheit*) is valuable, and a development of the emotional life (*Entfaltung des Affektlebens*) is valuable; but these are opposed 'values', or at least capable of competing. Intemperance, ἀκολασία, and insensitiveness, ἀναισθησία, are opposed disvalues. The virtue of σωφροσύνη or temperance should somehow combine self-control with the development of the emotional life. But since there is a kinship between insensitiveness and a self-control that is not combined with the contrasted 'value', the Stoics made insensitiveness itself into a virtue; and because of the likeness between intemperance and development of the emotional life uncombined with self-control, the emotions have sometimes been rejected altogether.

Strict parallelism here would require Hartmann rather to point to some who had made intemperance into a virtue; perhaps Polus in the *Gorgias* might be cited in this sense; or Alfred Barratt, who said that 'the highest virtue consists in being led, not by one desire, but by all', the cause of repentance being 'never the attainment of some pleasure, but always the non-attainment of more: not the satisfaction of one desire, but the inability to satisfy all'; though, very inconsistently, he called the highest virtue, as just defined, 'the complete organization of the moral nature'.[1] But I do not wish to press this as a criticism, nor yet to ask how far anything like what Hartmann has said in regard to courage and temperance could be paralleled for all the virtues in Aristotle's table. That to which I wish to direct attention is Hartmann's suggestion of a synthesis of 'values' being involved in the Aristotelian mean; for a synthesis of values is very different from a mean of 'disvalues' or κακίαι.

I think that Hartmann's observation is a good one, but that it points to the need for a more thoroughgoing criticism or restatement of the Aristotelian doctrine than his. In the

---

[1] Cited by C. M. Williams, *A Review of the Systems of Ethics founded on the Theory of Evolution*, p. 117 (Macmillan, 1893).

'doctrine of the mean' Aristotle seems to me to have been trying, and failing, to improve on the account of virtue offered by his master Plato. Assuming what I have to say on this head to be sound, it would follow that the necessity for a synthesis of opposed 'elements of value', to which Hartmann draws attention, is a special case of a more pervading necessity. I believe that no action is obligatory independently of relation to any good, but that this good may be, and in the last resort is, connected with a life to be lived, to the form of goodness in which the particular obligatory action is necessary. If so, a man's particular actions should be such as will together make a life in which this goodness can be realized; their 'values' are connected with the goodness of the whole; and the synthesis of *Wertelemente* which Hartmann requires in a particular action is really the suiting of the particular action to the wider plan of life to which it belongs, in a situation of a sort that seems sometimes to call for exercise of one and sometimes for exercise of the other of two 'opposed' virtues.

It is Plato's teaching that you cannot unexceptionably define any virtue by naming the sort of acts it requires of you. A man's courage should not always make him stand in the ranks and fight, nor his justice always make him restore what he owes. The statement indeed that justice, in the widest sense of that word, will make him do his proper job, τὰ αὑτοῦ πράττειν, may seem open to an objection just the contrary of what lies against the attempt to define virtues by naming their works; for while one method assigns to a virtue acts which do not belong to it, the other fails to say what do. But Plato tries to meet this objection by describing the life of a good State and the constitution of the soul. By the first description we are helped to divine the particular acts that should be done; by the second to see through the development of what capacities in us and through what inner discipline we may do the acts belonging to us in the life of the State, and not other acts. This

Y

discipline and development bear fruit in all right actions, and the 'inward and spiritual grace' from which the 'outward and visible' deed issues is different because of them from what it would be if the agent were not thus 'just', even though the outward and visible deeds might yet be on occasion the same. In that sense, virtue is one; though this unity involves, as Plato is careful to maintain, distinguishable constituent excellences in distinguishable forms or parts (εἴδη or μέρη) of the soul; and though also we may distinguish many virtues, according to the kinds of situation that repeatedly occur and the kinds of deed which for the most part are required in them. But that such deeds are right in such situations is true only for the most part; that is why the virtues cannot be unexceptionably defined by naming the sorts of acts they require of us.

Now Aristotle was more interested in the multiplicity of virtues than in the unity of virtue. To this we owe it that he devoted a book and a half of the *Nicomachean Ethics* to the detailed description of a number of particular moral virtues, and the vices alternative to them in their several fields. These are so many 'values' and 'disvalues', *Werte* and *Unwerte*, in the phrase of Hartmann and other exponents of 'axiology'. If all these 'values' ought to be actualized, are *seinsollend*, and certain situations allow of one's actualizing more than one, but only alternatively, then antithetic relations and 'antinomies' arise, and the need for 'synthesis'. If, however, virtue is one, it should not require of us incompatibles. That is why the synthesis of antithetic 'values' which Hartmann finds to be involved in some moral virtue described by Aristotle as a μεσότης or mean is only a particular case of what must be always necessary for determining the right act in a given situation, if the unity of virtue is to be sustained against the multiplicity of the particular virtues.

And Aristotle, though more interested in the multiplicity, does not deny that unity, the belief in which led

Plato to offer a definition of justice 'in the soul' which would make the just man the man of complete moral virtue. Only he will not give to this all-pervading unity the name *justice*. If we ask ourselves whether anything corresponds in the *Nicomachean Ethics* to the Platonic distinction between justice in the State and justice in the soul, we must, I think, admit that the distinction between ὅλη Δικαιοσύνη, complete justice, and ἠθικὴ ἀρετή, moral virtue, as the generic identity of the various particular virtues in his table, so corresponds. Aristotle himself really says as much; for justice, in this comprehensive sense, is, he says, not a part of virtue, but the whole, οὐ μέρος ἀρετῆς ἀλλ' ὅλη ἀρετή: all virtue is contained in it, as the proverb says; the man thus just has 'fulfilled the law'.[1] And then, in the last section of the chapter, he gives its relation to moral virtue. They are the same thing differently regarded; i.e. what this same is, as justice and as virtue, are not the same; in relation to other men, it is justice; merely as a disposition in the soul of the man who is just, it is virtue.[2]

This is not really different from what Plato had written in the fourth book of his *Republic*, at the end of the passage in which, assuming that we mean the same when we call a State and when we call a man just, he has gone on to analyse the soul, and shown how the three sorts of excellence, whose display by different men holding different functions in the State makes the actions just which we regard as corporate acts of the State, enter also into every action of a just man. Therefore they enter—and this, if we are to understand Plato, we must never forget—into those very actions of different men, by which they co-operate in a corporate act of the State. The statesman whose

---

[1] *Eth. Nic.* v. i. 12–19, 1129 b 11–1130 a 10.

[2] Ibid., § 20, 1130 a 10: τί Δὲ Διαφέρει ἡ ἀρετὴ καὶ ἡ Δικαιοσύνη αὕτη, Δῆλον ἐκ τῶν εἰρημένων· ἔστι μὲν γὰρ ἡ αὐτή, τὸ Δ' εἶναι οὐ τὸ αὐτό, ἀλλ' ᾗ μὲν πρὸς ἕτερον, Δικαιοσύνη, ᾗ Δὲ τοιάΔε ἕξις ἁπλῶς, ἀρετή.

wisdom, the soldier whose courage, the others also whose
temperance contribute to make a corporate act of the State
just, will each make his contribution as he should only
because, in so ordering his own soul and his own life that
he may do so, he displays all three excellences. The justice
of the State, therefore, is an expression of the justice in the
souls of those whose several actions are concerned together
in what we call the State's acts; for Plato knew that only
individuals act. And this is what he says in the passage
to which I am referring.

'Something of this sort is in truth, it seems, what justice was'—
the justice of which he has been so long speaking—'concerned not
with the outward doing of one's own *duties*, but the inward:[1] in
very truth with a man himself and what is his, that he should not
allow the kinds[2] within his soul to do each another's *work* in him,
nor to interfere one with another, but having verily set aright what
is his and gained rule himself over himself, having ordered and come
to friendship with himself and conciliated *these kinds* in their triplicity, just as if it were three strings in a scale, top and bottom and
middle, and any there may be between, having bound all these
together and become out of many one, temperate and ordered, so
at length should act, if he do some action whether concerned with
getting money or with the care of his body or with some affair of
State or transaction of private *life*, in all these counting and calling
just and noble whatever action preserves and helps to complete in
him this disposition, and wisdom the knowledge that presides over
this action, and *likewise* unjust whatever action at any time undoes
this *disposition*, and folly the opinion presiding over this.'[3]

Such is Plato's account of the disposition which is
virtue, in whatever particular sort of virtuous action and

---

[1] I italicize words supplied in translation, as above, pp. 156-7. The Greek
—οὐ περὶ τὴν ἔξω πρᾶξιν τῶν αὑτοῦ ἀλλὰ περὶ τὴν ἐντός—is ambiguous;
for τῶν αὑτοῦ may be either one's own duties, or the 'parts' of one's own
soul; in the next words—ὡς ἀληθῶς περὶ ἑαυτὸν καὶ τὰ ἑαυτοῦ—it is the
latter; but there is probably a shift of meaning (one might almost say a play
upon the words) indicated by ὡς ἀληθῶς.

[2] γένη: i.e. what are also called the εἴδη, or μέρη, parts, of the soul.

[3] *Rep.* iv. 443 c 9–444 a 2.

in whatever dealings with others it is shown. Aristotle, in the passage cited above, as often elsewhere, has but put into a succinct phrase or formula what Plato had set out at length. He does the same when he contrasts appetite and purpose, saying that a man's purpose may be contrary to his appetite, but that he cannot have contrary appetites at once.[1] This statement sums up the result of the argument by which Socrates, in *Republic* iv. 436 b 5–439 e 1, convinces Glaucon that what makes it possible for a man to refrain from gratifying an appetite which he does not cease to feel, and so to be contrarily affected in himself towards the same thing at the same time, is that there is a rational or considerative as well as an appetitive principle or part or form or kind in his soul. It is of course to similar experiences of contrariety within the soul that Socrates appeals in arguing further for a principle of spirit distinguishable alike from the appetitive and the considerative forms of the soul's being.

It is not necessary here to expound the reasoning by which this account of the soul is commended, nor to discuss the value of the account.[2] All that I wish to do is to consider how Aristotle's definition of moral virtue is related to Plato's definition, based on this account, of 'justice in the soul'. I have suggested that the most famous feature of Aristotle's definition, the doctrine of the mean, expresses an attempt—I think an ill-advised attempt—to improve upon Plato's account of the part which 'temperance' plays in 'justice in the soul'. I have so far offered reason for saying that any one looking for Aristotle's treatment of the facts to which Plato directed our attention, when expounding justice in the soul and its relation to justice in the State, would expect to find it in the definition of moral virtue, ἠθικὴ ἀρετή, and the exposition of the relation of this to ὅλη Δικαιοσύνη or complete justice.

But we cannot judge this question fairly without bearing

---

[1] *Eth. Nic.* iii. ii. 5, 1111 b 15: καὶ προαιρέσει μὲν ἐπιθυμία ἐναντιοῦται, ἐπιθυμία δ' ἐπιθυμίᾳ οὔ.   [2] Cf. for this Essay III above.

in mind what Plato never points out in so many words, though the *Republic* contains several definite statements implying it, viz. that the three forms or parts of the soul are not merely co-ordinate: that the division as it were does double duty, and, though not a 'physical', is not merely a 'logical' division.[1] To speak of parts suggests that the unity of the soul is by way of addition to an appetitive principle of the other principles. But the spirited and rational are not merely added to the appetitive, as an appetite for grass might have been added in Nebuchadnezzar to his existing appetites for other foods, instead of being substituted for them. The appetitive is itself modified by the presence of the other two, as the spirited also is modified by the presence of the rational. Besides this, in any action they are all involved; to crave, to be angry, or even indignant, to consider or approve, none of these is to act. And the co-operation of them in action—how the soul is at once in some respects the same in all action, in other respects differs according as a man acts more or less justly —this is one-half of Plato's teaching; that we may understand this is one purpose of his division; and so far as the human soul shows its being in all these modes at once, we might call the division metaphysical. But the appetites which Socrates, in *Republic* iv. 436 a 11, describes as for the pleasures of nourishment and procreation and their like, though, if the soul were merely appetitive, they would be the only sort of desire it would feel, are by no means this in fact. Desires of other kinds belong to it as spirited, and of yet others as rational. This is most explicitly asserted in ix. 580 d 7–8. Socrates there offers, as a further proof that a man's soul may be divided according to three 'kinds', this: that there are pleasures of three kinds, each proper to one mode of the soul's being, and likewise desires and principles.[2] There are, that is to say, desires that belong to

---

[1] Cf. *supra*, pp. 79–80.
[2] Τήνδε· τριῶν ὄντων τριτταὶ καὶ ἡδοναί μοι φαίνονται, ἑνὸς ἑκάστου

a soul as spirited, and again as rational, not only those which belong to it as appetitive; so that ἐπιθυμία has a generic as well as a specific sense, and so far as the soul is an ἀρχή, or initiates change, the threefold division is a logical division into three principles in virtue of which it does so.[1]

The importance of all this is as follows: The function of the rational or considerative 'part' in the soul is not merely to regulate the appetites, i.e. the activities of the appetitive 'part', from which, at the outset of his analysis, by calling attention to its withholding a man from the gratification of his appetites, Socrates proves that it is distinct. It has to regulate all a man's desires, including those of which it makes him capable itself, like desire of knowledge, and those, like desire of power, whereof the spirited 'part' makes him capable. Similarly, the function of the spirited 'part' is not only to hold a man steadfast to an approved course when this course involves rejecting the gratification of some appetite, but equally when it involves refusal to gratify a desire of which the spirited 'part' itself, or even the rational, makes him capable; for a man may on occasion judge it right, in the interests of the community or of his own soul, that he should sacrifice some pursuit of power or knowledge.

Though it lies aside from my main thesis, it may perhaps be worth while to suggest here that this distinction between the generic and the specific senses of ἐπιθυμία might well be borne in mind by Freudian psychologists when they speak of the *libido*. When the direction of a man's energies

---

μία ἰδία. ἐπιθυμίαι τε ὡσαύτως καὶ ἀρχαί. ἀρχαί here presumably are movers to action; they 'take the initiative'.

[1] Aristotle again finds a way of expressing this, by distinguishing in the genus ὄρεξις the three species βούλησις, θυμός and ἐπιθυμία. *Vide De Anima*, III. ix. 432 b 5–6; cf. *Magn. Mor.* I. xii. 1187 b 36: ὀρέξεως δ' ἐστὶν εἴδη τρία, ἐπιθυμία, θυμός, βούλησις When Aristotle says, *De Anima*, III.ix. 432 b 6–7, criticizing Plato for dividing the soul into parts, εἰ δὲ τρία ἡ ψυχή, ἐν ἑκάστῳ ἔσται ὄρεξις, he says what Plato would have readily admitted.

into some other channel than the gratification of sexual appetite is described as a sublimation of the *libido*, it seems often thought that this appetite is being somehow transformed, say into a devotion to good works. But though such devotion may fill a larger part in the life of a man who has been disappointed in love, or in whom sexual appetite has been repressed, than otherwise it would have done, it is not itself a transformation of the specific appetite, but an alternative manifestation of the generic capacity of desire, and one of which another 'form' of the soul than the appetitive makes him capable. To suppose that sublimation of the *libido* is transformation of appetite is like supposing that to draw a circle is to transform a drawing of a triangle.

The soul then, according to Plato's account, as rational or considerative, has at any moment, if it is to act justly, to divine what would be best in the situation and act accordingly. But it has in it all sorts of impulses to action, some springing from its appetitive, some from its spirited, some from its rational nature. Any of these may move it towards doing something of which as rational it disapproves, or from doing something of which as rational it approves. What Plato calls courage, the excellence of the spirited 'part' as this functions in all action, will sustain him in following his judgement, when thus moved contrarily. But the man of formed and settled 'justice' will not be moved by appetite towards that of which 'consideration' would never approve pursuit,[1] and his desires for what in different circumstances he would approve pursuing, in whichever 'part' of the soul they originate, will not be so strong as to make it difficult for him to hold fast to the course approved by him. To determine, however, what place in the scheme of his life the indulgence of any particular desire, the development of any particular interest, the devotion to any particular occupation, should hold is

---

[1] Or, as Plato says, *Rep.* ix. 571 b 5, by παράνομοι ἐπιθυμίαι.

to determine that scheme; and it is the task of his rational nature, of the λογιστικόν. The inclusion in or omission from that scheme of any interest or occupation, the indulgence or disregard of any desire, must be so determined as may make his life the best that it can be; though what this is again cannot be settled without regard to what is best for the community of lives in which his must take its place; and there are of course, as Plato recognizes, certain 'necessary' appetites, without whose indulgence the individual cannot live, and the race cannot continue. But some men in some situations ought to reject the indulgence even of these. No rule can be given by which to determine either when their indulgence should be altogether rejected, or how largely any desire, interest, or occupation admitted to have place in the scheme of a man's life should be allowed to bulk there.[1] That is what a man's wisdom, the excellence of his rational or considerative nature, is to enable him to decide, or at least to recognize when a wiser than he has indicated it for him. And that his divers desires and interests should be developed in such mutual adjustment and relations of degree as the scheme that his wisdom approves requires is what Plato calls σωφροσύνη, or temperance: an excellence, as he says, not of the appetitive alone but of the whole soul, just because it involves desires or moving powers, ἐπιθυμίαι τε καὶ ἀρχαί, belonging to each of its 'parts' or 'forms'.

Now how far does Aristotle recognize all this in his definition of moral virtue? Does he too see in moral virtue the union of three sorts of excellence, wisdom, courage, and temperance? It seems to me that he does, but with a profound difference in his view of the last; and that this difference is shown in his doctrine of the mean.

He defines moral virtue as a disposition displaying pur-

---

[1] It will be noted that the question *when* a desire should or should not be indulged is the question ὅτε Δεῖ, whereas *how largely* is ὅσον Δεῖ, and only the latter is a question of degree.

pose, in a mean relative to the agent and determined by a
rule, whereby a wise man would determine it.[1] That it is

[1] *Eth. Nic.* II. vi. 15, 1106 b 36: ἕξις προαιρετική, ἐν μεσότητι οὖσα τῇ
πρὸς ἡμᾶς, ὡρισμένη λόγῳ καὶ ᾧ ἂν ὁ φρόνιμος ὁρίσειεν. Burnet, who took
the mean to be a 'ratio between opposites' (*Ethics of Aristotle*, p. 71: cf. *supra*,
p. 156), says in a note on II. ii. 2 'that the least misleading translation' of κατὰ
τὸν ὀρθὸν λόγον 'is "according to the right rule". The phrase comes from
the Academy . . . and was too familiar to need explanation.' We, however,
need explanation of it. On p. 247, though repeating this translation, he
also calls the 'right rule' 'the form of goodness', presumably because the
immanent activity of such a rule in conduct would make that good. Presumably, again, the right rule would prescribe or maintain the correct ratio
between opposites. We are therefore brought to what is the fundamental
question, viz. how Aristotle conceived any ratio between opposites. Now
on p. 71 Burnet writes: 'The form which is the cause of all becoming is
always a ratio (λόγος) or mean (μεσότης) between the two opposites, it is a
definite 'interval' as musicians call it, a fixed proportion in which the opposites neutralize one another and give rise to a new product. If Aristotle had
only known the theories of modern chemistry, they would have seemed to
him a most perfect exemplification of the principle; for what the modern
chemist calls atomic weights are just of this nature, and a chemical formula
like H_2O is the most typical instance of what he calls a λόγος or μεσότης.'
I submit, with respect, that this is rather loose thinking. Two tones at any
interval are not contraries and do not neutralize each other. The same
may be said of substances of different atomic weight, and of atoms of
different elements which in any definite multiple proportion compose a
molecule. The modern chemist supposes that the qualities of chemical
compounds depend on the proportion in which certain ἁπλᾶ σώματα, or
elementary bodies, combine. Aristotle tried to carry his explanation further
back. His ἁπλᾶ σώματα, the 'four elements' earth, air, fire, and water, depended for their natures on the proportion in which certain ultimate contrary qualities, the hot and the cold, the moist and the dry, combined in
pairs. Fire was the hot-dry, earth the cold-dry, air the hot-moist, water
the cold-moist; and when the simple bodies are combined, if they possess
contrary qualities, these begin somehow to destroy one the other, and convert it into its contrary. It is difficult to see how the notion of a definite
proportion is to be understood in a blend of contrary qualities of which either
can convert its contrary into itself. If so much hot remained hot when
combined with so much cold, and the cold remained cold, we could say
that the hot and the cold were combined in a definite ratio. But if the
body becomes of one temperature, we cannot say this. A bath may be
brought to 98° by mixing so much boiling water with so much water at
40°, but equally by mixing in some other proportion water at 120° and
water at 80°, and so on. A definite degree of warmth could only be regarded as depending on a ratio of contraries if these were absolute heat
and absolute cold. Perhaps the hot and the cold were so thought of by

a disposition, ἕξις, agrees with Plato's language about justice in the soul, which he speaks of as ταύτην τὴν ἕξιν. And in calling it ἕξις προαιρετική, a disposition displaying purpose, Aristotle recognizes in it the factor which in justice in the soul Plato called courage, ἀνδρεία. For Plato defines this courage as a holding fast in everything to a right and lawful opinion concerning what is and is not to be feared.[1] By this he means that the just man, whatever loss or suffering or unpleasantness may threaten him from the

Aristotle, but if so his thought was far from that of a modern chemist. It was nearer to that of Kant, when he said that the definite degree or 'intensive magnitude' of a sensation or quality united the two moments of reality and negation or zero, and again that in body the contrary forces of attraction and repulsion are somehow combined. It is true that a modern chemist offers no explanation of the difference between the sensible qualities of a chemical compound and those of its elements, while Aristotle tried to explain certain of the sensible qualities of his ἁπλᾶ σώματα, and of the ὁμοιομερῆ which they formed through μῖξις, by the proportion between the primary contraries in these simple bodies. But his theory was scientifically unfruitful and is metaphysically obscure. Nor is it any better as applied to moral virtue, if we suppose the λόγος by which the μεσότης here is determined to be a ratio of contrary impulses. For these impulses would themselves be capable of varying in degree of strength, and it is difficult to see how the ratio in which they are to be combined, in order to secure the 'mean' required, can be fixed unless the strength of each is first fixed. Yet this strength might in turn be regarded as involving a combination of contraries in a certain ratio, and so *ad infinitum*. Others have interpreted λόγος to mean 'reason', i.e. the faculty, τὸ λογιστικόν or (as Aristotle calls it) τὸ λόγον ἔχον. Apart from the question whether λόγος ever means this in Aristotle's writings, it seems a fatal objection to such an interpretation here, that it would make the last six words of the definition redundant. For a fool misuses the same faculty as a wise man uses, when he (the fool) misjudges the mean. Moreover, § 7 of the chapter, 1106 a 36–b 5, where Aristotle illustrates what he intends by a μεσότης πρὸς ἡμᾶς, supports the interpretation 'rule'; rules for training, it seems to be meant, would fix limits that an athlete should not overstep in either direction to the amount of food or exercise to be taken; but for particular athletes the precisely right amounts will fall at different points between these limits, and these niceties cannot be fixed by the rule. The late J. Cook Wilson held that ὀρθὸς λόγος in Aristotle's *Ethics* meant 'right reason'; but Professor J. A. Smith, another eminent Aristotelian, has argued strongly for the interpretation 'rule', and I have borrowed the last argument from him.

[1] *Rep.* iv. 430 b 2: σωτηρίαν διὰ παντὸς δόξης ὀρθῆς τε καὶ νομίμου δεινῶν τε πέρι καὶ μή.

course which he approves, will by courage hold fast to the right opinion that these are less terrible than not to do what he approves. And when Aristotle says that moral virtue displays purpose, he means that a virtuous man abides in action by the judgement he has formed after deliberation, ἐμμένει τοῖς γνωσθεῖσιν,[1] whatever there may be moving him to act otherwise, though of course it is not this resoluteness that makes his judgement correct; and thus to abide comes, in his opinion, of courage.

Further, Aristotle assigns a part to wisdom in the constitution of moral virtue, as Plato does in that of justice in the soul. For the mean is determined by a rule, namely, by that whereby the wise man, the φρόνιμος, would determine it. It is true that a man may be virtuous without being capable of discovering the rule for himself; he may rely on the wisdom of some teacher or confessor; but at least he must have wisdom enough to accept the rule and think it correct; ἐμμένειν τοῖς Δόξασιν[2] is ἐμμένειν τοῖς αὐτῷ Δόξασιν. And in this Aristotle is not differing from Plato, who says that courage is holding not knowledge fast but a right and lawful opinion, Δόξα. For very few *know* good and evil; and if a man did really know what is good, he could not, in Plato's belief, voluntarily do what he did not think its attainment required of him; though on this question, which is the question of incontinence or ἀκρασία, Aristotle's view is not so clear. There is, it is true, a very important difference between Plato and Aristotle regarding the wisdom involved in moral virtue or justice in the soul. For Plato thought that it was the same intellectual

---

[1] *Eth. Nic.* III. i. 9, 1110 a 31, in the discussion of ἀνΔρεία; cf. *inter alia,* ibid. VII. ix, where ἐμμένειν τῇ προαιρέσει, ἐμμένειν τοῖς Δόξασι also occur. The weak or incontinent man, ὁ ἀκρατής, under the influence of the desire or impulse of the moment, fails to abide by his resolve or purpose; the virtuous man, in whom it is necessary τόν τε λόγον ἀληθῆ εἶναι καὶ τὴν ὄρεξιν ὀρθήν, εἴπερ ἡ προαίρεσις σπουΔαία (ibid. VI. ii. 2, 1139 a 24), will abide by his purpose.

[2] Cf. *Eth. Nic.* VII. ix. 1–4, 1151 a 29–b 22.

excellence as is shown in science or speculative philosophy, whereas Aristotle did not, and consequently drew a distinction, unknown to Platonic usage, between φρόνησις and σοφία. But this difference does not affect the fact that they agree in holding wisdom, an excellence of the λογιστικόν or λόγον ἔχον μέρος in the soul, to be a factor or moment in what the one calls justice in the soul and the other moral virtue.

There remains the question whether Aristotle recognizes as the third factor or moment 'temperance' or σωφροσύνη. And it seems to me that he does so, but takes a different view from Plato's of what this factor is, when he says that this disposition is in a mean relative to the agent, ἐν μεσότητι τῇ πρὸς ἡμᾶς; and also that in this he is not, as I take him to have believed he was, improving upon, but spoiling the analysis which he follows.

It is, of course, no objection to this conjecture that temperance, σωφροσύνη, figures in Aristotle's table of particular virtues, as one among a number of means or μεσότητες. For it is quite consistent with the unity of virtue implied in Plato's account of justice in the soul that this disposition can show itself in, and give a special character to, some group of a man's actions distinguished by their being concerned with a special kind of appetite or desire, or a special kind of situation. So Aristotle distinguishes one particular virtue from another by reference to what kind of affection or action, πάθος or πρᾶξις, displays the general character of being in a mean. And there is no more difficulty in giving the name σωφροσύνη both to a factor in all virtuous action and to a particular virtue than there is in admitting, as Aristotle does, a distinction between justice as a whole, ὅλη Δικαιοσύνη, and particular justice, ἡ κατὰ μέρος Δικαιοσύνη. Nor is the double use of the words mere equivocation; it points to a peculiar complexity in the facts.

We saw that, according to Plato, measure or moderation

must be imposed on each appetite, interest, and desire; but that in what measure each should work or be indulged in a man's life depended on the plan, or form, of that life as a whole; and that such a dependence affords no rule by which to determine its measure, or in accordance with which to moderate it. For what life is just for a man can only be known by knowing what pursuits, indulgences, and occupations are to be included in it; since, till this is known, the life to be pronounced just or unjust is not before us for judgement. Rules indeed there may be that hold good for the most part; but in the cases where they hold no longer, this is because of what else is required of a man—actions of other kinds than fall under the rule and constitute the field of the particular virtue in question. Such rules therefore are not criteria. The only criterion would be the just life; but what that is cannot be known until we know what ought to be done in the case for which a criterion is sought, and therefore the just life cannot be a criterion.

I conjecture that Aristotle was dissatisfied with this position, as we all may well be, even if the matter really stands so; and that he sought to go further, and show that the matter is susceptible of a more exact treatment than this, though he admitted that the exactness possible in moral questions falls very far short of what is to be demanded in mathematics. To secure this greater exactness or precision, he substituted for the notion that the measure, μετριότης, required in action or indulgence or emotion of any kind is to be determined by reference to the whole scheme of a good life, the notion that it can be determined to a certain place upon a scale of quantity or degree, on which all actions, indulgences, or emotions of the kind in question must have a place; and he suggested that there may be rules, by help of which we may limit the range upon the scale within which that place falls for the agent concerned. It seemed to him easier to fix the mean by reference to contrary extremes or vices displayable in the same kind of action, indulgence, or emotion than by reference to anything so vague and hard to seize as the form or plan of life to which the required action must belong.[1]

The doctrine of the mean has been often criticized. To one criticism Aristotle himself points out the answer. It does not imply that the difference between virtue and vice is one of degree. Characters not differing among themselves in degree may be grounded in conditions that do differ in degree or quantity, as beauty and ugliness of visible form depend on ratios between the quantities of the several parts of what is beautiful or ugly. It is a more serious objection that the differences in which virtuous and vicious acts are grounded are many of them not of degree or quantity, according to Aristotle's own account. The even-tempered man, or πρᾶος, will show anger not only in the right degree, but with the right persons; the generous man will give not only as much as but to whom and when he should. Such conditions fit well enough into Plato's account of 'temperance', but not into the theory of the mean.[2] Again, even if differences of quantity or degree more pervasively distinguished the 'matter' of actions in the mean from those in either extreme than in fact they do, it would be a mistake to think that by directing attention to this Aristotle helps us to discover what is right in a given situation. No doubt if we knew already what was too much or too little, that knowledge would help us towards knowledge of what virtue requires, and the more so, the less difference there was between the excess and the defect.

[1] On p. 158 and p. 170, n. 1 above I have given reasons for rejecting the view that λόγος is a ratio of contraries. But I may point out here that, if we adopt this interpretation of it, the contrast here suggested between Plato's conception of what σωφροσύνη is in justice, and Aristotle's of what the mean is in moral virtue remains substantially unaffected. Aristotle will still be trying to fix what is correct in some πάθος or πρᾶξις by reference to a ratio between contrary factors involved *in it*, not by reference to a plan of life into which it enters along with other πάθη and πράξεις.

[2] Cf. *supra*, p. 169, n. 1.

But in fact the knowledge that this would be too much and that too little is often reached through recognizing something else than either to be right or nearly right. And right rules are no better guides because they determine a mean than if they were like the commandments, 'Do not kill', 'Do not steal', 'Do not lie'. These hold good for the most part; but our difficulties arise when taking life, or ignoring rights of property, or saying what is false, seems the least evil course in the circumstances; and a rule does not help us to know when it should be broken.[1] So also a rule that fixes limits beyond which one should not go in either direction holds good only for the most part; the mean may fall between them for most agents in most situations; but relatively to a particular agent in a particular situation the rule may fail.

For if we consider a virtue that is especially patient of being presented as depending on the degree of certain impulses or πάθη, viz. courage, we must admit that there are situations in which the courageous man should avoid all danger, or again none. And we remember the man to whom Jesus said, 'Sell all that thou hast and give to the poor'. If then the limits between which, when we consider all occasions for a certain sort of action or affection,[2] we must admit that the mean may lie are all and nothing, there is the same range for the virtue which is in the mean and for the vices which are not. We may have rules, as has been said, holding good for the most part, but so much is compatible with Plato's exposition. If we want more, and ask to what we should look when the rules do not apply, Plato has at least something to say. We should look to what other acts, indulgences, pursuits seem required of us or commendable in our course of life. This will not tell us how to act now; but it will direct our attention to that of which

---

[1] Cf. *infra*, p. 267.

[2] Aristotle says that his μεσότητες are περὶ πάθη καὶ πράξεις, and the particular virtues differ according to the sort of πάθη and πράξεις they concern.

consideration is necessary, if we are to reach a judgement. Aristotle substitutes for this reference to the play which should be allowed in one's life to other impulses, desires, and interests a reference to the different possible extents of play that may be allowed to the one whose part is in question; and in consequence he has nothing to say regarding cases where a rule applicable for the most part should not be observed.

And in the *Eudemian Ethics* this is acknowledged: 'When a man's action is rightly irregular, it is in the mean; for in a way the extremes fall within the mean.'[1] Nothing is now left of the doctrine of the mean, except that there are useful rules of conduct, to be followed for the most part. What was intended, as I believe, to give more precision to that part of the analysis of moral virtue which concerns the description of the 'acts and affections', approved by wisdom and sustained by courage, than Plato's account of σωφροσύνη gave, has turned out to give less. Indeed, it affords no guidance whatever. For if I were to ask what scope I ought to give in my life to the indulgence of my love of music (say), or travel, it is of some use to be told: Look beyond that activity, and consider what else there is for you to do and enjoy in life, how different determinations of your question will affect the rest of your life, and with which adjustment you think you will be living best. But it is of no use to be told: The degree or extent of scope to be given it must lie in a mean, and the mean lies between giving it none at all, and giving it all possible scope and the first place in your consideration.

For these reasons, while I think that Aristotle in his definition of moral virtue was following and trying to improve upon Plato's analysis of justice in the soul, I also think that by the modification he made in it, viz. by introducing the doctrine of the mean, he in fact largely spoilt it.

---

[1] III. vii. 1234 b 4: ὅταν μὲν γὰρ καλῶς ἀνώμαλοι ὦσιν, οἱ μέσοι γίνονται· ἐν τῷ μέσῳ γάρ ἐστί πως τὰ ἄκρα.

VII

PURPOSIVE ACTION

I DESIRE in this paper to consider what we mean, or should mean, by purposive action.

The better to develop my position, I shall refer by way of contrast more particularly to two works, one of great and ancient fame, the *Nicomachean Ethics* of Aristotle, the other a recent volume by Professor J. L. Stocks, *The Limits of Purpose and Other Essays*,[1] where the view taken of purposive action is, I think, in substance Aristotle's; and it seems to me to involve both writers in grave difficulties. The clearest statement of it by Professor Stocks is in the words: 'Purpose involves by general agreement, a distinction between the means and the end'.[2] This is what I wish to question. I do not deny that Aristotle can be quoted to the same effect, though he says much that is inconsistent with it. But nothing else in his great work is, I think, the source of so many of its defects.

We may spend a little time, first of all, in considering examples of ordinary usage. We have the transitive verb, *to purpose* this or that; and the noun. When 'purpose' is a noun, I suppose it stands either for the act of purposing, and may take epithets referring to the character of the agent, as when we say a man is of resolute or unstable purpose; or it may stand for what is purposed. To purpose is, etymologically, to set before, *proponere*, propose; if it be asked 'before what?', two answers are conceivable. I may set this before that, health before riches, riches before honesty; or I may set this or that before myself. No doubt the latter is intended; the former we call *preferring*. *Mihi est propositum in taberna mori*; there is no suggestion here of alternatives 'postponed', though doubtless they exist. So Tennyson's Ulysses says:

---

[1] Ernest Benn, 1932.　　　　[2] Op. cit., p. 22.

My purpose holds
To sail beyond the sunset, and the baths
Of all the western stars, until I die.

In neither of these cases is the *propositum* either a means, or the end of a means, though, when I take means to an end, I might be said to have set either before me. No doubt it is often asked 'With what purpose did you do this?' The question presupposes that what was done was done as a means; but not that only what is done as a means is done purposively. Again, we should, I think, naturally say that when we choose we act purposively, or (to use another word which will need our attention) deliberately. But choosing has certainly no necessary connexion with taking means to an end.

But that to act purposively is to take means to a desired end is the express doctrine of certain well-known chapters of the *Nicomachean Ethics*, where Aristotle, having distinguished between the voluntary and the involuntary, proceeds to discuss προαίρεσις: for which I think purposing, or purpose, is the best English equivalent. Purpose comes next for discussion, he says, because it seems particularly germane to virtue, and to be a better criterion of a man's character than his actions are.[1] Yet he goes on to give such an exposition and definition of it as would make it no criterion of character at all.

For it is Aristotle's express teaching that acting purposively, προαίρεσις, is taking means to an end, as his whole discussion of deliberation shows. We wish for some end; we deliberate on the means; and the purposed is the same on which we deliberated. He makes the matter more abundantly clear by comparing the search of a man deliberating to that of some one pursuing the analytic method in geometry.[2] The comparison means this. The

[1] *Eth. Nic.* iii. ii. 1, 1111 b 4–6. The most important chapters are ii and iii, but iv and v also contain remarks bearing on the question.
[2] Ibid. iii. 11–12, 1112 b 20–4.

geometer has to determine whether some construction can be made, or how some theoretical question can be decided. For example, is an angle in a semicircle always a right angle? He asks himself, if what else were true, would that be? and again this (when he has discovered it), if what else? and so on, until he reaches something which he already knows to be true. Here he can say: If the angle in a semicircle were always equal to the other two angles of the triangle, it would be a right angle; and that it would be, if always divisible into two angles each equal to one of the other two; but he can show, by drawing a radius from the centre of the circle to the apex of the triangle, that the angle *is* always so divisible; and he now proceeds back to the demonstration of what was in question. So in deliberation it is a question whether I can bring about some end desired, say my election to some office. I ask, if what were brought about should I be elected, and that if what, and so forth: until I discover something in my own power to bring about, which therefore I now desire to bring about, and do. Perhaps if X's vote could be secured I should be elected; and X would vote for me on condition that a job was given to his son; and Y would give the son a job if he knew that otherwise some past misdeed of his would be made public; and it is in my power to make it public. I therefore proceed to secure my election by way of blackmailing Y.

That is Aristotle's account of purposive action; and if so, to purpose well is no more than to take after deliberation the effective means to what is desired. No question is raised—at least primarily—concerning the purposed act except whether it will lead to the desired result. True, if it appear to a man that he may secure this by several ways, he looks by which he may 'best and most easily' secure it— πῶς ῥᾷστα καὶ κάλλιστα.[1] But in the whole account that is

---

[1] Ibid. III. iii. 11, 1112 b 16–19. Incidentally this passage shows that the προαιρετόν need not be chosen from among alternatives, and therefore that προαίρεσις is not 'choice'.

the only suggestion that in considering what he shall do, and so coming to act purposively, he will ask what is good, or noble. Nor does Aristotle appear to see that when a man turns from seeking means in his power to an end desired, and asks instead by which discovered means it may be best, or even most easily, brought about, the deliberation now involved is not comparable to the geometer's search. But of this more presently.

Aristotle holds that purpose, προαίρεσις, is what distinguishes man from the beasts—in them we can only distinguish what is voluntary from what is involuntary; and again the grown man in whom his rational nature is fully developed from the child in whom it is not. And he opposes purposive action to what is determined by appetite or impulse of anger—ἐπιθυμία or θυμός: as Professor Stocks, describing what I think he is presenting as the general view, and himself wishes rather to supplement than to reject, says that 'below purpose we have the more obscure states called impulse, instinct, appetite, and so on'. These, he says, are 'directed to nearer ends, and not necessarily involving consciousness even of these'.[1] But I doubt whether the possible absence of consciousness is their distinguishing mark, and feel certain that nearness of end is not.

I do not question that purpose is the distinguishing mark of rational action, though it is hard to say where the first germs of this are to be recognized. What I do question is the assumption that purpose involves a distinction of means and end. Doubtless where that enters there is rationality; but it is a very different thing to say that there is no rationality without it.

The latter view leads to the position that the difference between a good and a bad man lies no way in them as rational but as desirous of this or of that. No doubt Aristotle, herein following Plato, says that it belongs to a

[1] *The Limits of Purpose*, p. 12.

man as rational to desire the good; but that is not consistent with holding that what makes action rational is being purposive, if purposive action is taking the means revealed by deliberation to a desired end.

And if it is that, why should a man's purpose be a better criterion of his character than his actions are? His purpose here must be what he purposes, not that he is purposing; for all action, properly so called, involves, in Aristotle's view, purposing. And if the purposed is the means to some end, not the end or desired result of those means, of two men pursuing similar ends, is it not the skill or cleverness, rather than the moral character, that is shown by what means they adopt? In the field of purpose, Professor Stocks says, 'action is discriminated by achievement and non-achievement, failure and success'.[1]

To this it is an obvious reply, that a man's character is pre-eminently shown just in his being prepared or not to achieve by such and such means the end he desires. Of course it is. If I can find no other way to keep my income at its present level than by adulterating the goods I sell, my readiness to adulterate them in order that my income may not be diminished does show my character. And you may impute to me accordingly an evil purpose. But you will be bound, if you do, to reject the analysis of the factors in purposive action just offered.

That analysis holds that in purposive action there are (i) desire, which may be right or wrong, of some end; (ii) deliberation, directed to discovering by what means the end may be brought about; (iii) adoption of the means. But if I rather give up the pursuit of the end desired than pursue it by the means which deliberation discovers, without either ceasing to desire the end or revising my judgement that the means are these, it must be because of something which this analysis has left out of account.

And this is surely that I ask myself whether it is right

---

[1] *The Limits of Purpose*, p. 92.

that I should maintain my income by adulterating the goods I sell, or else, which state of life that could be mine is better, that in which I continue to enjoy the same income but adulterate the goods I sell to get it, or that in which I continue to sell unadulterated goods but suffer a diminution of income. I put it these two ways, because I do not wish here to raise the issue of the ultimate relations of right and good. But whichever be the question I ask myself, will not my answer be deliberate and my action purposive? Only, my deliberation will not be about the means to an end, and the purposed will either include the end to which I discovered that the means was adulteration, or exclude the means discovered to the end that I desired.

Let it be that purposive action is action after deliberation, or considered in distinction from impulsive or instinctive action; and so far as we think *before* we act, not merely in acting, I suppose that is true. But is deliberation always about means to an end? That is one of the capital mistakes that trouble Aristotle's treatise.

There are, as every reader of it knows, other statements in it completely irreconcilable with the view that I have been displaying. In a passage that might be quoted in commentary on the statement that a man's character is shown rather in his purpose than in his actions, we read that deeds that are of virtue are justly or temperately done, not because of what they themselves are, but of the agent's disposition; he must have acted knowingly and purposing them, and purposing them for their own sakes, and with a settled disposition.[1] And elsewhere we are told that a man may do what is just without being just; he may do what the law commands unwillingly, or in ignorance of what he is doing, or for something further and not for itself; but he *may* do it all so as to be a good man, i.e. purposively and for the sake of what is done.[2] In both these places a man is said to do purposively what he does for its own sake,

---

[1] *Eth. Nic.* II. iv. 3, 1105 a 28.   [2] Ibid. VI. xii. 7, 1144 a 13–20.

or on its own account, not as a means to an end. Moreover we are repeatedly told that what is done of virtue is done for its nobleness, τοῦ καλοῦ ἕνεκα. This nobleness is no effect to which what is done is a means. And in spite of the famous generalization with which the treatise opens, that every art and investigation, action and purpose, seems to aim at some good—a statement immediately followed by a discussion of certain differences among the ends (τέλη) aimed at—the end is shortly afterwards said to be acting well. This acting well cannot be for the sake of some further acting well, or there would be a *progressus in infinitum*; therefore it must be thought of either as something from which the distinction of means and end has disappeared, or as including both; it can no longer be said that we only desire the end and only do what will bring it about.

The view that purposive action is taking means to an end is connected, I think, in Aristotle's mind with the mistake of treating an 'apparent good', φαινόμενον ἀγαθόν, that this or that man desires, as means to the real good that every rational being desires. And it has its source in overlooking half the field of deliberative thinking.

If we wish to determine the field of deliberative thinking, we must ask from what other thinking it is to be distinguished. And Aristotle is surely correct in distinguishing it from scientific, or demonstrative, thinking. There may be thinking which is neither demonstrative nor deliberative; but we shall admit that the conclusions of deliberation are not demonstrated. We are not said to deliberate what tensile strength and section of girders to be used in building a bridge will carry a given maximum load with a specified margin of safety; but we may deliberate what margin of safety to specify. When questions are submitted to deliberation, scientific thinking is in constant demand; but in the last resort we come to issues that cannot be scientifically settled, or the parties would agree; these are matters, as we say, for judgement; and the wise counsellor is the man of good judgement. And these are the real subjects of deliberation.[1] Now, such questions seem to be of two main sorts. Of one sort is the question, what is going to happen, either if I do nothing—what therefore have I to provide against?—or if I do thus or thus? This field of deliberation Aristotle recognizes, and describes it as that where it is not clear, or not determined, how a matter will turn out, though we know what generally happens.[2] A statesman or a deliberative assembly is constantly engaged on such problems, and acting or voting for action on the best judgement he or it can form on them. What will be the results of starting reflation? Will France declare war if called upon to withdraw from Fashoda? Will a strike in this situation succeed? Here there is no question what result is desired—that is taken as agreed—but whether a certain means will bring it about. We may, however, be agreed about this, and dispute whether to take the means and achieve the result is preferable to not doing so. Will the results of reflation be better than the present state? Is a successful strike worth all the suffering involved? This is the other field of deliberation. Here, too, there is no demonstration, and judgements will differ. But here the problem is not to discover means to an end; and the thinking involved is not analogous to the analytical investigation of a geometrical problem.

Aristotle, when he discusses deliberation in the *Ethics*, takes no account of this second field. Why a great thinker overlooks what becomes obvious afterwards to others, we cannot always rightly tell; but in this case I think we may point to a connected error which makes the oversight more intelligible.

This error is regarding as a means to some whole its contributory or constituent factors. That Aristotle did this cannot, I think, be disputed; and it is still very commonly

[1] Cf. *Eth. Nic.* vi. i. 5–6, 1139 a 3–15.   [2] Ibid. iii. iii. 10, 1112 b 8.

done.[1] So soon as he has said that every art and investigation, action and purpose seems to aim at *some good*, he goes on to speak of *the good* as not indicated amiss by those who said it was what all things aimed at.[2] How is *some good* related to *the good*? As a constituent, or as a means? If as a constituent, what particulars are to be admitted into the constitution of the good? If as a means, must means to the good be themselves good? Such questions did not escape Aristotle's notice, but he never gets clear about them. He says that we do one thing for the sake of another, and conceives that there may be a long series of subordination, but that there must come something on account of which everything else is chosen, and which itself is chosen on account of nothing further, for else there would be a process *in infinitum*, and all desire would be vain; this thing is the good, and men call it happiness, but that is to give it a name only, and we want to know what it is.[3] Here the good is thought of as reached at the end of a series of actions, and if it is one, of all a man's actions; yet Aristotle rejects the doctrine that you cannot call a man's life happy till the end.[4] And he says happiness is something that abides,[5] and (as we know) that it is acting well; yet if so, how can one's actions be means to it? Again, if actions, though means to the good, are also themselves good, together they are preferable to either alone; yet we are told that happiness, the most choiceworthy of all things, is not to be counted along with any others, just because it and they together would else be better.[6] Either then no action is itself good, or no good action is a means to happiness. Again, since different actions are plainly means to different ends, what becomes of the notion of a *finis ultimus*? It must really comprehend and not lie beyond these particular ends.

---

[1] e.g., F. H. Bradley seems to do it, *Collected Essays*, vol. II, pp. 451, 527-9.   [2] *Eth. Nic.* I. i. 1, 1094 a 2.

[3] Ib. I. iv. 2, 1095 a 17-22, after I. i. 3-ii. 1.

[4] Ib. I. x. 1-2, 1100 a 10-14.   [5] Ib. I. x. 7, 1100 b 2-7.

[6] Ib. I. vii. 8, 1097 b 16-20.

Once more, if we desire the good, or happiness, without knowing in what it consists, and do whatever we do for the sake of and as means to it, the comparison of deliberation to geometrical analysis breaks down. If you do not know to what determinate question in geometry you seek an answer, how can you tell what it is from which an answer, one way or the other, would follow? And if you do not know the determinate nature of your end, how can you know what means would bring it about? You wish for the good which you call happiness; you are to deliberate about the means to its attainment; but before any such deliberation can get under way, you must settle in what it consists. This you do not know by wishing for it, and men are nowise agreed about it. What are you to call the process of thinking by which you reach agreement with others, or at least resolve your own doubts? If deliberation, such deliberation is to discover constituents, not means. And will the good, which is your end, include any actions, or only be a result of actions? If the latter, then indeed all purposive activity will be taking means, and no acting will be itself good, and we may say, as I heard a late distinguished philosopher say, that all effort is evil; and presumably only states of feeling will be desired, and be good, and for their sake only shall we act, or take means. But if the end includes actions, these will not be means; or at least, even though there will be, and we know it, results of them that will be also factors in the whole that we call happiness, they will be done as well on their own account as for the sake of those results. Are they purposively done only so far as done for the sake of their results? I can see no reason for saying so.

Nothing of this is new. Yet the confusion between means and constituents still haunts us; and if we are to be quit of it, I think we must break completely with the view that the essence of purposive action is taking means towards an end. That view will always generate trouble; and

it has done so for Professor Stocks, as I will try to show by
reference to certain passages of his essays, before offering
a different account of purposive action.

Thus, after a brief account of what is meant, I think, as
the Aristotelian view, he admits that men to-day have
begun to question it.

'The conception of a single ultimate end is also doubtful. It is, in
fact, not much favoured by modern thought. . . . But this does not
mean that the conception of human action as essentially purposive has
been surrendered. . . . We do not say "There is no moral ideal;
there is no single purpose in which every purpose is fulfilled". . . .
The clear-cut Greek conception of a *summum bonum* is not surrendered. . . . The unification of the moral life in a single distinctive
ultimate purpose seems to remain in the form of a "mere idea" or
unrealisable ideal.'[1]

Now I contend that the Greek, if that means Aristotle's,
conception of a *summum bonum* is anything but clear-cut,
because he is never clear whether virtuous actions are
means to it or constituents of it; or rather, he is equally
clear that they are each, in different places, and the views
are irreconcilable. And what Professor Stocks says here is
only sound if they are constituents, but he professes that
they are means. Only so would the moral life be unified
in an *ultimate* purpose; but who thinks it is, unless we are
to do everything with a view to some result after death?
Again, the more distant results, it is said, will unify more
of a life; and doubtless the purposes which unify more of
a life will be completely realized only at a later date. If a
man's purpose were in all things to do what he thought
right, I suppose he would never have exhausted the execution of it. But would he not be achieving it all the time?
Can it be called ultimate? It is true that where the relation
of means and end enters, and what is done as means would
not be done at all except for the sake of some result, there
the more distant results commonly unify more of our

---

[1] *The Limits of Purpose*, pp. 12–13.

activities, being more distant just because they can only be brought about by a number of actions spread over a series of years; I say 'commonly', since it does not take much longer (say) to plant and keep cleared until established a slow-growing than a quick-growing tree, for the sake of its maturation hereafter; and the more distant maturation will not unify more of a life. Purposive activity, according to Professor Stocks, is such taking of means to an end beyond; it 'has no value for itself, but implies an ideal in which it is wholly superseded, a state of affairs in which all our ends are realised without activity on our part'.[1] But if so, do we want a single distinctive ultimate purpose?[2]

And what makes a distinctive ultimate purpose single? Would the establishment in this country of a classless society and the maturation in it of a *Sequoia gigantea* be equally single? The first comprises a great many changes, to none of which would all that needed doing be a means, nor are they all means to one result beyond them; and the divers actions in my power may lead some to one and some to another of these components. If it is nevertheless one purpose, there must be a reason for including in it just these components; and is not that inclusion purposive, though it is not taking means? Unless we are to deny that the *differentia* of acting rationally is being purposive—and Professor Stocks says that 'man first shows his reasonableness in action by making action purposive'[3]—we must abandon altogether the view that acting purposively is always means-taking. That is but one form of it.

[1] Ibid., p. 82.

[2] It may be noticed that our 'purpose' is here the 'end', while it is the means that are said by Aristotle to be purposed. This may be taken as an indication that where means and end enter, purposive action may regard both.

[3] Ibid., p. 80. On pp. 71–2 it is recognized that action may be described as purposive in respect that it is conformed to the requirements of morality, and 'if you choose to extend the term purpose to include all open-eyed activity, then you will be justified in calling art and morality purposive, and you will have to invent another word to represent concentration on ends'. Why not 'means-taking'?

If the field of morality is purposive activity, and that is always taking means to an end, then, since moral differences are shown in action, they must be shown in taking means. So 'the goodness of a good man does not depend on this, that he has a different end from a bad man, or a clearer view of the same end, or a single end where he has many.'[1] Morality, in fact, like art, has no purposes—i.e. no ends—of its own.

This is said explicitly of art. 'Art is essentially parasitic upon purpose. It exists by adopting a purpose foreign to itself and exploiting the medium by which that purpose is achieved.'[2] But in working out this doctrine the sense of the word 'means' is altered, and the identification of purposive activity with means-taking unconsciously abandoned. And the first of the statements quoted in this paragraph will not, I think, prove true. Let me illustrate this. We must bear in mind that, according to Professor Stocks, 'in purpose means and end necessarily fall apart'.[3]

In 'any process carried out by the human muscles under the direction of human intelligence . . . purpose sees only the result and all else in terms of it as means: the energy spent will be wasted unless it brings in a proportionate return. Art glorifies the means.'[4] An example is taken elsewhere from riding a bicycle.[5] This I might, e.g., do as a means to being at a certain destination by a certain time, and with that purpose ride; but I may delight in the expertness with which I manage the machine. But herein there is no new purpose; only conscious enjoyment 'of the means and methods by which the work is done'. But why is it not a new purpose, to ride my bicycle well? Do I not do so 'on purpose'? And is there not a confusion between

---

[1] Ibid., p. 65. [2] Ibid., p. 21. [3] Ibid., p. 80.
[4] Ibid., p. 31. The sentence runs: 'glorifies the means, brings them to light, and thereby also makes the expenditure of energy self-justifying'. So far as it is self-justified, it is not regarded as means. It is against the neglect of this in Professor Stocks's main contention that I wish to protest.
[5] Ibid., p. 19.

means and constituents in speaking of 'the means and methods by which the work is done'? For the work done is the riding, and it is not the means to this that I enjoy; the riding is means to being at my destination to time, which is not the work done. There is the same confusion in the passage quoted above about exploiting the *medium* by which the purpose is achieved. What is exploited is not the medium of that to which it is means.

This confusion reappears in other statements about art.

'The artist destroys the mere means, abolishes the indifferent or equally good, and in so doing makes of the whole complex of means and end for the first time a real organic unity. . . . Every scrap of material used must be completely used up. . . . So far as art masters the purpose on which it supervenes, it makes each smallest detail of the execution significant; it provides a reason of its own for every choice left open by the purpose or theme . . . the transformation effected by the artistic interest is nothing less than the achievement of individuality. What purpose aims at is and must be defined in general terms.'[1]

But if means and end are related like riding a bicycle and being at a given place to time—and that is the professed doctrine of their relation—art does not make of them a unity. My riding a bicycle and my being at my destination to time cannot form an organic unity any more if I ride well than if I ride clumsily. I may submit to a surgical operation in order to be rid of a disease. If the surgeon is unskilful, the cure may not come about; but if he is skilful, the operation and the cure do not achieve a single individuality. Art can never surmount the distinction of means and end characteristic (according to Professor Stocks) of the level of purpose. The purpose or end is not a theme. Nor need what purpose aims at be defined in general terms. I may tell a builder I want a ten-roomed house; and that will leave him much latitude in the operations of building. But I may also give him complete

[1] Ibid., pp. 24–5.

drawings and specifications, and say, 'Build that'. If the effect for the production of which I desire to discover means, or actions in my power, is forged currency notes, my chances of passing them without detection are very small so long as I only define to myself what I aim at in general terms.

Professor Stocks has slipped unconsciously from thinking of the relation between means-taking activities and their results, which are what he says are brought into an organic unity when art masters the former, to thinking of the relation between designing and the complete design, or between the parts of a work of art and the whole work. I may tell an architect in general terms the sort of house I want, and he may presently produce me a complete design satisfying those conditions, and he may have a reason for every detail. But the way in which my requirements are satisfied is not means, nor the 'purpose or theme' a result. Even the designing activity, though purposive, is not means to its own completion, except in the sense in which growing is a means to being full-grown. That the artist engaged in such activity is not seeking means to an end is shown by reverting to Aristotle's analysis of that seeking. That starts, as we saw, from a knowledge of the result to be brought about, and seeks actions in our power, the doing which would cause that result. But the artist does not start from the knowledge that 'this is the design of the house to be built', and consider by what process of thinking he may come to the apprehension of this design.

The operations of building are a means to the being of a house; and a house in being is a means to the keeping warm and dry of its occupants and contents. But it is not to these relations that we must look to verify what Professor Stocks says about the function of art. We must look to the relation between the materials of the house and the beauty and serviceableness of the house. Materials are not means, and serviceableness is not the desired condition of the thing served; nor is the beauty of a house a means to its occupants and contents being kept warm and dry. The beautiful house has uses beyond its beauty, but for which it would not have been built, though this is not true of all beautiful things. Not every work of art has a use distinct from its beauty; or if it contributes to the worth of the artist's life, or of other men's, that is not in its capacity as means to the worth as an effect. We are told that:

'First there was the demand for representations and a trade which arose to meet it. Then this trade transformed itself into art, and continues today to transform itself into art, to the extent to which in any given instance of its use the craftsman's delight in the medium mastered and penetrated the product.'[1]

This can hardly be true of the earliest known works of art, the prehistoric rock-drawings of animals; and as before, the 'medium' is not *means* to the 'product'. But no doubt it is true for many works by which artists seek to earn a living. And in that sense art adopts a purpose foreign to itself. But it does not follow that 'art has no aim of its own',[2] though, of course, it has not all *one* aim. Artistic activities are many, each unified by its own purpose, and just because of this the artist may be hampered by another purpose on which his art is parasitic. For, as Plato said, an art, so far as it is perfect, seeks nothing but to make its own subject-matter as perfect as possible.[3] In so seeking, it is purposive, but is not taking means to the achievement of the purpose on which it is parasitic. In taking means to this, it is utilitarian; and just because it has a purpose distinct from the utilitarian, its having the latter often destroys the singleness of the artist's aim.

Professor Stocks thinks that what he has said of the artistic act and interest may equally be said of the moral act and the moral interest. The moral interest supervenes upon purposes independently given. But since the artistic

[1] Ibid., p. 21.　　　　[2] Ibid., p. 25.
[3] *Rep.* i. 341 d 10–11, 342 b 1–6.

interest transforms the means, he has difficulty in finding a place for a further and moral transformation.

'Purpose proposed an end and construed all else with sole reference to it; art brought the means to life and made them justify themselves. What room is left, then, for morality? Means and end between them exhaust the act.'[1]

The answer is surprising, and, I think, untenable.

'Purpose, when fully developed and expressed, is action, and the embroidery of art, if incidental to purpose, is incidental to action; but "action" none the less is a term foreign to the vocabulary equally of art and of purpose.'[2]

I would allow that of every purposive activity, either merely means-taking or otherwise, one may ask whether it is good, and whether one ought to engage in it. But that is not to say that those activities are not actions, nor that purposes are only supplied to and not by the moral interest.

'Suppose one rejects a possible way of making money', says Professor Stocks, 'on moral grounds. This will not mean that one gives up the purpose of making money where one decently can' ... or 'that one has thought of another and a better way of making money'.[3] Making money is 'only an end, like any other, a possible result of action, and ... falls, with all other ends, under the inflexible moral rule that it may not be pursued by any and every means'.[4]

Our ends—this seems to be the argument—are no more supplied by the moral than by the artistic interest; but each of these interests in its way controls the means-taking. Yet supposing I were to substitute for making money in the above illustration the death of a rival; is it only certain means to achieving this purpose that I must reject on moral grounds? And if ends are provided to the moral interest extraneously, and making money is one of them, must not my maxim be *rem, si possis, recte; si non, quocunque modo rem*? Making money when one decently can may be sometimes right; but sometimes a man ought to abandon it altogether. You cannot take the ends to which in fact

[1] Ibid., p. 27.   [2] Ibid., p. 30.   [3] Ibid., p. 27.   [4] Ibid., p. 29.

and independently of moral considerations men's means-taking activities are directed, and say that morality is concerned only with the means to be used in attaining them.

'Morality', says Professor Stocks,[1] 'may call on a man at any moment to surrender the most promising avenue to his own moral perfection'; again speaking as if the end were furnished to it extraneously, and it were only concerned with the means. And doubtless it may be a man's duty to abandon his career and fight, though his career was a better school of moral perfection than war commonly is. But that is really to say that morality may call on a man to reject or postpone some contemplated end, not revise the means to it. Only if we call the good which a man can realize in, or make of, his life his end, is there an end which the moral interest may not call on him to reject; and that is because this interest itself provides it. And if that is what is meant by his moral perfection, his moral perfection is not an end in the sense of something to which what he does is means. I will not discuss here the view that the moral interest is regardless altogether of any good to be realized either as a result or in the doing of the action it prescribes. According to this view, which I do not share, though acting from a sense of duty is morally good, what it is my duty to do need neither itself be good, nor be expected to have any good result. Without subscribing to this, I would maintain that nothing properly to be called an end, nothing of a nature determinate enough for us to seek means to it, is given to the moral interest as what must be accepted as an end, with no moral question except concerning the means by which it should be sought. Of any such end, the moral interest may lead me to say 'In no way this'.

The moral interest does not indeed provide all ends. But neither, when ends are furnished to it, is there left to it only the task of controlling means.

'It does not matter, so far as I can see' (I quote again), 'in what

[1] Ibid., p. 29.

terms the purposive attitude is conceived, whether as directed to self-interest, one's own happiness, or to the greatest happiness of the greatest number, or even as self-realization: in each case this limitation stands, that the end is "constituted by Nature and supposed" in the purposive activity.'[1]

But surely it is a moral question whether I should direct my activities to my own happiness, or the greatest happiness of the greatest number, or self-realization (which, I agree, turns out on examination to be 'a purely formal conception'[2]). Further, there is the question in what they severally consist. The purposive attitude is shown in deliberately including these components and rejecting those; and the moral interest enters also here. Of the various ends which human nature sets a man desiring or seeking after, the moral interest makes him consider which to include in his life; and this not without regard to the character of the means by which they might be brought into being. And such regard to the means is treating them not indeed as ends, but as right or wrong, good or evil, and so fit or unfit to be components of his life; and if admitted as components or constituents of a virtuous or good life, though they are not admitted as means to its virtuousness or goodness, yet they are purposely admitted, in that way of purposiveness which is not means-taking. That the conception of 'a continuing form finding its changing embodiment in the changing situations of life' is 'at the foundation of all effort and every purpose'[3] I largely agree. But the whole effort to embody this form in one's life is purposive, and every activity in which this is done is *pro tanto* a purposive activity, though it need not be means-taking. We must conceive purposive action more widely than that.

Perhaps we may be helped to determine how we ought to conceive purposive action if we ask ourselves why we think such action to be distinctively rational. And, to answer this question, we may consider with what pur-

---

[1] Ibid., pp. 81–2.   [2] Ibid., p. 91.   [3] Ibid., pp. 75–6.

posive action is to be contrasted. I suppose with what is impulsive, instinctive, or reflex. A question may be raised about the instinctive; for in many of their instinctive activities animals have been thought to exhibit purpose or design. But in so thinking are we not challenging the opposition of instinct and intelligence, and holding that there is more in such activities than the conceptions with which the physical sciences work will cover?

A completely physical interpretation of what we call the actions of men or other animals would hold that the conscious states of desire, aversion, fear, pleasure, pain, and all thinking and imagining are irrelevant; an adequate account of the changes that occur in any process carried out by animal muscles could be given without reference to them. It is allowed that we cannot always at present give such explanations. But though explanations have still to be offered in which these conscious states and activities are treated as playing a part, it is often such a part that the whole process may still be covered by the conceptions of physical science. Thus that the sight or scent of food determines an animal in a certain physical state to the motions of approach, seizure and ingestion is such an explanation; and though the effect of these motions is the removal of both the physical state and the conscious discomfort called hunger, we need no more say that they are means taken with that end in view than we say that mountain ranges cool the warm moisture-laden air from the ocean in order to help the vegetation in the plains below. Such a schema of explanation as may be thus applied to feeding may be extended to the more complex setting of ideo-motor action. Not scents nor sights, but images of these in the mind, or sounds (whether of words or otherwise) that call up such images may come to cause the movements which in turn cause the result that might have been described as their end. But so long as what is loosely called the association of ideas is all that is involved, we are still within the field of scientific conceptions. The so-called association of ideas (I do not say everything which that has been held to cover) is really a linkage of unit-activities that comes about in the animal in virtue of such activities having been provoked together by stimulus from without, so that hereafter when one is provoked again it will serve as stimulus for the other. Much else would have to be said to make this account complete. The same unit-activity may have been provoked along with divers others, and have acquired linkage with them all; and there must be some reason why on a subsequent occasion its renewed provocation leads on to this rather than that other. Moreover, much happens in a mind which, though some psychologists have referred it to association, others have shown to involve far more than such linkage of unit-activities. But that alone in principle can distinguish what Hobbes called the 'wild ranging of the mind' from rational discourse, or what Locke called the association of ideas from the following out of that 'natural correspondence and connexion' of them[1] which he said it was 'the office and excellency of our reason to trace'. That again is the principle of the conditioned reflex; and those who would explain as the establishment of a conditioned reflex an animal's learning by trial and error to find its way out of a maze, or to unfasten without random movements the door of a cage separating it from its food, are really supposing such an association of unit-activities to arise. The word 'activity' here must, of course, be taken to include hearing a particular sound, smelling a particular odour, seeing a particular shape or colour or coloured shape, feeling fear, hate, or anger, desiring or imagining thus or thus and so forth, as well as executing a particular movement. The

---

[1] Really, of that of which we are thinking; Locke confuses, in his contrast (*Essay concerning Human Understanding*, II. xxxiii. 5), *idea* as = a thought or other 'state of mind' with *idea* as = 'whatsoever is the object of the understanding when a man thinks'.

Gestalt school have pointed out how much even of animal behaviour seems irreducible to such linkage of unit-activities, unless *Gestalten* can be regarded as particular stimuli, and the apprehensions of them as unit-activities produced in response. Unfortunately, as Dr. Bruno Peter-mann has shown,[1] in their conception of a physical *Gestalt* they proceed as if it could be so regarded, and thereby fatally blur the distinction between changes that fall under the conceptions of physical science and those which mani-fest reason.

Ideo-motor connexions are established in men, although something else than an ideo-motor connexion may be re-quired to set them working. A pianist purposely starts playing; but, as he plays, the sight of a printed note deter-mines the movement by which a certain key is struck. The 'secondarily automatic' conforms to the association schema; though, unless it is somehow controlled in a manner that does not, purposes may not be carried out. And within a secondarily automatic series we do not speak of means and end, though there are relations of cause and effect. We do not say that a pianist looks at the score as a means to moving his hand in a certain direction. This, perhaps, we should not say even before the activity had become secondarily automatic, since the movement of his hand is as much in his own power as the looking. But neither should we say, when the activity has become so, that he moves his hand as a means to the sounding of the note. The whole activity is to be called purposive because the details are adjusted to one another so as together to consti-tute the whole designed, rather than because of relations of means and ends.

The user of an adding-machine, reading the digits in the items to be added, for each digit-reading presses a particu-lar key. Here is sequence of unit-activities. There emerge

[1] *The Gestalt Theory and the Problem of Configuration.* Kegan Paul, 1932.

printed digits giving the total; and nothing has happened inside the machine that cannot be brought under the conception of a linkage of unit-activities. The machine has not thought, nor acted purposively. But its designer, who determined how the unit-activities must be linkable so that this could happen, thought and acted purposively in thinking. And this thinking was not such a linkage of unit-activities as goes on in the machine.

What human activities cannot be brought within the schema of explanation that covers reflex, impulsive, and conditionedly reflex action, when ideo-motor and other associative connexions are added? Determination by desire can be brought within it; and if the action in my power is not itself that of which the thought or imagination excites desire, but only causes that when done, still the action will fall under the schema. But so far it would not be a means-taking action, but only one producing the effect desired. To justify calling it a means-taking, there must be not only the thought or imagination of z causing the thought or imagination of that movement in my power y which would cause z; the thought that y is a means to z must be added. And this is not merely that the thought of z should lead by unit-linkage to the thought of y as well as to desire, and these by ideo-motor connexion to the movement y; nor even that besides this the thought that y will cause z should arise. This last thought must not only arise but be another factor helping to cause y. Now how can this be? I have already the thought or imagination of z and of y; I must now think of causing. But that is not enough; for that I can think of without thinking that y will cause z. To bring together the thoughts of a and of b and of a relation R is not to think that a is in the relation R to b. Even if it were held that I cannot think of two terms and a relation without thinking of them as related by it—which is not true—there would be nothing to determine, if the relation were asymmetrical like cause, which term should fall into which place. To think then of causing is not enough. Moreover, why should it happen? Unit-linkage cannot connect the thought of a term with that of a relation as it may connect it with that of another term; for the terms may be imaged, but the relation not. This was the difficulty that troubled Hume, and led him to resolve the thought that a causes b into the thought of the sequence of b on a; but all that he really accounted for, even so, on his principles of unit-linkage, was the sequence of the thought of b on that of a; not until after which, even on his principles, could I have the 'idea' of the sequence.

Genuine means-taking activity seems to me beyond the range of the non-rational. Whether it occurs in animals other than man I do not know. But I submit that the explanations frequently offered of what are called means-taking activities in them leave out what alone could justify so calling them. Many activities both of theirs and ours can be brought under a schema merely of desired-effect-producing.

Now means-taking activities are, as we have seen, identified by some, both anciently and to-day, with purposive. But they are in no wise the only human activities which fail to conform to the schema of unit-linkage. Suppose I desire my house-door to shine with a particular colour. The unit-linkage schema might explain my covering it with a certain pigment, as a desired-effect-producing movement. But it would not explain my desiring it because I thought it beautiful any more than my painting it as a means-taking movement. For beauty is not a particular imaginable, like a house-door shining thus; and the desired shining of the house-door is neither a means to beauty nor produces beauty as an effect, but (as I may think) is beautiful. Precisely the same argument applies if what I desire is thought of as good, or as choiceworthy. Yet every one would accept, as a reason why I desired my door to shine with this colour, that I thought it would be beautiful, or as a reason why I desired to know something, that I thought the knowledge good; I am not saying, morally good. And my so thinking is not unconnected with my activity being rational; but it is unconnected with any relation of means and end.

I pass to cases where it is yet more obvious that the rationality from which I have distinguished conformity to the unit-linkage schema has nothing to do with means-taking. Though you might approve my painting of my door because the colour chosen is beautiful, it would hardly be beautiful independently of its relation to the surrounding colours. Anyhow, artistic activity is commonly shown in the production of parts so adjusted to one another that the whole is beautiful. In this adjusting, as distinct from producing the parts, there is no means-taking; and the process of deliberation described by Aristotle could never discover how the adjustment is to be secured, a 'theme' developed, a design completed or reached. Take the case of a building. It is not a question how stable foundations may be constructed, how the materials required may be transported, cut up, shaped and erected, but what the materials, their shapes and relative situations shall be. Or in dancing, not how the dancer's muscles may be supple and trained, but what the movements shall be. There is plenty of means-taking considered in deciding the one sort of question, but not in deciding the other. Each detail in the design of building or of dance is deliberated on, and included with reference to the rest with which it forms a whole: unless, indeed, the whole springs before the mind at once, as Professor A. E. Housman[1] says has occurred to him with at least whole stanzas of a poem; and even then each detail is to be justified and retained with such reference. But no detail is a means, producing, as an effect beyond or apart from it, either another detail or the whole.

[1] *The Name and Nature of Poetry*, Cambridge University Press, 1933, pp. 49–50.

Yet is not the activity rational? Is not each detail purposively included? Is not its relation to the rest and to the
whole a reason why it is included in the design, and, where
design and execution are different (as they commonly are,
though not, for example, when a man completes a poem 'in
his head'), why it is included in the execution, just as much
as its causing the 'end' is a reason why a man takes the
means in his power? The process of discovering such
relations can no more be brought under the schema of
scientific explanation than can the discovery of means; and
the thought of them no more determines action according
to the principles of unit-linkage than does the thought that
something is a means. And I cannot see that these non-
means-taking activities are less rational or less purposive
than the means-taking are.

It seems to me that an action is purposive so far as in
doing it the agent looks beyond the action itself or its
qualities to something the apprehension of which, or of
its relation to which, is a reason or among the reasons for
his doing it. This statement needs certain elucidations or
qualifications which will appear in the course of illustrating
different ways in which this general character of purposiveness may show itself. But one, since it concerns them all, I
will set down at once. It is that the apprehension of that
beyond the action itself which furnishes a reason for doing
it may be implicit only. This is so even in means-taking.

Purposiveness is means-taking, when that to which the
agent looks beyond the action is some effect expected to be
caused by the change which the action brings about. The
dancer of a *pas seul*, in taking each step with reference to
others beyond it, is acting purposively; but because those
other steps are equally actions in the dancer's power and
not effects of the step in question, it is not a means to them,
and the purposiveness is not means-taking. But a physician
healing himself, though he takes one action with reference
to others of his to follow, waits for effects of the one to

arise in his body through causes outside his control; and so far his purposiveness is means-taking. I have suggested above that the connexion between the action in one's power and the effect for the sake of which it is done may be so uniform and unquestioned that one does not attend to the distinction between them; such is the connexion between the movements of a pianist's fingers over the keyboard and the sounds that follow. We may as fairly say that a man gives a rendering of a sonata on the piano as of a song with the voice, and not that he takes means to the production of the former music. But his actions at every moment are purposive in respect of the relation between each of them and the rest as constituents in playing the sonata; they are means-taking only in respect of the causal connexion between striking a key and the sound resulting. Let me give another illustration of the distinction. If the reasons for my action lie in the expected actions of others, but these enter with mine as constituents into the execution of a single and common whole, my action, though purposive with reference to them, is so far not means-taking. I say *so far*, because of course the whole activity to which both it and they belong, like my whole activity of playing a sonata, may be means-taking in relation to an effect expected to follow from it; and each particular component action may be said to participate in this means-taking purposiveness. But if, though my action has reference to the action of another, yet this is by way of changes to be produced by my action in the situation in which another has to act, then the purposiveness in my action is means-taking, just as in the instance of a physician healing himself. The other's action, again, may be expected to be done with reference to the same comprehensive activity as mine; or it may be expected to be done in execution of a different purpose to mine, but to further in some way the realization of mine. In the latter case, though not in the former, my action is means-taking with reference to the other man's action, as well as to the change in the situation which it is expected immediately to effect.

So much for means-taking, which is but a special case of what seems to me one main form of purposiveness, viz. when that to which the agent looks, beyond the act itself or its qualities, is something else particular to which it is related. That something else may be an effect desired, and then the action is means-taking. But it may be other actions contributory, or expected to contribute, to the same total activity or its result; and these other actions may be either my own or of others. Or it may be the whole to which the action or its result is expected to contribute, though no thought of what other actions are necessary besides is present to the mind. Thus a man acts purposively when he does what he thinks will 'augment his happiness'; and this is different from taking means to the production of a particular desired pleasure. The latter also is purposive; though merely to be determined to action by the pleasure accompanying the imagination of some not present state, and of the movements the imagination of which is linked with the former imagination by the 'association of ideas', is not purposive. And I suppose that in many of our most characteristically purposive activities, we do each action with reference rather to the whole to which our various co-operating actions contribute than to other contributories. This is especially noticeable where our apprehension of what beyond the action furnishes a reason for doing it is only implicit. For in carrying out a difficult task, when a man is as we say wholly absorbed in what he is at the moment doing, he may be said to forget altogether in doing one action the others done or awaiting doing, but never altogether to forget the one purpose or task, in the execution of which they are all components.

Let me repeat that the whole which requires the particular action for its completion need not be, like dancing or chamber music, a mere whole of action. It may be something which the whole of action is to leave behind it as its product; and in this case there is a means-taking relation to the product to be left behind. But the apprehension of the relation between the particular action and the whole of action or other contributory particulars, and of that between what it is to produce and the whole product, or other parts of it, to be left behind, also makes the particular action purposive.

The other main form of purposiveness in action—and this form does not have means-taking as a special case—seems to me to be shown when the action would not have been done, but for the agent thinking that he ought to do it, or that it or its result—or some whole of which it or its result is a constituent—is good or beautiful. These considerations are neither of means nor of specific qualities in the action or its result; for that I ought to do an action is not a quality of it, and to be good or beautiful is not a specific quality of what is so; that for which it is held that I ought to do one action, or that one action or its result is good or beautiful, is not that for which I so think of another. Here, too, I think that we somehow look beyond the particular action, and but for this should not do it. And, though we may also look to a particular result, which is something else to which the action is related, the essential feature is that we look to what is no such particular: to duty or good or beauty. No doubt I do the action because I ought to do *it*; because *this* is good or beautiful. But I have regard to a universal principle of obligation; to a goodness or beauty that cannot be identified with what makes this good or beautiful.

And this perhaps is why, even if we were erroneously to call the system, by their relations to which, and to one another in which, our actions are purposive, the end of those actions, yet there is no *finis ultimus*. So far as it is possible for a man to unify all his activities by way of one purpose, it is by making them not means (unless it were to a result to come about after death), but constituents of a good for the sake of which they are done. 'By what means', asks Carlyle, at the close of his *Life of Sterling*, 'is a noble life still possible for me here?' He is thinking of such unification; but he should have asked 'By how living?' not 'By what means?' Yet even so, the goodness realized in a noble life cannot be identified with it, but falls also, as it were, beyond it; though it is no particular to which such a life is related as, in the first main form of purposiveness, a particular action is related to something else particular beyond it.

There remains a field not yet spoken of, that of the rational activity displayed in thought. I find it difficult not to admit purposiveness there also. It appears to me clear that the whole effort of trying to understand, the mind's voyage of intellectual discovery, is internally purposive. And the same holds of an artist's effort of thought in discovering the design he wants to achieve, the poem he wants to write, and so forth. Each detail of his thought has reference to a whole beyond it. Only he is not explicitly aware of this Beyond, of the design to which the detail has reference, until afterwards. Yet surely it, or the thought of it, must somehow work in determining what comes into the mind, and the incorporation of this into the design, as in purposive action the thought of a beyond works in a man's decision; particularly, as the thought of a good works, which some action may help to articulate and constitute.

If so, purposiveness is the distinguishing characteristic of the working of intelligence, whether in speculative discovery or artistic creation, or practice; but not means-taking: that is but a special case of one form of purposiveness. Those who speak of the limits of purpose may be asking themselves where human activity rises above purposiveness, or else where we can find what is not yet in any way purposive. To my mind, while in the higher direction there are no limits of purpose until bare 'contemplation' is reached, such as is conceived for example to characterize the beatific vision, in the lower they are exceedingly hard to draw. On the one hand, there may be irruptions of unpurposive behaviour in man; on the other, it is difficult to believe that there is nothing but unpurposive behaviour in other animals. The Cartesian belief that these are unconscious machines is scarcely held to-day; but are they altogether machines, though conscious? No mere complex of non-purposive component activities can be purposive; nor do I see how the purposive can develop from the non-purposive. But where and how the capacity for purposiveness first appears—that seems to me to be the question of the limits of purpose.

VIII

A COMPARISON OF KANT'S IDEALISM WITH THAT OF BERKELEY

WHEN I reflect how much is said and written, and how little certainty is reached, on questions of philosophy, I can but doubt the wisdom of the invitation with which I have been honoured, to lecture before you to-day.[1] Great indeed must be the attraction of our problems, and the interest of our pursuit, to support us in the endurance of so many disappointments.

We have seen in recent years an active output of new philosophical theories, and much of it has claimed the name of realism. When I was an undergraduate there were very few teachers in Oxford who did not regard the case for realism as finally disposed of: for realism, I mean, in the sense that the things we perceive, or with which science is concerned, are independent of any knowing mind. That things known are independent of mind is asserted on all sides to-day.

Some who assert it are primarily interested in maintaining what is rather different, that the object of any man's knowledge is what it is and what he knows it to be, independently of any knowing of it. To maintain this, if mind is active in some other way than knowing, is not to maintain that the thing known is independent of mind in every way. Others are primarily interested in bringing the mind within the sweep of scientific, and particularly of biological, investigation; but that is an old story. Others, among whom are the so-called New Realists, take a more original position. They assert to be independent of mind the very objects of apprehension which in the idealist tradition were held most obviously dependent: sounds,

[1] This Essay was delivered at the British Academy, as the Annual Philosophical Lecture on the Henriette Hertz Trust, in 1929.

E e

colours, scents, and what we distinguish, as the shifting appearances of the same thing to different observers, from the supposed identical thing. These sense-data or sensa, they say, are no otherwise mental than a man is a French citizen, by membership of a particular aggregate. He can lose his citizenship but remain the same man; and a sensum can lose the relations to others which make it mental, and still remain the same item. What collects certain of those items into minds, and at other times or even at the same time into bodies, is not clear; and certainly is not made clearer by what we are told about processes of logical construction, since products of construction can hardly do the constructing. *Mutatis mutandis*, Bradley's question is still pertinent: 'Mr. Bain collects that the mind is a collection; has he ever thought who collects Mr. Bain?'[1]

No philosopher has more uncompromisingly rejected realism, in the sense in which I am taking the word, than Berkeley, and none has claimed more confidently to have refuted Berkeley than Kant. Kant's *Refutation of Idealism* in the second edition of the *Critique of Pure Reason* is notoriously at variance with much of his teaching elsewhere; particularly with passages of the first edition which he omitted from the second. Some find in it an abandonment of the fundamental doctrine that our knowledge is only of appearances, not of things by themselves; another sees in its 'realistic theory of the independent existence of material nature' the ripening of the germinal ideas which give to the critical philosophy its real originality and value.[2] To me it seems that the argument of it is singularly weak. But if we reject it, what are we to say of the relation of Berkeley's thought to Kant's? That is the question which I wish to discuss, for it seems to me to have some points of interest which I have not found worked out.

Let us first examine Kant's *Refutation*. It runs as fol-

---

[1] *Ethical Studies*, 2nd ed., p. 39.
[2] N. K. Smith, *A Commentary on Kant's Critique of Pure Reason*, p. 315.

lows: 'The bare, but empirically determined consciousness of my own existence proves the existence of objects in space outside me.' That is his thesis; here is his proof. It is not long.

'I am conscious of my existence as determined in time. All time-determination presupposes something permanent in perception. But this permanent cannot be something in me, just because my existence in time cannot be determined except through it. Therefore the perception of this permanent is possible only through *a thing* without me, not through the bare *presentation* of a thing without me. Consequently the determination of my existence in time is possible only through the existence of real things which I perceive outside myself. Now consciousness in time is necessarily connected with consciousness of the possibility of this time-determination; therefore it is also necessarily connected with the existence of things outside me, as a condition of time-determination, i.e. the consciousness of my own existence is at the same time an immediate consciousness of the existence of other things outside me.'[1]

The general character of the argument is this: that consciousness of one thing, A (my existence in time), is impossible without consciousness of another, B (things outside me); the consciousness of A being admitted, that of B, and therefore the existence of B, must be admitted also. This is why Kant concludes a proof of the *existence* of objects in

[1] B. 275–6. The *Refutation* professes to be directed against the 'problematic idealism' of which Kant takes Descartes as spokesman, not the 'dogmatic idealism' of Berkeley; that, Kant says, is unavoidable, if space be supposed to be a property of things; but his doctrine, that space is a form of our sensibility, has removed the ground for it. The removal, however, of an assumption whose truth would make idealism necessary still leaves it possible that idealism may be established on other grounds; and the *Refutation* must have rather had in mind Berkeley, who explicitly rejected the reality of material substance, and is elsewhere by Kant taken as an outstanding exponent of idealism, than Descartes, who, though denying that we *immediately* apprehend bodies in space, taught that we had conclusive reasons for asserting their existence. Kant's *Refutation* professes to show that our apprehension of them is immediate; so far, therefore, it contradicts Descartes; but if sound it would on the main point refute rather Hume and Berkeley, who did deny the reality of material substance, than Descartes who did not.

space outside me with the statement that my consciousness of my own existence in time is at the same time an *immediate consciousness* of their existence.[1] His procedure is reflection, and really dogmatic; but none the worse for that. But let us turn to the detail.

The statement that I am conscious of my existence as determined in time must mean, I think, merely that I am conscious that my states, or what Kant elsewhere calls the phenomena of my inner sense, are successive; time-relation is a form of relatedness in which they occur. But the interpretation of the next sentence, 'All time-determination presupposes something permanent in perception', is more difficult. If, as Kant is trying to prove, there are real things outside me which may exist and change unperceived, their existence is also determined in time; but as their existence, and so the time-relatedness involved in their existence, do not presuppose perception, they do not presuppose anything permanent in perception. Of their relatedness in time, therefore, the sentence would not be true, and Kant must have meant here by time-determination perception or consciousness of time-determination. But what did he mean by saying that it presupposes something permanent in perception: that it presupposes something permanent in perceiving, or perceiving something permanent? The first alternative may draw support from empirical psychology. We are told that the apprehension of change in our states is possible only if there is some unchanging state with which their changes may be noticed to contrast. The somatic consciousness, or coenaesthesia, is said to furnish the contrast required; and when anything occurs to interrupt the continuous qualitative identity of this state of feeling it is said that profound psychical disturbances arise. But whatever be the empirical facts about coenaes-

---

[1] It is also why he describes his argument as a refutation of the problematic idealism of Descartes, which rests on the denial that our consciousness of their existence is immediate.

thesia, it hardly provides an unchanging state of feeling, nor anything with the permanence that Kant's argument on this interpretation of it would require. Moreover, not only had Kant denied, in the first edition,[1] that any empirical state is thus unchanging, but the next sentence seems to exclude such an interpretation, for it says that 'this permanent cannot be something in me'; and 'something in me' should mean some state of myself of which I am conscious, some phenomenon of my inner sense. Kant must therefore be taken to have meant that the consciousness of the time-determination of my states presupposes the perception of something permanent; and this permanent is not in me—that is, it is not one of my states; for if it were, it would be merely one of the items, the consciousness of which presupposes that of something else. But why may not the permanent be the self which is not any of its states? Until this is shown, the argument cannot proceed. It is fair enough to say that the perception of this permanent is not possible through the bare *presentation* of a thing without me. For the bare presentation, or *Vorstellung*, would be a state in me; and when Kant argues that the consciousness of my successive states is only possible through something permanent in perception, i.e. (as we have seen) through perceiving something permanent, he means through being aware of a permanent that is none of my states. But why must it therefore be a *thing without me*? Why may it not be myself? This is the crucial point. The rest of the proof seems only to say that if consciousness of A is not possible without consciousness of B, I am immediately, and not subsequently and inferentially, conscious of B in being conscious of A.

It would seem that Kant was uneasy about assuming *sub silentio* that it is not enough, in order to be conscious of succession in my states, to be aware of the permanence of my actively conscious self. For in the first two *Remarks*

[1] *Kritik der reinen Vernunft*, A. 107.

that follow the *Proof*, he alleges, without establishing, its insufficiency; indeed, in the second *Remark* he states that we can only set before ourselves[1] (or, according to another text, perceive) a time-determination through the movement of something permanent in space. No doubt we measure durations this way; but consciousness of succession is possible without it, as in hearing a tune. The doctrine of the synthetic unity of apperception teaches that I could not be conscious of any relatedness among my presentations—and therefore not of my existence in time —if the 'I think' could not accompany them all: if, that is, I could not be conscious of the one self whose they all are. This permanent is therefore apprehended. Kant indeed warns me against ascribing to it any further permanence than is needed in order that it may be the correlative of my successive states; that would be to make a transcendent use of the conception of the self. But equally the permanence of the permanent in space is only correlative with experience.

Nor is it of any use to point out that the self is not an object of empirical intuition (which was the reason why Hume rejected it); for equally what is permanent in space, as distinguished from its changing qualities, which Kant regards, at least from one point of view, as presentations, or states in me, is not an object of empirical intuition. It is true that he alleges impenetrability to serve thus as the intuitable in our apprehension of matter. But impenetrability is not really sensible. As he points out elsewhere, a body may seem to disappear, e.g. when consumed by fire;[2] and not empirical intuition, but only the conviction that there is something permanent which changes, makes us confident that it has not disappeared. True, we go on to say that it has been *dispersed*; i.e. we think of its parts, if taken small enough, as unchanged. But this is to make figure, rather than impenetrability, the sensible to be sub-

---

[1] B. 277, *vornehmen*: Grille conjectures *wahrnehmen*.   [2] A. 185 = B. 228.

mitted to the conception of permanence; and even figure
only serves on the supposition that there are atoms of unchanging shape preserved in all their movements. Some
have believed that bodies, however small, may change
shape as well as place. If that were so, there would be no
sensible correlate for permanence at all ; and if it be not
so, there is still a great difficulty presented by the question
of the atom's real and permanent size. That only the
permanent can change, as maintained by Kant elsewhere,
is a proposition in metaphysics;[1] it cannot be verified by
observation any more of things without me than of myself.
There may be reasons, and I believe there are, for assigning to things without me a reality which Berkeley denies
them. But they are not produced in the argument before us.

The *Refutation of Idealism* therefore, I think, fails. Kant
has not succeeded here in dragging the root of his doctrine
to light. Yet I believe we may discover the thought that
guided him, and that we may be helped to this discovery
by a comparison of his teaching with Berkeley's. I put
aside any considerations which rest upon discarded passages of the first edition, as that, whereas Kant says, in the
Fourth Paralogism,[2] that space itself, with all its appearances, as presentations, is only in me, Berkeley in his
Siris[3] says that 'those who would penetrate into the real
and true causes' will 'speak of the world as contained by
the soul, and not the soul by the world'. I shall take
Kantian doctrine that is unwithdrawn, and (as I think) for
Kant fundamental. I wish to call attention to a remarkable
agreement between their accounts of what the reality of
things consists in, and again of their distinctions between
reality and illusion within experience; and at the same time
to call attention to certain connected differences in their
doctrines.

Berkeley finds the reality of things in the order and con-

---

[1] Or in transcendental philosophy: cf., e.g., A. 184–5 = B. 227–8.
[2] A.375.   [3] *Siris*, § 285.

nexion of our ideas.[1] 'Mechanical laws of nature or motion direct us how to act, and teach us what to expect.'[2] 'Natural philosophers excel, as they are more or less acquainted with the laws and methods observed by the Author of Nature,'[3] but observed, if we would speak strictly, in causing men's ideas. For a spirit is the only real cause; what we call the relation of cause and effect in nature is properly a relation of sign and thing signified. 'Ideas are not anyhow and at random produced.'[4] But they are not produced by bodies. 'We are chained to a body,' says Philonous; 'that is to say, our perceptions are connected with corporeal motions. By the law of our nature, we are affected upon every alteration in the nervous parts of our sensible body; which sensible body', he however continues, 'is nothing but a complexion of such qualities or ideas as have no existence distinct from being perceived by a mind; so that this connexion of sensations with corporeal motions means no more than a correspondence in the order of nature between two sets of ideas, or things immediately perceivable.'[5] This system of signs he calls the Language of the Author of Nature. But it should be noted that there is a certain confusion in his use of that metaphor. He first employs it in his *New Theory of Vision*, where he speaks of a visual language.[6] But tangibles are there treated as 'without the mind', and the metaphor, on this basis, is appropriate enough. Afterwards sign and thing signified are equally ideas; but in language words do not stand for one another. Hence he also treats the order of ideas in its entirety as a language in which the Author of Nature declares to us himself; and what they signify is not one another but their Author.[7] The meta-

---

[1] *Principles of Human Knowledge*, §§ 60–6.
[2] *Siris*, § 234.   [3] Ibid., § 243.
[4] *Principles of Human Knowledge*, § 64.
[5] *Works*, vol. i, p. 459, ed. Oxford, 1901: *Dialogues between Hylas and Philonous*, III.
[6] *New Theory*, § 147, cf. *Principles of Human Knowledge*, § 44, &c.
[7] e.g. *Siris*, § 254.

phor is now at fault; for it is the words of a language that have meaning, not a language in its entirety. This failure of the metaphor is, as we shall see, important. It betrays a failure to think out the necessities of his doctrine.

Meanwhile it is clear what answer Berkeley held himself entitled to give to any one asking him how he distinguished between real and illusory perception. If I really see a man before me, the occurrence of my present visual idea is connected with that of other ideas in my own mind, such as I might indicate by saying that I heard the sound of his approaching footsteps, saw his footmarks, shook him by the hand, and so forth; it is connected again with the occurrence in other finite minds of ideas more or less like mine, and with the possibility of such ideas in other finite minds as might be indicated by saying that they saw the reflection of his body in the cornea of my eye. But if I merely have the illusion of seeing him, then the occurrence of the same present visual idea is connected with that of none of those others; but only perhaps with that of some past emotional ideas, hopes, and fears of mine, and with future ideas in other minds that might be indicated by saying that they saw marks of disease in my brain at a post mortem. Now what is Kant's doctrine? 'To know the *reality* of things requires *perception*, and consequently sensation, of which one is conscious: conscious not indeed immediately of the object whose existence is to be known, but yet of its connexion with some real perception according to the analogies of experience; it is these which exhibit to us in general all real connexion in an experience.'[1] The analogies of experience require us to regard our presentations as occurring in connexion with physiological conditions; these are events in nature; and nature we must conceive as a system of bodies in space, determining changes one in another according to laws or rules. To perceive something real, therefore, is to have a presentation or *Vorstellung* (the word

---

[1] *Kritik der reinen Vernunft*, B. 272.

is equivalent here to Berkeley's 'idea'), whose occurrence is connected according to the order of nature with that of other presentations, our own or other people's. The illusory, as before, would be differently connected. If we ask what difference there is between the two doctrines in their cash value (to use William James's phrase), the answer is—none.

But, it will be said, there is this great difference, that Berkeley allows nothing except the cash of ideas and the Author of Nature; Kant distinguishes our perceptions or ideas alike from things by themselves (what he sometimes calls the transcendental object, an unknown x) and from objects of experience—real things in space without me. In his system, the cash of ideas will buy goods that can be delivered.

Doubtless he thought so. But when we consider how Berkeley's account needs supplementing, if it is to be made intelligible, and what Kant tells us of the real nature of the goods, or phenomena, the difference between them will appear less great.

About the nature of phenomena, and their distinction from our presentations on the one hand, and things by themselves on the other, Kant makes so many inconsistent statements that any account of what he really meant is disputable. I will be bold enough to offer an account of what I believe he wanted to say, though he never quite succeeded in saying it. It concerns chiefly his theory of causation.

Time-order in our presentations is, according to Kant, the mind's work, a result of synthesis, and so is the imagination of time-order among them. But that one presentation precedes another in my apprehension is not that I apprehend a cause followed by its effect; nor is a sequence of ideas in imagination the thought of a causal sequence. This is Kant's starting-point, his demonstration of the failure of Hume's derivation of the idea of cause and effect from the principles of association. For if Hume were right, to think that A causes B is merely that the impression or idea A is followed in the imagination by the idea B; but by the principles of association, the impression or idea B is as readily followed by the idea A; and I ought, when that happens, to be thinking that B causes A—when, for example, a sound calls up the idea of a swinging bell I ought to think that the sound rings the bell. Except on the presupposition that in nature all succession is determined in accordance with some rule, I could never come by the thought of an order of events to which more belongs than the series of my own presentations, whether impressions or ideas; whereas I manifestly do. That is the answer to any empiricist theory of causality; to J. S. Mill's, for example, when he alleges that we directly know that there is uniformity of succession among by far the greater number of phenomena.[1] If phenomena be our presentations, the statement is patently false; and in his *Examination of the Philosophy of Sir William Hamilton* he allows that the uniform antecedent of a phenomenon is generally only a possible perception.[2] But possible perceptions are not directly known; we cannot appeal for their occurrence to experience, as Mill understands experience. The belief in rules of causality then is not the result either of custom or induction. That all events in nature conform to some rule is an *a priori* principle.

But it is also synthetic; and therefore cannot, according to Kant, be asserted of a nature independent of mind—of things by themselves. It is true, because nature is con-

---

[1] *System of Logic*, III. xxi. 4.

[2] 'As already remarked, the constant antecedent of a sensation is seldom another sensation, or set of sensations, actually felt. It is much oftener the existence of a group of possibilities, not necessarily including any actual sensations, except such as are required to show that the possibilities are really present. Nor are actual sensations indispensable even for this purpose, for the presence of the object (which is nothing more than the immediate presence of the possibilities) may be made known to us by the very sensation which we refer to it as its effect.' Ch. xi, 5th ed., 1878, p. 237.

formed to the principles of synthesis demanded by the understanding. How is this conformity possible?

The conformity is possible, because these principles are exhibited in a manifold that is permeated by relations of space and time, and relatedness in space and time is the result of work done, in the synthesis of sense, by the same mind that understands. If the sensible did not exhibit relatedness in space and time, it would not even be sensible. We may say also that what exhibited neither quality nor quantity would not even be sensible; it would be for us nothing. That is why these categories are said to determine objects, but those of relation and modality the existence of objects.[1] A presentation is an object of the inner sense; but I do not apprehend anything real, an existing object, or phenomenon, unless it is connected with other such according to the laws of a possible experience. Now, since the mind is to give to the manifold of sense its relatedness in space and time, it may do so under the direction of the understanding, and so as to suit its requirements; and only because the synthesis of understanding works through that of sense can it secure the conformity of nature to its requirements. Any arrangement of the sensible in time and space must consist with the forms of temporal and spatial order. But time and space are not like other forms of order, which are constituted by the natures of the terms ordered in them, so that in them it is absurd to suggest that a given term might be related to others of the order in more than one way; that 7, for example, might not come between 6 and 8, or that the blue of a forget-me-not might be darker than that of a star-gentian, and yet both be the colours they are. Time and space each provide an order of places, but are indifferent to the quality of what shall occupy them. And it is upon the qualities of what is ordered in space and time that the exhibition of regularity in nature depends. Even our modern physicists, who most of all abstract from qual-

[1] *Kritik der reinen Vernunft*, B. 110, 199.

ity, must admit this. For if there were no more by which to distinguish one body from another than there is by which to distinguish one place from another, they must declare the motion of one body among others a phrase as meaningless as the motion of one body in otherwise empty space.

The mind indeed is not responsible, according to Kant, for quality, nor for differences of quality, in the sensible, beyond the formal condition that all quality must exhibit degree. The rest, what he calls the material character, is given: it depends somehow on the thing by itself, the unknowable x. But given it is. What then is the task of understanding, in directing the synthesis of sense? To fill the places in the time-scheme of sense with presentations so qualitied that it may be able to regard their occurrence as connected with events in nature whose succession is determined, in this very time, always in accordance with some rule. The order of my presentations will then, and only then, be understandable; and it will be so because we can then regard them as events, connected according to rules with other events that are not presentations, but are phenomena whose occurrence conforms to other rules. Taken apart from their connexion with these phenomena, the order of my presentations would appear to conform to no rules among themselves; there is no empirical regularity in the succession of my ideas. That they have such an order that, when taken in connexion with the phenomena, they are seen to conform in their occurrence to rules, is the work of the understanding, which gave them the order that such connexion would require of them. Whatever may be said about the reality of the phenomena on this view, the thought of them has been real; for it has guided the mind, though blindly and unconsciously, in its synthesis of sense.

Let us now return to Berkeley. The function divided by Kant between mind working in us and the thing by itself is assigned by Berkeley altogether to the Author of Nature. It is a mistake to call God in his system a *deus ex machina*,

any more than is *Bewusstsein überhaupt* in Kant's, or Spirit
in Hegel's. Also it is true that Berkeley became a Bishop;
but when he published his *New Theory of Vision* he had only
just become a deacon, and he must have thought out his
main position while yet an innocent layman.

There is, according to Berkeley, no cause but a spirit.
Finite spirits can produce in themselves imaginations; but
ideas or things sensible are produced in them only by God.
This however not at random, but in a regular course, arbitrary indeed, yet consistent. Ideas in finite minds must be
conceived therefore to occur in connexions which these rules
require; and whereas each of us perceives only his own
ideas, the complete system with which the several ideas of
all finite conscious beings are connected is eternally known
to God. 'All objects are eternally known by God or, which
is the same thing, have an eternal existence in His mind:
but when things, before imperceptible to creatures, are, by
a decree of God, perceptible to them, then are they said to
begin a relative existence with respect to created minds.'[1]
'There is an *omnipresent, eternal mind*, which knows and
comprehends all things, and exhibits them to our view in
such a manner, and according to such rules, as He Himself hath ordained, and are by us termed the *Laws of
Nature*.'[2]

But we are not to suppose that world to exist in the
eternal mind as if this mind perceived it from all points
of view at once. It is not such a 'logical construction' of
'private worlds' as Mr. Russell would have it to be. 'To
know everything knowable is certainly a perfection; but
to endure, or suffer, or feel anything by sense, is an im-
perfection. The former, I say, agrees to God, but not the
latter. God knows or hath ideas; but His ideas are not
conveyed to Him by sense, as ours are'.[3] So in *Siris*: 'God
knoweth all things, as pure mind or intellect; but nothing

---

[1] *Dialogues between Hylas and Philonous*, III: *Works*, i. 472.
[2] Ibid., *Works*, i. 447.   [3] Ibid., *Works*, i. 459.

by sense, nor in nor through a sensory.'[1] 'As understanding perceiveth not, . . . so sense knoweth not . . . sense or soul, so far forth as sensitive, knoweth nothing.'[2]

How are we to put this theory to ourselves? that God conceives a system of bodies in space, variously composed and interacting according to laws, with definite time-relations between the events therein; and that at such times at which certain events are conceived to occur therein in a particular sensory, he exhibits some idea to a particular finite mind. It will be noted that time, on this view, must be allowed a singleness and reality which Berkeley denies to it, when he says that it is merely the succession of ideas, so that there is no more a single or common time than there are ideas common to different minds.[3]

Now Kant would object to such a theory at the outset, that space and time are inconceivable to a being whose ideas are not conveyed to him by sense, and therefore pure intellect could not conceive this scheme. The objection is formidable; yet does it not recoil upon himself? for the understanding that directs the synthesis of sense is equally called upon to conceive such a scheme. It is true that Kant speaks in this connexion of the productive *imagination*, and imagination is sensuous. The mind in its synthetic activities, he may have thought, is one: it is at once sensuous and understands. But a blending of the activity directed with that directing it is not easy to realize; and we have a problem here which neither Berkeley nor Kant has solved, nor perhaps any one else.

In any case they are agreed so far as this, that our several ideas, or presentations, occur in such an order as they would, if their occurrence were connected according to laws with events in sensories which are themselves bodies along with other bodies in space and time, mutually affecting each other according to rules which we call laws of nature. I

---

[1] *Siris*, § 289.   [2] Ibid., § 305.
[3] *Principles of Human Knowledge*, §§ 97, 98.

perceive something real, i.e. my idea or presentation is an idea or presentation of an object, not a mere state in me, if its occurrence can be thus interpreted. But if asked whether this object has a reality independent of mind, they both must answer no. Berkeley will reply that it exists in the divine mind; it belongs to a scheme conceived by God to guide him in producing the cash of our ideas. Kant, notwithstanding the *Refutation of Idealism*, will reply that it belongs to a scheme that mind in each one of us is bound to think, in order so to order his presentations that he can say that through them he has experience. To ascribe other reality to it than this would be to make it a thing by itself, no longer transcendentally ideal.

And this is really a remarkable extent of agreement. But when we look for the differences, we find them, I think, to be partly to Berkeley's disadvantage, and partly to Kant's. Berkeley does not see that he has not shown how we should ever discover the plan in accordance with which our several ideas are produced. 'Without a regular course nature could never be understood';[1] but what directs my mind to the discovery of this regular course? It is here that his metaphor of the language of nature betrays him. He calls nature the language, and either God or else nature again what the language tells us of; whereas he unconsciously thinks of nature as telling us of herself in the language of ideas. But mere observation of the order of my ideas, as we have seen, would never discover to me nature and her regular course. Unless it belongs to finite minds to think with the divine mind, so far at least as to conceive the general principles of orderliness in nature which God conceives, they would never find out the detailed rules observed by the Author of Nature. And here Kant has the advantage over Berkeley; for the categories are principles, the conception of which is native to mind, to that *Bewusstsein überhaupt* which is one in us all. The mind works in accordance with them in that

[1] *Siris*, § 160.

blind synthesis, through which it comes about that there is at the outset of consciousness an order of its presentations. Small wonder if in considering these it becomes conscious of the plan on which it has worked unconsciously.

But on another count the advantage seems to rest with Berkeley. Kant claims to have shown that the principle of causality, and other categories, are valid for all possible experience. We may allow this for the mathematical categories, as he calls them, of quality and quantity. Of what has neither quality nor quantity, as we have seen, there can be no perception at all, and we can never be troubled with the intrusion of such nonconforming items into the order of our presentations. But the other categories, the dynamical, require that there be set in relations of time and space sensibles of definite kinds. It is not enough that the sensibles should merely conform to the forms of spatial and temporal order. That they might do, whatever their sensible qualities. If grapes grew on thorns, and figs on thistles, there would be no more breach of the rules of Euclidean geometry than if a wag had hung them there. Our presentations in their order exhibit to us events in nature only if the quality of what is sensible now and here is such as the laws of nature require. Now such sensible quality is given, and is not due to the synthetic activity of mind. If the order of my presentations is to be such that I can suppose them connected in their occurrence with events in nature determined according to rules, I ought after seeing a flash (say) to hear a sound of definite quality. Allow that the mind can give duration and date, and some degree of its quality, whatever that quality be, to material of sense that would not otherwise have them; yet how am I to be sure that the material will be such that what is sensible to me at the date and for the time in question shall be a sound of the sort required? Unless the unknown x responsible for this given factor which analysis discovers in the objects of sense is, as it were, sympathetic to mind, this need not be. Kant does indeed suggest that what lies at the base of external phenomena, what 'so affects our sensibility, that it acquires presentations of space, matter, figure, and so forth', may be also at the same time the subject thinking in us.[1] In the *Kritik of Pure Reason* such remarks occur mainly in the section on the *Paralogisms* discarded from the second edition; but they are frequent again in the *Kritik of Judgement*. In the second Remark appended there to § 57, for example, it is said that the supersensible which underlies the sensible may be the intelligible substrate of nature both without and within us. But he cannot afford to leave this an open question. If it be not so, the task of the understanding in giving to what would otherwise be mere manifold of sense the form of objects of experience is like that of a man called upon to arrange in sentences that shall express his thought letters which he must take as they are given; the task may be impossible of fulfilment.

Now this particular difficulty does not arise on Berkeley's theory; for God, to whom the formative function belongs which Kant assigns to mind in us, determines also the sensible characters for which mind in us is not held by Kant to be responsible; as a man who can determine not only the order but the quality of the articulate sounds he utters is free to form the sentences required to express his thought.

We may now summarize the results of our comparison. Both Berkeley and Kant deny that there is a world of bodies in space independent of mind. Both affirm our sensible experience to be such as would arise if there were such a world, and to be only intelligible to us, only not a mere flux of feeling, when we think of it as connected with the events of such a world. Berkeley accounts for this by supposing that God, to whom the thought of such a world is eternally present, excites in finite minds those sensible experiences

---

[1] *Kritik der reinen Vernunft*, A. 358.

which a world, the scheme of which God thinks of, would require; but he leaves unexplained how this world becomes the object also of their thought. Kant imputes to the spontaneity of mind in finite beings both the fact that the scheme of such a world is an object of their thought, and an activity in ordering their sensible experiences accordingly; but he fails to explain how the material of these experiences is such as to admit of being so ordered. Kant, it may be said, asks of mind in us more than, on his theory, it could achieve; Berkeley, in a sense, asks too little. Kant should have allowed to the principle which is not in us more kinship with the intelligence which is; Berkeley to us more kinship with the intelligence which is not. But there is not such difference between them as might justify Kant's half-pitying disparagement of the 'man in Ireland'.

What, however, is the importance of showing the extent of their agreement, if it is only agreement in error? Are not both, if what has been said is true, unable to defend the ascription of any reality to nature, even when their doctrines have been developed in the ways suggested? Though the *Refutation of Idealism* may have failed to prove it, is it not a fact that we are as immediately aware of a world of things in space as we are of our own states?

I think we must say that we are immediately aware of a world of things in space. By calling our awareness immediate I do not mean that it comes at once, or is unconditioned. But the conditions which might be assigned are of two sorts. There are, first, what may be called the empirical conditions: a body, physiological stimuli, intercourse with other persons; but all these belong to the world of which we become aware, and our awareness of them must not be held privileged above that of what else belongs to this world. We cannot take them for granted in attempting to account for our awareness of the rest. But secondly, there are the metaphysical—or what perhaps we may call in Kantian language the transcendental—conditions. To know these would be to know the nature of that reality within which our life and knowledge arise and to which the world in space and its history belong. And if we can discover them, it can only be by reflective thinking, which thinking itself is not the least notable matter with whose possibility our account of this reality must be consistent. It would be foolish therefore to offer an account which would make of this reflective thinking something incapable of discovering them. I suppose that what I am calling reflective thinking is (at least in its employment upon the problem of the conditions of our knowledge of the physical world) what Kant meant by criticism; but he was surely mistaken in the antithesis he drew between criticism and dogmatism. Dogmatism is an ugly word, because it suggests assertion without reflection; but when we reflect, we have no better or worse reason to give for the assertions reached than that we apprehend the truth of them.

Now this activity of reflective thinking seems to me different in nature both from the thinking by which knowledge advances either in the inductive sciences or in mathematics and from what is called logical construction.[1] Logical construction, if I understand rightly, is supposed to bring us to the thought of those objects whose relations are then investigated in inductive or mathematical science; but it brings us to the thought of them by somehow constructing them out of sense-data. I cannot recognize, in such construction, a process of development; and the transition from the sensitiveness of infancy to that awareness of objects without which neither inductive nor mathematical thinking can begin seems to me to be a process of development. Until this has taken place, reflection also cannot begin.

Reflection, as I have said, may be directed to the question what that reality can be, within which our life and knowledge arise, and to which the world in space and its history belong. But it may also be directed to questions

---

[1] By Lord Russell and others of his way of thinking.

short of that. For example, reflection shows (and there too, the activity might be called critical) that my belief in other selves cannot have come about, as Berkeley[1] and others have supposed, by an argument from analogy; and that no complication of psychological associations, no logical construction, nor yet any inference in which we could distinguish premises and conclusion, could suffice to lead us from a knowledge of sense-data and their temporal and qualitative relations to a knowledge, or apprehension, of bodies in space. It is for this reason that I call such knowledge or apprehension immediate.

It would surely be a mere misdescription of the facts to put all so-called *sensa* on one level, and say that when we feel pain or hear sounds, and when we see or touch, what occurs can equally well be described as apprehending phenomena of the inner sense. The relation of what we feel or hear to the feeling or hearing it is not the same with that of what we see or touch to the seeing or touching it. Where the apprehension of figure and space-relation enters, there enters the thought of a difference between what is and how it appears to us, which is immediate; this, and not 'the consciousness of my existence as determined in time' (as Kant's *Refutation of Idealism* would have it), is what presupposes the existence of 'things outside me'.

And there one is tempted to leave the matter, and say that these things are real and independent of mind, and that we come along and get to know them. Yet we cannot be so easily quit of the idealist. In the first place there are the difficulties (to be mentioned again) about the infinity and continuity of space, and what distinguishes a body from a geometrical solid; and secondly there is this difficulty. In that immediate apprehension, in which is involved the distinction between what is and how it appears to us, we seem to apprehend bodies of sensible magnitude and continuous surface. The real figure of what looks

---

[1] *Principles of Human Knowledge*, §145; cf. *Alciphron*, Dialogue IV, § 4.

differently to observers from different angles or at different distances is, we say, a cube when we look at a tea-chest, a disk when we look at a penny. But when we investigate the empirical conditions of our awareness of these real things without us, we are driven to give quite a new account of them. We seemed immediately aware of something continuous and cubic or discoid, appearing diversely from different points of view; and now we are told there is only a collection of separate minute particles, whose shapes are unknown, darting about with unimaginable rapidity at intervals vast in comparison of their diameters, though like these minute in comparison of any length sensible to us. And when the physicists tell us that mass may disappear in radiant energy, material substance is wearing very thin. There is some plausibility in the distinction between space and the impenetrable body that fills a volume of it, so long as we think of mass as quantity of matter or of what fills space; but what is there extensive about energy? Is it not intensive rather?

Our common-sense realism is thus rudely shaken, and we cannot leave the matter where we were tempted to leave it. The bodies in space of which I seemed to be conscious in the same act of seeing or touching which involved the apprehension of what seemed private to myself, some phenomenon of my inner sense, have been dissipated into something extraordinarily unlike them. I am left indeed with space, but with nothing in it that really has the real shapes of which I seemed to be conscious in that perception, wherein was involved the distinction of the real body and its shape from how they appeared. Even space is being as it were rebuilt by the physicists and mathematicians: with what justification cannot be discussed now. And space is an unsatisfactory thing by itself, and not made satisfactory by having bodies in it. For it is infinite and infinitely divisible, and therefore neither a genuine whole nor with genuine unit-parts. No portion of it therefore, nor body occupying any portion, has a size that can be stated as being any fraction of the spatial whole or multiple of the spatial unit; we can only state its ratio to some other portion; and to such ratio size is indifferent. The intelligible ratio is displayed in something, the apprehension of which is bound up with sense, if not merely sensuous, and whose being, I confess, seems to be inseverable from the being of sensuous or imaginative mind. Certainly the real things without me are not private like the pains I feel or the sounds I hear. But perhaps, as these are bound up with my feeling or hearing them, so are those with the being of knowing and perceiving minds. The empirical conditions of the apprehension of them by finite minds, and the development in finite minds of that apprehension, may depend together upon a reality or intelligence which shows itself in nature to itself in minds. This is of course an old theory or, if you will, romance; for truly it has not been made understandable in detail. And if anything easier can be shown sufficient, well and good. Meanwhile all that I ask you to consider to-day is whether it be not true that something of this sort emerges both from Berkeley's doctrine, and from Kant's who thought himself and Berkeley so opposed, when we supplement them in certain ways which their weaknesses seem to require—from Berkeley's, if it is to be made intelligible that we should divine in common the system of nature to which our several private courses of ideas all point; from Kant's, if it is to be made intelligible that the understanding working in us all alike should not be baffled in its activity by the alien nature of that with which it has to busy itself.

IX

THE SYNTHESES OF SENSE AND UNDERSTANDING IN KANT'S *KRITIK OF PURE REASON*

A MAN, according to Hume, is 'nothing but a bundle or collection of different perceptions, which succeed each other with an inconceivable rapidity, and are in a perpetual flux and movement'. Though he says also that 'the mind is a kind of theatre' where these perceptions 'successively make their appearance', yet he adds that 'the comparison of the theatre must not mislead us. They are the successive perceptions only, that constitute the mind.'[1] This 'psychological theory of the mind', as he called it, much attracted J. S. Mill. But, as Hume had noticed in us a great 'propension to ascribe an identity to these successive perceptions', so Mill admitted that 'if we speak of the Mind as a series of feelings, we are obliged to complete the statement by calling it a series of feelings which is aware of itself as past and future'. He reasonably regarded that as a paradox; yet he shrank from the alternative 'of believing that the Mind, or Ego, is something different from any series of feelings', and preferred to accept the paradox 'as an inexplicable fact, without any theory of how it takes place'.[2]

Herbert Spencer, in his *Principles of Psychology*, has a theory to offer. 'Evolution is primarily a progressing integration'; and the mind evolves. Its proximate components are feelings, and relations between feelings. A relation indeed 'under an ultimate analysis ... proves to be itself a kind of feeling', one momentary, or occupying 'no appreciable part of consciousness'; it 'may in fact be regarded as one of those nervous shocks which we suspect to be the units of composition of feelings'. But we are

---

[1] *A Treatise of Human Nature. Of the Understanding*, Part iv, § vi.
[2] *An Examination of the Philosophy of Sir William Hamilton*, ch. xii, *ad fin.*, p. 248.

justified in distinguishing between such an indecompos-
able relational feeling and a feeling proper, which is 'an
aggregate of related like parts' that occupy time, or space,
or both. Further,

> 'Feelings and the relations between feelings respectively corre-
> spond to nerve-corpuscles and the fibres which connect them; or
> rather, to the molecular changes of which nerve-corpuscles are the
> seats, and the molecular changes transmitted through fibres. . . .
> The fact that, as elements of consciousness, the relations between
> feelings are very short in comparison with the feelings they unite,
> has thus its physiological equivalent in the fact that the transmission
> of a wave of change through a nerve fibre, is very rapid in compari-
> son with the transformation it sets up in a nerve centre.'

We find 'conclusive proof', in the instance of sounds, that
'when a rapid succession of such waves [of molecular
change] yield a rapid succession of such units of feeling,
there results the continuous feeling known as a sensation'.
We may suppose that the same holds good among primary
feelings of other orders. A sensation, then, 'is really
generated by the perpetual assimilation of a new pulse of
feeling to pulses of feeling immediately preceding it'; it is
'an integrated series of nervous shocks or units of feeling'.
When, similarly, 'each sensation is assimilated to the faint
forms of antecedent like sensations', mind is constituted;
'by integration of like sensations, there arises the knowledge of a sensation as such or such'.[1]

Fundamentally the view of the mind, which some of our
New Realists and Neutral Monists take to-day, does not
differ from Herbert Spencer's. It is true that his distinction between the terms involved in a physiological and
those involved in a psychical process, with the resulting
doctrine of parallelism or correspondence, has been
dropped; what to Hume was the monstrous fiction of a

---

[1] *Principles of Psychology*, vol. i, part ii, ch. ii: 'The Composition of
Mind'. The quotations are from § 65, pp. 163–5, and §§ 74–6, pp. 184–
90. I have much compressed Spencer's statements.

perception having a continued existence without the mind does not seem monstrous to a Neutral Monist; these perceptions, or *sensa*, aggregated in certain ways, are bodies; aggregated in other ways, and with images in the collection, they are minds. William James, one of the founders of Neutral Monism, had already in his *Principles of Psychology*[1] distinguished the substantive and the transitive parts of the stream of thought, as those to which objects and relations between objects respectively are known. 'If there be such things as feelings at all, then *so surely as relations between objects exist in rerum naturâ, so surely, and more surely, do feelings exist to which these relations are known.*' In later life he rejected this distinction of objects and relations from the feelings to which they are known. 'My thesis is that if we start with the supposition that there is only one primal stuff or material in the world, a stuff of which everything is composed, and if we call that stuff "pure experience", then knowing can easily be explained as a particular sort of relation towards one another into which portions of pure experience may enter.'[2] As an identical point can be on two lines, if situated at their intersection, so the same presentation, say the seen room in which I sit, belongs in one context to the history of a house, in another to that of my mind.[3] In the first, it is objective, represented; in the second, subjective, and represents.[4] Knower and known are here 'the self-same piece of experience taken twice over in different contexts';[5] but in other cases, between two pieces of *actual* experience, there are 'definite tracts of conjunctive transitional experience', and in the definitely felt transition from one to another, the first acquires the function of meaning or knowing the last.[5] 'Knowledge of sensible realities thus comes to life inside

---

[1] Ch. ix, vol. i, pp. 243–5: italics in original.
[2] *Essays in Radical Empiricism*, 'Does Consciousness Exist?', p. 4.
[3] Ibid., pp. 12–13.
[4] Ibid., p. 23.
[5] Ibid., 'A World of Pure Experience', p. 53.

the tissue of experience.'[1] But what James calls a felt transition must, by his account, be itself a feeling; for if it be said that it is a relation between feelings, we must recall that relations are transitive items in the stream of feelings. It is by some peculiar aggregation, therefore, of items in the primal stuff of the world that minds are formed; and this will still be a correct statement of William James's view, though we bear in mind that the items for aggregation are supposed—perhaps not very consistently—to have arisen by way of differentiation in a primitive flux that somehow tends to 'fill itself with emphases', and exhibit 'salient parts' which 'become identified and fixed and abstracted'.[2] How or by what agency they become identified does not appear, any more than it appears in the writings of more mathematically trained writers of the same camp, how and by what agency so many things are 'correlated'.

Had Kant been as easy-going as these philosophers, there would have been no *Kritik of Pure Reason*. But to him the apprehension of a manifold was a problem requiring solution. He was not content to leave it as a 'final inexplicability', nor would it have seemed to him any solution to say that feelings exist to which relations are known, or which correspond to the transmission of a wave of change through a nerve-fibre as less transient feelings correspond to processes in the nerve-centres. For a manifold series of feelings is not the apprehension of a manifold. If A apprehended α, B β, and so on, neither A nor B nor any other *one* would apprehend α and β and the rest. Plato long ago called attention to the issue. If the eyes saw and the ears heard, that which saw would not hear and that which heard would not see. That which is aware both of colours and of sounds is the one soul, or whatever we are to call it.[3] So Kant said that if a manifold is to be united in

[1] Ibid., pp. 56–7.   [2] Ibid., 'The Thing and its Relations', pp. 93–4.
[3] *Theaet.* 184 b 4–185 a 7.

apprehension with the unity of a self, there must be a synthetic unity of apperception. But in saying this he went beyond Plato. For the phrase indicates that, if there is to be apprehension of a manifold, it is not enough that the conscious subject should be one. It must apprehend the items of the manifold to be related; and more, to do this it must have itself given them the relatedness which it apprehends.

That it must apprehend them to be related seems clearly true. For if it passed from apprehending α to apprehending β without apprehending any relation whatever between them, it would merely change from being conscious of α to being conscious of β. To be conscious of them as many, as 'α and β', it must distinguish them, and even to distinguish is to apprehend as somehow related. Some writers to-day speak of an 'and' relation. This seems to be a mistake. For there is no one relation indicated by the word 'and' to hold between whatever items, the names whereof we link by 'and' when we enumerate them. Left and right, to-day and to-morrow, means and end, agent and patient —the members of these several pairs do not all stand in one same 'and' relation, but in different relations; and if I pick out one term from each pair, and think and speak of left and to-morrow and means and patient, it is as merely differing, not as related by any 'and' relation, that I think of them, though indeed I seldom consider together subjects so heterogeneous. Nevertheless, though there is no 'and' relation, and though also I should describe the universe very inadequately if I said that it was a manifold of terms diversely related, it is true that some form of relatedness must be displayed by the members of any manifold which I am to apprehend as one manifold—even if it be only so meagre a manifold as an aggregate.

The forms of relatedness, according to Kant, which must be apprehended in any manifold, if one and the same subject is to be conscious of it, are of two kinds. For a manifold to be sensible, for one and the same *perceiver* to be conscious of a multiplicity perceived, 'the manifold of intuition must be subject to the formal conditions of space and time'.[1] Kant does indeed in certain passages suggest that there may be other forms of relatedness through which a manifold can be sensible, in an intuition unlike ours;[2] but we cannot conceive what such objects might be. Perhaps his reason for the suggestion was that he had no explanation to offer, why it is by spatial and temporal relations that the manifold of what we perceive (or intuit) is unified, and therefore thought himself unable to deny that a manifold might become sensible by virtue of being somehow otherwise related. With the forms of relatedness of the other kind he believed the case was different.

These are such by which a manifold becomes an object not of sense (or intuition) but of understanding. 'The supreme principle of the possibility of all intuition . . . in its relation to understanding is that all the manifold of intuition should be subject to conditions of the original synthetic unity of apperception'.[3] Kant had in mind that we do not merely hear and see, feel, taste, and smell; we think or judge about what we thus 'intuit'. To judge is to 'subsume a percept under a concept'. That is seen in the linguistic form of the categorical proposition, *B is A*.[4] Kant notices that what is subsumed is never a bare 'this'; 'since no presentation except only intuition is directed immediately to an object, a concept is never related immediately to an object, but to some other presentation of it, whether intuition, or one that is itself already a concept'.[5] Thus if, looking out to sea, I said 'That ship is dismasted', I should relate the concept 'dismasted' to an object already

[1] *Kr. d. r. V.*, B. 136.
[2] Ibid., B. 148; cf. A. 27=B. 43, A. 42 = B. 59.
[3] Ibid., B. 136.
[4] Or in negation, *B is not A*: here we reject such a subsumption; the thought of it is therefore still involved.
[5] *Kr. d. r. V.*, A. 68 = B. 93.

conceived as a ship. If, however, I merely said 'That is a ship', I should relate the concept 'ship' to an object not already anyhow conceived, but nevertheless intuited, i.e. to what is sensibly presented. But if I merely look, without thinking what that is which I see, then an object is presented, and nothing mediates between it and its appearing. I might point, and say 'that'; but if asked 'That what?' I must either bring it under some concept, applying to it a general name, or remain silent. If from inability to 'subsume' it I remained silent, I should not cease to see or 'intuit' it; but I should not judge or think.[1] For me to do this, 'that intuited' and no bare 'that' must become the subject of judgement. But intuiting is not judging; it is not subsuming a bare 'that' under its appearance. How could this be possible? For nothing can be subsumed under a concept except because the concept has first been found exemplified, along with other characters, in what is subsumed under it;[2] and in a bare 'that' nothing is found,

---

[1] I might of course be trying to judge or think about it, and so have passed beyond mere sense, which is, of course, inarticulate, though as we pass out of it we may notice that we were barely perceiving what we now make the subject of a (perhaps unspoken) judgement.

[2] *Kr. d. r. V.*, B. 133–4 (footnote). Kant's contention here is unaffected by the question whether every categorical proposition affirms or denies an attribute of its subject. Lord Russell and others have made it a charge against the traditional logic that it recognized no form of union between the subject of affirmation and what was affirmed of it except that of a subject with its attribute. The charge is not true. Aristotle thought that in science we demonstrate an attribute of a substance; but in ordinary discourse the subject of affirmation need not be a substance, and what is affirmed need not be an attribute, though it will at least be an accident of the subject, if the affirmation is true. Thus, whether I say 'That dog is intelligent' or 'That dog is bigger than mine', I ascribe to a subject already brought under the concept 'dog' an accident; but while to be intelligent is an attribute of a dog, to be bigger than mine is not. It is true that Leibniz believed whatever could be truly affirmed of any substance to be an attribute of it. For the same reasons he denied the reality of relations. But neither the traditional logic nor Kant agreed. Whitehead and Russell, in their account of 'atomic propositions', in effect go to the opposite extreme. The meaning of such propositions is to assert some kind of relation between terms which are each a bare 'this' or 'that': but the relation is of some kind, and

and there could be no reason to subsume it under one concept more than under any other.

The concepts under which, in the above examples, a subject has been subsumed, viz. 'ship' and 'dismasted', are empirical concepts. But there are, according to Kant, certain 'pure concepts of the understanding', or categories, under which, if I am to judge about and understand it, a sensible object must be subsumable. These are not alternative to empirical concepts, as one empirical concept is alternative to another. They are as it were the patterns on which empirical concepts are formed, and under which therefore empirical concepts are themselves subsumable. For as 'that' is a ship, so a ship is a body of a certain size, and a body is a substance with certain attributes; and if the ship is dismasted, it has been acted on and changed by other bodies; and so forth. Spatial and temporal related-ness must be exhibited in what I am merely to intuit or sense;[1] but to apprehend anything as existing in time and space I must conceive the sensible (in which these forms of relatedness are exhibited) as sensible characters of some substance which, or whose component parts, persist, and changes in it as connected according to some law with other changes, in it or in other substances. The connexion of sensible characters with the substance in which they inhere, or their connexion as effects with what causes them, is not intuitable like the relation of above and below or of earlier and later; it is conceivable or understandable. But there can be no connexion without something to connect, no

---

not bare. Thus, in the notation $R_2(x, y)$—x has the dyadic relation R_2 to y—the symbol R_2 has intension, but the symbols x and y have none. And propositions, like 'that is red', are dealt with by the fiction of a 'one-term relation', and by using the notation $R_1(x)$, which means 'x has the predicate R_1', R_1 being also a symbol for a term with intension, and x for a bare 'this', or 'logically proper name'. See *Principia Mathematica*[2], I. xv. It was Kant's opinion that a predicate can only relate to a subject which is not thus bare, and therefore by mediation of another concept, or of intuition.

[1] I have previously written 'perceive' as equivalent to *anschauen*; but the word often implies some thinking about what is *angeschaut*.

relation without *relata*; and unless in sensible intuition we became acquainted with terms between which these conceived relations could be thought to hold, the concepts would be without sense or meaning.[1]

[1] *Kr. d. r. V.*, B. 149. 'Unsere sinnliche und empirische Anschauung kann ihnen allein Sinn und Bedeutung verschaffen'. Kant seems to think they would remain as 'mere forms of thought' or 'pure concepts of understanding', but empty (*leer*). It may be questioned whether purely formal thinking is possible. Kant believed that in logic (or what he calls general logic) we abstract from everything that can distinguish one subject of thought from another, and considering subjects of thought in general discover what belongs to them barely as such. Now the activity of thinking is shown in judgement; and he found judgements traditionally divided on four different bases, of quantity, quality, relation, and modality, so that any judgement was either singular, particular, or universal; either affirmative, negative, or limitative; either categorical, hypothetical, or disjunctive; either assertoric, problematic, or apodeictic. He thought that these differences arose by differentiation of the activity of thinking; and that this activity is controlled by the so-called 'laws of thought', viz. the laws of Identity, Contradiction, and Excluded Middle. Therefore, though thus to distinguish judgements involves concepts of an aggregate and its members (for Kant interpreted distinctions of quantity in extension), of subsistence and inherence, of condition and consequent, of mutual exclusion between alternatives, of actuality, necessity, and possibility, he supposed that we could come by the thought of these through studying the activity of thinking. He then treated them as applicable to whatever is to be thought about—to objects of thought in general; but to say this was not to assert that by thinking we can discover the nature of the independent real, although formal logic, unlike mathematics and science, held good not only of phenomena but of *Dinge an sich*. This inconsistency was only possible because the 'pure concepts' were called forms of thought, and not of what is thought about. It would have been well if he had remembered Aristotle's discussion of the Law of Contradiction in the *Metaphysics* (Γ. iii–vi, esp. iii. 1005 b 11–34). That the same predicate cannot at once belong and not belong to the same subject in the same respect or part of it is there treated as a principle of being, and only secondarily as a principle controlling thought, inasmuch as if I thought otherwise I should and should not be of the same opinion at once. To say that it is *merely* a law of thought would be to say that, although indeed one cannot think *x* at once to be and not be *y*, *x* itself, for all that is known, may not be thus restricted, but may be and not be *y* at once. But if one thinks this, one is thinking precisely what to call it a law of thought alleges that one cannot think. If the 'laws of thought' then are *only* laws of thought, they are *not* laws of thought. To assert them is, as Aristotle saw, to make assertions about everything that is, without regard to what in particular distinguishes one thing that is

In what is sensible then to one mind, if any distinctions
are to be possible within it, the items of the manifold that

from another. They concern, as he said, τὸ ὂν ᾗ ὄν; and we are 'dogmatic',
not 'critical', philosophers in maintaining their truth. Kant held them true
of things in themselves; but how, on his principles, are we justified in saying
even thus much of a reality independent of mind? Only because, as he
supposed, we are saying only how we must think about it, not how it must
be; and so it was, according to him, with the pure concepts of the understanding. But had he realized that what he called forms of thought are
really what we think the object to be, he must either have admitted that
thinking gives us knowledge, so far, of 'things in themselves', or have made
the forms of thought, no less than those of sense, applicable only to 'phenomena'. There have been philosophers, like Herbert Spencer and William
James, who have in effect held that, because in knowing anything I must
think of it, therefore perhaps I cannot know it as it is. (Cf. J. Cook Wilson's
Inaugural Lecture on *An Evolutionary Theory of Axioms*, B. H. Blackwell,
Oxford, 1889; W. James, *Principles of Psychology*, ii. xxviii.)

The fact is that there can be no purely formal logic, if that means one
in which abstraction is made from everything that can distinguish one object of thought from another. It is noteworthy that some logicians who
have pressed hardest the view that logic is purely formal have rejected as
'extra-logical' the distinctions of 'relation' among judgements. Indeed, if
we are really to ignore all differences in what is thought of, and in judgements so far as they differ in virtue of differences in what is thought of, it
would seem that only the difference between affirming and denying will
be left us, as grounded merely in the differentiation of the activity of
thinking. And even this may be challenged; if the distinction between
affirming and denying arises because we apprehend a difference in the object of thought between its being this and its not being that, it also is in
some sense extra-logical. Plato argued long ago in the *Sophist* that there
is a sense in which being and not being both are; if so, the distinction
between them is, relatively to their both being, 'material'. The attempt
sometimes made to reduce negation to affirmation by re-writing *B is not A*
as *B is not-A*, perhaps betrays a suspicion that the ordinary form points
beyond difference in the act of thought to difference in what is thought of.

It may be doubted whether Kant's view that logic is purely formal is
consistent with his contention that mathematical knowledge requires intuition. A prevalent philosophy of mathematics teaches that mathematics is
nothing but formal logic. For this purpose it has to treat as belonging to
formal logic the notions of *class*, and *member of a class*. So Dedekind, in
his attempt to explain number, thinks himself entitled to assume the notions
of aggregate and unit, under the names *System* and *Element*, as if they were
not already numerical. But all these are particular objects of thought, and
what we discover from consideration of them is not discovered from studying the activity of thinking. If it were, a study of that activity might suffice,

are distinguished must be unified by relations of space and time into spatial and temporal wholes. And in what is an object of thought or understanding to one mind, they must be further unified by relations that make them subsumable under 'pure concepts of the understanding'. These are the two kinds, to one or other of which belong the forms of relatedness, consciousness of which in a manifold makes the apprehension of it compatible with the unity of the apprehending subject. But whereas Kant made no attempt to deduce from the nature of sense that the relatedness in what is sensible must be that involved in being spatial or temporal, he did attempt to deduce from the nature of thought what forms of relatedness must be conceived among the parts of a manifold, if one mind is to understand it. That attempt took the form (1) of assuming that the fourfold classification of judgements, with the *differentiae* on each basis of division, was grounded in the nature of thought itself, without any reference to what is thought of, and was manifestly correct and complete; (2) of deriving the not intuited but conceived connexions, whose exemplification in the multiplicity of the spatial and temporal world seemed to him to make it understandable, from the 'pure concepts' involved in the differentiation of judgements. It is fairly generally admitted to-day that this deduction is a failure, and into that question we need not enter. Nevertheless, in his initial contention Kant was right, viz. that a manifold can be the object of our consciousness only if whatever is distinguishable in it appears somehow related, and that unless elements were distinguished in it, it would not seem to be a manifold.

But Kant held further that the one mind which apprehends these forms of relatedness in the manifold of which

without intuition, to reveal mathematical truth. And then, if we press the distinction between logic, as a study of thinking, and experience of the given, we may find ourselves tempted to say, with some philosophers of mathematics, that mathematical necessity is no more than the necessity of following the rules of the game.

it is conscious must be itself responsible for that manifold's having them. This indeed is the central tenet of the critical philosophy, and because of it he maintained that our knowledge is only of phenomena, not of things in themselves. What has to be said about it?

Kant thought it furnished him with an answer to the question how synthetic judgements *a priori* are possible. By what right can we make universal statements, in mathematics and in physics,—i.e. statements that cover not only particulars of which we have had experience, so that we can have discovered that they hold good concerning these, but all particulars of which we or any one else may ever have or might have had experience? The answer is that these statements are true universally because they state certain forms of relatedness in the manifold which are due to the same mind which makes them.

But how far does this answer take us? The synthetic activity, which gives to the manifold these forms of relatedness, must precede the making of the judgements whose truth it guarantees. The synthesis of sense, by which there come to be spatial and temporal sensibles, issues in our intuiting spatially and temporally ordered wholes, not in our knowing the geometrical and numerical necessities in the being of the whole intuited. And the synthesis of thought or understanding issues in what is perceived conforming to certain principles of connexion, not in our knowing the principles to which it conforms. If the synthesis thus precedes the judgements, it is not these judgements. How then do we come to make these judgements, to think of those general propositions in which these principles or those of arithmetic and geometry are formulated? And how do we come further to know that they are true?

To the first question Kant nowhere gives an express answer; perhaps he thought one implied in calling the knowledge *a priori*. But to know anything *a priori* meant originally that our knowledge of it depended on our knowing something prior to it, in the sense that it was as we knew it to be because the other (called prior) was, and not vice versa. For example, if I know universally that the angles of a triangle are equal to two right angles, or that events have a cause, I know that the angles of the triangle whose apices are the centres at this moment of the sun, moon, and earth are equal to two right angles, or that my death will have a cause. If I did not know the general principles, I should not know these particular facts; but I might not know these, and none the less might know the general principles.[1] Thus not the general principle but what followed from it was known *a priori*; and conversely, if I did not infer some particular fact from a general principle, but took some general proposition to be true because its truth would account for observed particular facts, I should reason *a posteriori*. But already before Kant's time usage had changed, and general principles, when believed to be necessary and universal, were said to be known *a priori*. The explanation of the change may possibly lie in the two ways of understanding a proposition of the form *All B is A*. It may be understood as an enumerative statement about all the B's, or as asserting a necessary connexion between being B and being A. If I know the connexion, I know consequently that anything which is B is A, and therefore that 'All B is A', as an enumerative statement, is true. And it is easy to shift from saying that I know the proposition in its enumerative sense *a priori*, to saying that I know it *a priori* when taken in the sense of asserting a necessary connexion. When the shift has occurred, and we say that we know *a priori* not the unexamined particular fact, knowledge of which depends on that of the general principle, but the general principle itself, we can no longer give to *a priori* its original sense. But because, in the

---

[1] Cf. Arist. *Cat.* xii. 14 a 34: πρότερον δὲ δοκεῖ τὸ τοιοῦτον εἶναι, ἀφ' οὗ μὴ ἀντιστρέφει ἡ τοῦ εἶναι ἀκολούθησις.

original sense of the term, its being *a priori* accounted for our having some piece of *a priori* knowledge, therefore it may have escaped Kant's notice that in the new sense of the term this was no longer so.

There are also passages where Kant seems to have thought of this knowledge of principles as *a priori* not because it presupposed other *knowledge*, but because it presupposed a *faculty* of synthesis. This perhaps comes out more clearly in the *Prolegomena to Every Future Metaphysic* than in the *Kritik*. Consider the following passages:

'In only one way, then, is it possible that my intuition should anticipate the reality of the object, and exist as *a priori* knowledge, viz. *that it should contain only the form of sensibility that precedes in me as subject all actual impressions affecting me from objects*. For that objects of sense can only be intuited in accordance with this form of sensibility, I can know *a priori*. . . .'

'Should one for a moment doubt that [space and time] are no determinations of things in themselves, but attach only to their relation to sensibility, I would gladly know how he can think it possible to know, before any acquaintance with things, i.e. before they are given to us, what the nature of the intuition of them must be; yet this is the case with Space and Time. The fact is however quite intelligible, so soon as they are taken for nothing more than formal conditions of our sensibility, and objects [are taken] for mere appearances; for then the form of the appearance, i.e. pure intuition, can quite well be presented out of ourselves, i.e. *a priori*. . . .

'They did not recognize that it is this space in our thought which makes possible physical space, i.e. the extension of matter; that space is no property of things in themselves, but only a form of our power of sensuous presentation; that all objects in space are mere appearances, i.e. not things in themselves, but presentations of our sensuous intuition; and that, since space, as the geometer thinks of it, is just the form of our sensuous intuition that we find in ourselves *a priori* and that contains the ground of the possibility of all outer appearances (so far as their form is concerned), these appearances must necessarily and exactly agree with the propositions which the geometer draws not from any concept of his own invention, but from the subjective ground of all outer appearances, viz. sensibility itself.'[1]

It would seem as if, when Kant spoke of 'this space in our thought', *dieser Raum in Gedanken*, and said that we find the form of appearances in ourselves *a priori*, he must have meant that our knowledge of the geometry of sensible things (which according to him are appearances) was *a priori* because derived from the nature of our sensibility. Yet this will not explain how, when we are said to find 'the form of our sensuous intuition in ourselves *a priori*', the phrase *a priori* is to be translated. Perhaps he regarded it as like *ab initio*, and took it as equivalent to something like 'in advance'.

But supposing that the form of our sensibility determines that objects of sense shall conform to the principles of geometry, yet how we come to formulate these principles and to know that objects of sense conform to them still remains unexplained. If it depends on intercourse with a man that a woman conceives, it will follow that no children will be born except after intercourse; but it will not follow that men and women should think of this principle, or know that births must conform to it; and in fact the Australian aborigines are alleged to have been ignorant of it. Kant starts by assuming that we know objects of sense to conform to certain geometrical laws; his doctrine, if true, would explain why they must conform, but not why we know that they must conform. What really follows from his doctrine is that, if we are to know them to conform, we must first know the truth of the Transcendental Aesthetic; whereas the Transcendental Aesthetic presupposes that we know them to conform, and professes to show why we do so.

Professor H. A. Prichard has therefore argued that geometrical 'judgements must be accepted as being what

[1] Op. cit., 1. Theil, § 9, ed. Hartenstein, iv. 31 (italics in original); § 11, iv. 32; Anm. 1, iv. 36.

we presuppose them to be in making them, viz. the direct apprehension of necessities of relation between real characteristics of real things'.[1] But we must admit that presupposing this does not explain how synthetic judgements *a priori* are possible, as Kant sought to explain it by supposing the universal and necessary forms of relatedness, the apprehension of which among the elements of a manifold makes it possible for one mind to perceive and know a manifold, to be themselves imposed by the mind.

If Kant had realized his failure here, he might perhaps, however, have modified his theory of knowledge in some such way as the following, instead of abandoning it altogether, as Professor Prichard holds that we must do. There are, he might have said, too many difficulties in the way of supposing that space and bodies in space are something real, to which the knowledge or perception of them is unnecessary, for us to accept that doctrine. No doubt we have knowledge, and *inter alia* of mathematical necessities; and when we are knowing, we cannot question it. Yet without questioning it we may ask what the possibility of it presupposes. Such an investigation may be called theory of knowledge, but it will not be open to the reproach which some have brought against all theory of knowledge. We cannot, they say, wait to admit that we really know anything in particular until we have first settled in general what the mind is competent to know; for if we can doubt whether the first be knowledge when we have it, we shall no more be sure that our account of the mind's powers in general is really knowledge.[2] Let us grant this and grant also that what we know cannot depend upon our knowledge of it for being as we know it to be. But to ask what the possibility of knowledge presupposes implies the rejection of neither of the theses granted. Now

---

[1] *Kant's Theory of Knowledge*, p. 65.

[2] Cf. L. Nelson, *Ueber das sogenannte Erkenntnisproblem*, Göttingen, 1908, § 3; J. Cook Wilson, *Statement and Inference*, ii, p. 872.

if for what there is to know and knowledge of it there is some common ground, so that the first could no more be without the second than vice versa, then our minds that know might be finding in the world the results not of their own fashioning activity, but of the fashioning or creative activity of an intelligence in whose nature our minds somehow participate.

There are in the first edition of the *Kritik* one or two suggestions pointing this way;[1] but Kant sheered off from developing this line of thought; and though it recurs in the *Kritik of Judgement*, yet if he found the world in any way accommodated to our powers of knowledge, he there too refused to draw from this any speculative conclusions.

A further objection may be made to Kant's doctrine. He holds that the mind gives to the manifold of sense its space and time relatedness. It does this unconsciously, for until the work is done there is nothing sensible; whatever is sensible is in space and time. But whether to a formless manifold form can be given may well be doubted. What Kant supposes is wholly different from that rearrangement of a manifold whose parts are already extended and in space-relations to one another with which we are all familiar, and different even from the production (for example) of a manifold of sounds in time which occurs whenever we speak. For that also presupposes a time, in which our acts occur.

It may perhaps be said that the conception which Kant, so far as it crossed his mind, rejected, of a creative intelligence through which the spatially and temporally related manifold comes to be, is less difficult than what he maintained, since it does not require us to suppose the existence of a formless matter. When he said that the matter of sense was 'given', and referred us for the giving of it to things in themselves, he made this abstraction. And he

[1] A. 358–9, 379–80. Cf. *supra*, p. 226.

involved himself thereby in a further fatal difficulty, to which attention has already been called in a previous essay.[1] The 'material' characters of different sensibles are equally patient of every variation in spatial and temporal order. Blue can as easily surround red as vice versa, and to vary the succession of the rainbow's concentric colour bands would conflict with no geometrical necessity. Nor does time prescribe what qualities of sound shall be successive or simultaneous. So far, then, as the synthesis of sense is concerned, if it is possible at all to give form to a formless matter, the mind's dependence on another source for the 'matter' whereto form is to be given introduces no new difficulty. But with the synthesis of understanding it is different. For the principle of causality requires not merely that every presented sensible should be in some relation of time and place to every other; how they are ordered in time and place must be bound up with what, in their 'material' variety, they are. The rainbow's colour bands must not be interchanged in their succession; the cuckoo must always repeat the same song with its falling note. But if the mind could secure only that sounds should be of some quality, and not of what quality they shall be, though it were to depend on the mind also in what order available notes shall be sounded, that will not guarantee the uniformity of the cuckoo's song, for the notes required may not be available. That there should be that in the given manifold which makes it possible to put a falling note where it is required in the time order does not depend upon the mind. Kant has overlooked two things. Firstly, that one cannot set about to give to anything order or conformity to law in general, but only a particular and determined order: secondly, that the order one sets about to give may prove incapable of being given because of what the material is to which one essays to give it.

Before developing these two points, however, we may

[1] Cf. *supra*, p. 225.

note one peculiarity of Kant's language sometimes criticized, which perhaps may be defended. He calls space
and time forms of the sensibility, as well as of what is
sensible. So in one of the passages quoted above space is
said to be a 'form of our power of sensuous presentation',
a 'form of our power of sensuous intuition that we find in
ourselves *a priori*'.[1] But we need not charge him with
supposing that a power of the mind is extended, or has
in it differences of earlier and later. Many examples can
be given where we ascribe the presence of a form in what
is sensible to some activity of ours; rhythm in speech or
movement, pattern in a dance, the shape of letters when
we write, are cases. The activities must be different where
results differ in form, and it is not unnatural to speak of
them as differing in form correspondingly. While we are
learning to write, or learning a dance, it helps us to have
before us something to copy, and for a time, after we have
dispensed with a sensible exemplar, we may be guided by
the imagination of it. But afterwards the activity proceeds
as if the apprehension of the form in an exemplar guided
it, without its being apprehended. So we may think of the
form as somehow immanent in the activity which it seems
unapprehended to control. When Aristotle said that in
the generation and growth of plants and animals the
specific form, to the realization of which in the material
of the organism the process of growth is directed, is also
the efficient cause of the process, he was speaking in somewhat the same way. He did not think that growth was
analysable into a mere interplay of atoms according to
what we should call physical and chemical laws. In that
there would be nothing purposive; but growth is somehow
controlled so as to reproduce the specific form. And if so,
according to what the specific form is which is to be
reproduced, so must the activity of control be different.
And if we were therefore to say that the form to be realized

[1] *Supra*, p. 245.

was the form of the activity, we should not be understood to mean that the activity of growth whereby (say) a tadpole becomes a frog is vertebrate and has four legs. But though we may so far justify Kant for speaking of forms of sensibility, the usages to which we have appealed in justification are not wholly analogous. The 'forms of activity' cited do not give form to a formless material. Either, as in speaking, the form and what it is displayed in are produced together, or, as in writing, a material such as ink already otherwise aggregated in space is brought into a new spatial arrangement; and this occurs also in growth.

Now, if this defence of calling space and time forms of the sensibility, and similarly the categories forms of the understanding, is sound—at any rate, if Kant meant by so calling them what has been suggested—the point is important in the following way. It implies that the syntheses of sense and of understanding proceed as if the mind conceived the forms of relatedness that are to appear in what is to be presented, and ordered the manifold accordingly. Kant held that natural causality proceeds according to laws, free causality according to the conception of a law.[1] It is perhaps a mistake to regard natural law and freedom as species of one genus causality. But if we use this language

---

[1] Cf. *Grundlegung zur Metaphysik der Sitten*, 2. Abschn., ed. Hartenstein, iv. 260: 'Ein jedes Ding der Natur wirkt nach Gesetzen. Nur ein vernünftiges Wesen hat das Vermögen, *nach der Vorstellung* der Gesetze, d. i. nach Principien zu handeln, oder einen *Willen*'; in *Kr. d. r. V.*, A. 444 = B.472, Thesis of the Third Antinomy, he opposes *die Kausalität nach Gesetzen der Natur* to *eine Kausalität durch Freiheit*; in *Kr.d.pr.V.*, ed. Hartenstein, v. 30, he opposes *Freiheit* to *das Naturgesetz der Erscheinungen, nämlich das Gesetz der Kausalität, beziehungsweise auf einander*; cf. ibid., p. 99, *Der Begriff der Kausalität, als Naturnotwendigkeit, zum Unterschiede derselben, als Freiheit*: ibid., p. 109, causality in the sensible world is *mechanisch-notwendig*, in the intelligible world *frei*; ibid., p. 120, *In der Antinomie der reinen spekulativen Vernunft findet sich ein ähnlicher Widerstreit zwischen Naturnotwendigkeit und Freiheit, in der Kausalität der Begebenheiten in der Welt*. (The page-references to T. K. Abbott's translation of the *Kr. d. pr. V.* in his *Kant's Theory of Ethics*, for the above quotations, are 116, 188, 198, 210.)

we must say that the syntheses of sense and understanding are akin rather to free than to natural causality. It is through them that it comes about that the sensible conforms to geometrical and temporal rules (Kant tries to derive from time the necessities of arithmetic), and that events conform to causal laws; and the conformity to law which arises through them in the material on which they are exercised cannot be presupposed to explain their working. They work purposively, and purposive activity cannot be assimilated to mechanical. No doubt a machine will execute a purpose, but only one which it is made to execute by some one acting purposively; it does not itself so act.[1] We are familiar in ourselves with purposive action unaccompanied by explicit consciousness of what is to be achieved,[2] and Kant seems to have ascribed such action to mind in its syntheses. It is not this at which we need boggle, but at the nature of the task assigned, viz. to give form to what is wholly formless.

We may now return to the consideration of the two points which it was said above[3] that Kant overlooked; and first and at most length to this, that one cannot set about to give to anything order—i.e. conformity to law—in general. We are concerned here with the thorny problem of what Kant meant in his deduction of the *Second Analogy of Experience*, that 'All alterations take place in conformity with the law of the connexion of cause and effect'.[4] So far as the synthesis of sense is concerned, it is anyhow a determinate order that is imposed: whatever is next in space or time to whatever else, the same principles of spatial and temporal order are satisfied. But the principle of causality would not be equally well satisfied, whatever is next in space or time to whatever else.

It is not possible to extract from Kant's obscurities and repetitions a statement of his doctrine on this central

---

[1] Cf. *supra*, p. 200. [2] Cf. *supra*, p. 207, and *infra*, pp. 296, 331-2.
[3] *Supra*, p. 249. [4] *Kr. d. r. V.*, B. 232.

problem of the *Kritik* which is demonstrably correct. Some of his statements seem to imply that my belief that I am perceiving a manifold of parts coexisting in space, which are not mere presentations or phenomena of the inner sense, is preceded by a stage in which nothing is presented simultaneously, but only successively; and the peculiar importance which he attaches in the section on the *Schematism of the Categories* to the synthesis of time is in the same vein. In studying this successively presented manifold I sometimes find that the order in which I can perceive the parts may be reversed, and sometimes that it cannot. Thus in the notorious illustration from 'the apprehension of the manifold in the appearance of a house which stands before me' and in that of 'a ship moving down stream',[1] we are told that no one will grant that 'the manifold of the house is also itself successive', although it is implied that there is in that case as well as in the other an apprehension of something successive, and not merely a succession of apprehensions; the difference between the two cases is that, whereas in both there are successive apprehended states of perception[2] A and B, in the first each may follow the other, in the second '*A* cannot follow upon *B* but only precede it'.[3] And it seems to be meant that I take note how the order of terms in some successions can be reversed if I please, but that in others not, and

[1] Ibid., A. 191–3 = B. 236–8.

[2] *Zustand der Wahrnehmung.*

[3] It is important not to misunderstand this last statement. Kant does not mean that when 'my perception of [the ship's] lower position follows upon the perception of its position higher up the stream', I am aware that no ship can move upstream. All that I am aware of is that I cannot here and now get the perception of the ship higher up after that of it lower down. On another occasion I might, if the ship were backing upstream or being towed up stern foremost. But here and now I can get the perception of the roof after that of the basement of a house, and vice versa. Kant argues as if the present empirical reversibility of my perceptions in the one case was used by me as evidence that there was a whole of coexistent parts in space, and the present empirical irreversibility of my perceptions in the other as evidence that something was happening.

so pass to thinking in the first case that there are bodies before me whose parts coexist in space, in the second that some event is happening before me. This notion seems also to underlie the extraordinary proof in the *Third Analogy* that 'all substances, in so far as they can be perceived to coexist in space, are in thorough-going reciprocity'.[1] The proof begins by saying that 'Things are coexistent if in empirical intuition the perceptions of them can follow upon one another reciprocally'; e.g. if I can perceive equally first the earth and then the moon and vice versa, then earth and moon are coexistent. But when the moon is on the horizon, cannot I see it and the earth at once and so apprehend their coexistence without the perceptions of them following upon one another reciprocally? Kant's language, however, implies that the thought that what I perceive is coexistent is always an inference from the reversibility of the temporal order of perceptions, in which there was no apprehension of space-relation. And by 'coexistent' he clearly means coexistent in space, not merely simultaneous, like the notes of a chord, though for all he says, when I sing 'Ding dong, ding dong, bell', the discovery that I can get the perceptions of the sounds *ding* and *dong* in either order should lead me to think them coexistent.[2] And the argument seems to be that as, in the instance of the ship, I attributed the empirical irreversibility of the time-order of my perceptions of it higher up and lower down the stream to

---

[1] Ibid., A. 211 = B. 256.

[2] It is interesting to note in certain sensationalist writers the same tendency to speak of coexistence when space-relatedness is meant. Thus James Mill writes of 'synchronous order, that is the order in space', and adds that 'it is necessary to carry along with us a correct idea of what is meant by synchronous order, that is the order of simultaneous, in contradistinction to that of successive existence. The synchronous order is much more complex than the successive. The successive order is all, as it were, in one direction. The synchronous is in every possible direction.' *Analysis of the Phenomena of the Human Mind*, ed. J. S. Mill, ii. 24–5. But the contrast of simultaneous and successive is not that of space and time.

something happening, wherein what was earlier determined what was later, so now I must attribute the empirical reversibility of the time-order of my perceptions to something happening wherein coexistents reciprocally determine each other.

'The relation of substances in which the one contains determinations, the ground of which is contained in the other, is the relation of influence; and when each[1] substance reciprocally contains the grounds of the determinations in the other, the relation is that of community or reciprocity. Thus the coexistence of substances in space cannot be known in experience save on the assumption of their reciprocal interaction.'[2]

But in fact there was never a time when the manifold I apprehended was of items only temporally related, and I never used my ability or inability to apprehend certain items in a reversed order of sequence as a ground for thinking there was, still less for apprehending, in the one case a whole of spatially related coexistent parts, in the other a sequence of events determined according to some law. This has been well pointed out by Professor Prichard.[3] And Kant can hardly have seen clearly that anything so remote from the facts is implied by his argument. For though he often implies it, he also speaks inconsistently with it. Thus (1) he implies it in the following statements. 'The apprehension of the manifold of appearance is always successive. The presentations of the parts follow one another. Whether they also follow one another in the object is a point which calls for further reflection, and which is not decided by the above statement.'[4] Here one would suppose him to mean that I might have a series of ideas or presentations without assuming that I was apprehending events, and this is confirmed by what shortly follows.

[1] Kant's text has *dieses: jede* is Wille's emendation.
[2] Ibid., A. 211 = B. 257-8.
[3] *Kant's Theory of Knowledge*, pp. 294-6. It will be evident that I owe much in this essay to the chapter in which the pages cited occur.
[4] *Kr. d. r. V.*, A. 189 = B. 234.

'Appearances, so far as merely as presentations they are thereby[1] objects of consciousness, are not different from the apprehension, that is the reception of them in the synthesis of imagination, and we must therefore say that the manifold of appearances is always produced successively in the mind.'[2] It will be noted that Kant speaks here of synthesis as involved in the apprehension of the successive appearances. He is supposing them to be presented to *one* mind, and not therefore contrasting a Humian stream of 'perceptions' with unitary consciousness of such a stream. What then can he be contrasting but a unitary consciousness of a mere stream of one's own successive states with apprehended spatial wholes and changes determined in them? Take also this:

'If then we experience that something happens, we thereby always presuppose that something precedes, on which it follows according to a rule. For without this I should not say of the object that it follows, since mere sequence in my apprehension, if not determined by a rule in relation to something preceding, justifies no sequence in the object. It is always then in reference to a rule, in accordance with which appearances are determined in their sequence (i.e. as they happen) through the preceding state, that I make my subjective sequence (viz. of apprehension) objective, and the very experience of something that happens is possible only under this presupposition.'[3]

If I make my subjective sequence objective by help of this

---

[1] *zugleich.* [2] Ibid., A. 190 = B. 235.

[3] *Kr. d. r. V.*, A. 195 = B. 240. *Object* here means not just 'object of consciousness', as in the previous quotation, but something which, though I may become conscious of it, I suppose to exist independently of my doing so. Kant is aware that he treats the presentations which he calls objects (of consciousness) as also indicating objects and that what he calls appearances are sometimes equated with these 'objects of consciousness' and sometimes with what they indicate (see the first sentence of B. 235 = A. 190). But he never justifies this, and seems often unconscious that he is shifting from one use of the word 'object' to the other. Thus, when he says (B. 110) that the categories of quantity and quality (which he calls *mathematical*) are concerned with (*gerichtet auf*) objects of intuition, those of relation and modality (which he calls *dynamical*) with the existence

presupposition, surely there must have been a 'mere sequence in my apprehension'.

But now (2) turn to the immediately succeeding paragraph, which is inconsistent with what these passages imply:

'It is true this seems to contradict all the observations that have at any time been made concerning how we proceed in the use of our understanding. According to these observations it is only through perceiving and comparing similar sequences in many events, that we are led for the first time to discover a rule, according to which certain events follow always upon certain appearances, and thereby for the first time are brought to construct for ourselves the concept of cause. . . . It is true that the logical clearness of this presentation, viz. of a rule determining the series of events, as a concept of cause, is not possible until we have made use of it in experience; but a reference to it as the condition of the synthetical unity of appearances in time was nevertheless the ground of experience itself, and therefore preceded it *a priori*.'

We need not insist that the synthetical unity of appearances in time, of which Kant here says that the concept of cause is the ground, is no more than unity of successive presentations as received in the imagination of one mind; he may be intending here to distinguish appearances from presentations. But he is clearly rejecting any view like Hume's or

of these objects, he shifts from meaning by 'object' a mere 'presentation' to meaning something existing whether or not presented to me. In all this he may be compared with Hume. Hume teaches that we know nothing except impressions and ideas, and certain relations between them which appear upon comparison of them. Consequently, when he defines a cause (*Treatise of Human Nature: Of the Understanding*, iii, § xv) as 'an object precedent and contiguous to another, and where all the objects resembling the former are plac'd in like relations of precedency and contiguity to those that resemble the latter', objects should be impressions or ideas. But he goes on to offer an alternative definition: 'A cause is an object precedent and contiguous to another, and so united with it, that the idea of the one determines the mind to form the idea of the other, and the impression of the one to form a more lively idea of the other.' Here objects are distinguished alike from ideas and impressions, which are said to be 'of' them. Kant endeavours at once to justify this distinction and to retain the view that in the last resort it does not exist.

Mill's,[1] that I can study the sequences in the stream of my perceptions or states of consciousness, and so be led to the notion of an order, not merely of these, in which the causal rule holds.

What explanation are we to offer of this inconstancy in Kant's exposition? Perhaps this. He saw very clearly that if I were without any particular thoughts implying that of an order of events which is not identical with the order of my presentations, and in which whatever happens exemplifies some law, I should be aware of nothing but a sequence of presentations; and that if I could take note of what presentations followed what in this subjective play, I should discover in it no regularity. J. S. Mill says of 'the law of the uniformity of succession'[2] in phenomena that 'we now know it directly to be true of far the greatest number of phenomena'. What he means is that we have discovered the laws exemplified in the occurrence of by far the greatest number of phenomena; though this is a gross overstatement. But this is only true if by 'phenomena' he understands events in nature, and he forgets that he has identified phenomena with 'states of consciousness'. If we asked him for instances of phenomena for which we know this conformity to law to be true, he might offer the tides, or the sound of thunder. But the very naming of these implies the thought of bodies in space whose changes depend on something not necessarily presented to me. It is monstrously false that I know directly—i.e. without appeal to the 'law of uniformity of succession'—that the ebb and flow of the sea follow uniformly on the shifting pull between the earth and the moon, or the sound of thunder on the impact of air-waves started in the clouds

[1] *System of Logic*, III. xxi.

[2] It is worth while noting that Mill speaks as if that every event exemplifies some law or other were itself a law exemplified. If there are principles of connexion, any one of them may be exemplified in a particular event; but that every event exemplifies some principle of connexion or other is not exemplified in any event. Cf. *infra*, p. 289.

upon an auditory nerve; but if I did, it would not be between states of my consciousness that I observed this regularity of succession. If it be asked what presentation uniformly precedes in my consciousness a sound of that peculiar quality which makes me call it thunder, the answer is, none. Thunder-claps intrude themselves abruptly into the series of my states of consciousness, and their immediate antecedent there may be anything you please; now a twinge of pain, now a squeaky noise, now a scent, and so on.[1] Even these suggestions, chosen because they do not involve mention of anything distinguished from all states of my consciousness, as to suggest the opening of a door or looking out of the window would, yet really imply the thought thereof. If I really were aware of nothing but a sequence of presentations, and had no thought of an order of events, I should not even have names for any of my presentations.

Now since to remove all thought of an order of events exemplifying laws would dissolve my experience into a phantasmagoria of presentations, it might be supposed that, starting with such a phantasmagoria, I could pass by introducing that thought to the experience which removing it would thus dissolve. And much of what Kant says seems to have been written as if he thought this were so. But it is not so. And he was at times conscious that what the thought of law in nature does for me is not this. It does not bring me from such a phantasmagoria to apprehending bodies and events, but from apprehending bodies and events without knowing the laws in accordance with which events in bodies are determined to knowing, or at any rate having opinion concerning, what these laws are. Yet this important distinction between the concept of cause and conceiving what causes what is no more clearly held to by Kant than it was by Hume. The passage quoted on p. 257 obviously refers to Hume. Kant ought to have pointed

---

[1] Cf. *supra*, p. 219 *init.*

out that perceiving and comparing similar sequences of events does not bring us to construct for the first time the concept of cause, but to conjecture what causes what, which we could not do unless we already had the concept of cause; and that, according to the theory which he is criticizing, it is similarity of sequences not in events but in 'perceptions' or presentations that leads us to the concept of cause. He is quite right in holding that the distinction of events from 'perceptions' presupposes it. He is wrong so far as his language implies that using it converts having sequences of 'perceptions' into perceiving sequences of events. And such a supposition is so far from the truth that he cannot bring himself to develop it thoroughly and consistently.

Why, then, does he use language that implies it? Because there is another conversion which his whole theory does require him to believe in and develop, but about which he never gets quite clear. This is a conversion not of a time-order of presentations into an experience of bodies and events, but of an unordered sensuous 'material' into an order of nature within which belong both bodies and the events befalling them and another kind of events, viz. our perceptions of bodies and of the events befalling them, or the presentations, to have which is to perceive them.

But for this conversion it would not be sufficient that the mind should use merely the concept of cause. If I already take myself to be perceiving bodies and events befalling them, I have the concept of cause; and the explicit use of it in the interpretation of my experience will lead me to theories regarding what causes what. But for the task which Kant assigns to this category it is necessary not only that the mind should have from the outset the concept of cause; it must have also the thought of what is to cause what, for every different sort of event.

It is fundamental to Kant's whole theory of synthesis as the work of the mind, that the synthesis of understanding works by directing the synthesis of sense. The synthesis of understanding brings it about that in what is intuited we find not only spatial and temporal relatedness of a manifold, but relatedness of other kinds, more particularly such in virtue of which we can regard what is intuited in space as a body or collection of bodies, whose sensible qualities are presented to us, and change only in definite ways connected with definite changes in other bodies. In thus regarding the intuited we subsume it under concepts—of substance and attribute, cause and effect, reciprocity. But nothing can be subsumed under a concept unless we find in *it* the character which, abstractly considered, we are said to conceive. Therefore, unless the intuited were a manifold whose parts of themselves, or at least independently of our subsuming, had these forms of relatedness, it would not be subsumable under these concepts, which the understanding brings to the consideration of it, and which are therefore *a priori*. Yet if its having them were independent of mind, we could not know how far it had them, and so could not assert that our concepts will always find exemplification in it. The mind, then, must give it these forms of relatedness which make it subsumable under our concepts, for we do know that our concepts will always find exemplification in it. Here we notice the same failure in Kant's defence of the principles which make a 'pure science of nature' possible as in that of those which make 'pure mathematic' possible.[1] He assumes that we know them to be true, and sets out to explain our knowing this; but if we accept the explanation, we did not know them to be true; for only the explanation shows them to be so.

But only by the precise way in which the qualitatively differing items of the manifold which we perceive are ordered in space and time can these conceived forms of relatedness be manifested. Everything perceived must be in space and time, in virtue of the synthesis of sense. But

[1] Cf. *supra*, pp. 246–7.

the spatial and temporal orders of sensibles are unlike all other sorts of order among sensibles in this, that they are indifferent to the sensible characters of what are ordered in them.[1] There is an order of pitch among tones, as well as of time; in pitch A must come between A♭ and A♯; in time it need not. There is an order of height among men in line, as well as of place; in height a man of 5 ft. 10 in. must come between one of 5 ft. 8 in. and one of 6 ft.; in place he need not. Hence to the synthesis of sense, which puts everything intuited in relations of space and time to everything else intuited, it is indifferent what qualities distinguish that which is intuited here and now, there and then, respectively. But to the synthesis of the understanding it is not indifferent. If I saw with the naked eye what looked like Saturn's rings when and where, in order to relate the presentation with others according to a rule, I needed to see the moon, the event in its relation to others would not be subsumable under the concept of effect and cause. If there were nothing directly or indirectly measurable of which the assumption that the amount was constant helped to explain observed changes in the sensible, the relations of the observed could not be taken as illustrating the principle that in all changes of appearance substance is permanent. And what makes terms in time and place relations illustrative of these principles is that they are sensibly what they are, not that whatever is sensible has time and place relations.

The understanding, then, is so to control the synthesis of sense in the time and space ordering which the latter gives to a mere unordered manifold, that the sensibly differing items of the manifold which come thereby to be presented in time and space relations shall be distributed to such times and places as will make the concepts of the understanding applicable to them in their relations. But if it is to do this, it will not suffice that it should bring only

[1] Cf. *supra*, p. 220.

pure concepts to the task. Not the thought of regularity in general is needed, but of what the laws of nature are to be which the presentation of this sensible here and that there, the occurrence of this precise change now and that then shall illustrate, if the sensible items of the manifold are to be so distributed in time and place as that the categories shall be applicable. The possibility of the task even so may be questioned. Kant seems to have connected the performance of it with the 'productive synthesis of the imagination'.[1] Certainly, if it occurs, it occurs unconsciously (as he supposed this to occur) and we are conscious only of the results, in the order of our presentations. But if it proceeded consciously, it is plain that we should be guided by the thought of what was to be connected with what, not merely of the need for principles of connexion; and if it proceeds unconsciously, it is equally that which must guide it. Consider a not wholly inadequate analogy. When I speak or write, certain sounds or visible signs come to be ordered in time or space; but that must happen whether I produce sense or nonsense. If it is to be sense, certain rules of accidence and syntax must be observed. I do not think of these rules in using my own language, though in using one of which my mastery is imperfect I may; none the less they control the activity, in the results of which I find them exemplified. But they are determinate rules, whether thought of or not. The mere unspecified thought that what I say or write should conform to rules of accidence and syntax, if I think of no rules in particular, could not guide my utterance; nor could that requirement working unconsciously control it, for it is indeterminate.[2]

---

[1] *Kr. d. r. V.*, A. 118=B. 152.

[2] Leibniz seems to have understood the matter better. That there should be order in a world he counted as a factor of excellence in it; but its presence required that God should have had certain 'principal designs' for it, i.e. should have conceived not order in general but what the laws should be in accordance with which the particular designs for the individuals in that world should be worked out.

It is clear, then, that we cannot set about to give to anything conformity to law in general. I may have the thought of such conformity in general and set about to discover what are the laws to which observed changes in things conform; and the concept may be called *a priori* inasmuch as to look for laws presupposes the thought of law. But Kant believed that our finding what we look for is made certain because we have put it there; and that the concepts which we bring *a priori* to the search guided us *a priori* in the synthesis which put there what we look for. They would not have sufficed. It is largely because he tried to work out his critical philosophy on the assumption that they would, that his exposition is so unconvincing. How could he make clear the necessity of that happening which could not happen?

It was said above[1] that Kant had overlooked two things: firstly, that one cannot set about to give to anything order or conformity to law in general; secondly, that the order one sets about to give may prove incapable of being given, because of what the material is to which one essays to give it. The first contention seemed worth developing at length. It is fundamental to any estimate of Kant's doctrine of *a priori* synthesis. On the second enough has perhaps been said in a previous essay in this volume.[2] It may be illustrated by continuing the analogy already used in illustrating the first contention. When I speak, I produce the word-sounds as well as their order, temporal and grammatical. But my power to do so depends on my control of my organs of speech. Paralysis of the throat, excision of the tongue, or some aphasic lesion in the brain, might make it impossible for me to talk sense, however clearly I remained conscious of what I wanted to say, though any noises I produced would still have a time-order. So the understanding, however much the laws to be exemplified in what should be

---

[1] p. 249.
[2] Essay VIII, pp. 225–6.

sensibly presented were consciously or unconsciously conceived, would be unable to secure that the spatially and
temporally ordered manifold should be one of which I
could 'make sense', if I could not count on having, for
allocation to these and those times and places, items of the
sensible character that the laws required. The categories
of relation might still be called valid for all possible experience; but only if by experience I mean the apprehension of
only such changes in the sensible as are so ordered that
the categories are valid for them.

X

THE SCHEMATISM OF THE CATEGORIES IN KANT'S *KRITIK OF PURE REASON*

In the second book of the *Transcendental Analytic* Kant comes to grips with the problem, by what right we use in our account of nature the pure concepts of the understanding or categories. To it he prefixes, after a few preliminary paragraphs, a short Introduction, 'Of the transcendental power of judgement in general'. The purport of this Introduction is somewhat as follows.

It is one thing to understand a concept, another to apply it correctly. The power to apply concepts correctly we may call power of judgement—*Urteilskraft*. This word, we may note, does not mean the power of judging, or of making judgements. Kant has already said elsewhere that we may regard understanding generally as a capacity to make judgements,[1] and what he here calls power of judgement he is distinguishing from this. What the power to make judgements or faculty of judgement is he indicates by contrasting it with that of intuition. Merely to see coloured expanses, to hear sounds, &c., without thinking that what one sees or hears is such and such, is to intuit. But I make a judgement when I think something about what I intuit. For example, I should make a judgement if I said, or thought, that the world was made by God; nevertheless, in Kant's opinion, I should thereby show myself lacking in power of judgement; for I ought not to relate anything sensible to the suprasensible as its cause. Again, consider the following statement: 'To argue that, because $a = b$ and $b = c$, therefore $a = c$ is to syllogize'. Here a concept is employed which has been brought to light in general

---

[1] 'Wir können aber alle Handlungen des Verstands auf Urteile zurückführen, so dass der Verstand überhaupt als ein Vermögen zu urteilen vorgestellt werden kann': *Kr. d. r. V.*, A. 69 = B. 94.

logic by reflection on the use of the reason in abstraction
from any question of the special content or *Inhalt* of arguments: viz. the concept of syllogism; and it is employed to
make a judgement, when the argument in question is said
to be syllogistic. But in fact the argument is not syllogistic,
and any one judging it to be what it is not is failing in
power of judgement.

Power of judgement is power not just to use concepts,
but to use them correctly. Kant points out that the understanding may be well furnished with concepts or rules, but
that to be so furnished does not enable one to apply the
rules correctly, nor to know what should be subsumed
under the concepts. This is true both of less general, or
less abstract, rules and concepts, like the concept of fraud
or the rule that one should obey one's lawful government,
and also of those, like syllogism, which, in Kant's opinion,
general logic discovers to belong to the form of thought in
general, as the above example illustrates. To apply rules
or concepts is a matter, says Kant, of talent or practice, and
no rules can be given for it. If I needed a rule instructing
me when to apply the original rules, I should equally need
a further rule instructing me when to apply that instruc-
tional rule. *Urteilskraft*, therefore, as power of judgement,
is a natural gift.[1]

But what Kant calls transcendental philosophy is, according to him, in the peculiar position, that it not only
reveals certain synthetic principles of pure understanding,
but does also assist the judgement in the use of them and
offer a rule for their application. It tells us *a priori* to what
the principles may be applied. The reason for this is that
these principles or concepts of the understanding must
relate to objects *a priori*; the question whether they so
relate or not is not one to be decided empirically. We must
therefore ask what is the condition of their thus necessarily

---

[1] Cf. what Bacon says, *Nov. Org.* i. 130, of the *vis propria et genuina
mentis.*

relating to objects—what is the condition, which being satisfied, we need not wait upon experience to know whether they so relate or not; and the use of them must be restricted to what satisfies this condition. Such is the rule which transcendental philosophy furnishes for the application of those other rules or principles or concepts which it reveals.

Transcendental philosophy has then two tasks to discharge in regard to the *Urteilskraft* or power of judgement. One is this of showing what the condition is, on which it depends that the 'pure concepts of the understanding' can be employed, i.e. that we are justified in subsuming anything under them. The other is to show how, when this condition is satisfied, certain synthetic judgements follow *a priori* from the application of these concepts to what is subsumable under them. The first task, with which alone we shall be here concerned, is held to be discharged in the section on the Schematism of the Categories.

But before examining this section we may point out that the transcendental *Urteilskraft* turns out not to do for us in its peculiar field what in other fields other *Urteilskraft* does for those gifted with it. In other fields to know whether this or that falls under some rule or concept, whether it is (as Kant says) *casus datae legis*, is to display sagacity in the details and particular problems belonging to the field in question. We might call the power 'good judgement'; it is the intellectual excellence shown, as Aristotle says,[1] in considering matters which happen now this way and now that, τὰ ἐνδεχόμενα ἄλλως ἔχειν, and called by him φρόνησις in application to questions of practice. It may be a sound rule for the stroke of a racing boat to spurt at the moment when the rival crew is on the verge of cracking; it requires good judgement to detect when that moment has arrived. A law which gives some officer discretion to grant or refuse applications of a certain sort

---

[1] *Eth. Nic.* vi. i. 5, 1139 a 6–8.

may add, that leave must not be unreasonably withheld; good judgement distinguishes the particular cases when it is reasonable to withhold leave. But in the transcendental field we find no such good judgement as this vouchsafed to us. All we find is a great range or class of cases, not individual cases, discriminated by the power of judgement as the field for the application of our concepts or rules. The range is the whole range of space and time; only to what is in space and time, but to everything that is so, are these concepts applicable. Transcendental power of judgement is no natural sagacity, like that 'right judgement in all things' for which in the collect we pray, and which Kant says truly enough cannot be taught but only assisted by practice. It does not inform the ordinary man, to whom his understanding suggests the concepts in question, what are the proper occasions of their use. It comes naturally to us all to employ these concepts, or categories, in our daily thought about what we perceive; but it comes equally naturally to us to extend their employment beyond what we perceive; the 'transcendental illusion' which Kant proposes to lay bare in the *Dialectic* is as common as the right use of these concepts. Transcendental power of judgement then is a matter not of talent and practice but of philosophical reflection; it is the critical philosopher who discriminates the cases to which the concepts apply from those to which they do not, and that in virtue of no such natural sagacity as *Urteilskraft* in general is said to be, but of a profound investigation most unlike its gift of recognizing immediately the *casus datae legis*. We may therefore dismiss, as a mere fragment of his 'architectonic', Kant's appeal to a special transcendental power of judgement in general, and examine on its own merits the doctrine of the *Schematism of the Categories*.

Kant begins his section on it by saying that if an object is to be subsumed under a concept, the presentation of the object must be homogeneous with the concept (*gleichartig*).

He offers as an example subsuming a plate under the concept 'circle'; the roundness thought in the second is seen in the first.

But the concept 'circle' is not a pure concept of the understanding; pure concepts of the understanding are not homogeneous with any empirical, or sensuous, intuition. How, then, can the sensuous be subsumed under them? How, for example, can the category of causality be applied to an appearance? Here is the difficulty which makes a transcendental doctrine of judgement requisite (and it will be noticed how far what Kant thinks requisite is from any natural sagacity); for where the concept through which the object is thought in general is not different from and heterogeneous with that which presents it *in concreto*, the application of the former to the latter needs no special discussion.[1]

Kant seems to have been puzzled here by two different problems which had exercised previous philosophers, and not clearly to have distinguished them. One concerns the nature of universals in mathematics, and the relation of universals to the particulars said to be 'subsumed' under them. The other is in principle the same with Hume's problem about the origin of the ideas of those relations which do not depend on the ideas which we compare together, but may be changed without any change in the ideas.[2]

What he says about the homogeneity between concept and presentation in his example of the circular plate shows a misunderstanding, which mathematical examples facilitate, of the nature of universals and their relation to their instances. It is not true that a plate is like the concept of a circle, i.e. circularity. It is like a geometrical circle; but a geometrical circle is not a concept. A geometrical circle

---

[1] Kant speaks of the *concept* which presents the object *in concreto*, because that which I judge circular may be already conceived as a plate, and not merely a something seen: cf. *supra*, pp. 237–8.

[2] *Treatise of Human Nature: Of the Understanding*, iii, § 1 *init.*

is as much a particular, whatever its form of being, as a plate is; but a plate imperfectly realizes circularity, and a geometrical circle perfectly. This confusion between the objects of mathematical study and universals is ancient and common. Yet it was cleared up by Plato, who distinguished τὰ μαθηματικά, the objects of mathematical study, alike from sensibles and from forms (εἴδη) or universals. Unlike sensibles, they are eternal and unchanging; unlike forms, they are many of the same kind; the mathematician considers intersecting circles, and a sum of twos, but there cannot be intersecting circularities nor a sum of twonesses.[1] We may call a geometrical circle homogeneous with a round plate, or a pair of mathematical units with a pair of gloves, because the former are both instances of circularity, and the latter both of twoness. But we cannot call any universal and its instances thus homogeneous. Kant is, in fact, a victim of the metaphor involved in calling a universal an exemplar or παράδειγμα, and exposes himself to the old objection. If the concept and the presentation which is to be subsumed under it are alike, must they not both be instances of some third?[2]

What is called subsuming is apprehending the *what* in

---

[1] Arist. *Metaph*. A. vi. 987 b 14 *et al*. Whether in the *Republic* Plato had clearly seized the distinction, at least in geometry, is uncertain. In *Rep*. vi. 510 d 5–e 1 he says quite truly that the geometer, though using visible figures, is thinking not of these but of what they resemble, what only the eye of the mind can see; but he offers as instances τὸ τετράγωνον αὐτὸ καὶ ἡ διάμετρος αὐτή, and these phrases would naturally mean squareness and diagonality, universals, not a geometrical square and its diagonal. The geometer, of course, is not concerned with squareness, but only with squares. On the other hand, in vii. 525 d 9–526 a 7, he points out that the arithmetician adds units that contain no parts (unlike sensibles used to represent them) and are all exactly equal; here it is not unity, but perfect examples of unity that he contrasts with sensibles: cf. *Phaedo*, 101 b 9–d 2, where unity is distinguished from any unit, and the sum of 1 and 1 from duality, and on the whole question, J. Cook Wilson, 'On the Platonist Doctrine of the ἀσύμβλητοὶ ἀριθμοί', ap. *Classical Review*, xviii. 5 (June 1904), pp. 247–59. Current philosophy of number tries to dispense with the acknowledgement of these forms of multiplicity.

[2] Cf. Plato, *Parmen*. 132 c 12–133 a 6.

the *that*. It may be a *what* already apprehended in some other *that*. If so, I may very likely have a name—a general name—applicable to that in which I now apprehend it. And it is this name, not the name of the concept, which I apply (*anwenden*) to the present *that*. I call what I am now seeing a cube or circular, not cubicity or circularity; but these are the names of the concepts. To subsume a presentation or an object under a concept is to recognize or think I recognize it (or it may be some feature of it) as a particular of some concept or universal, and therefore homogeneous with *any other particular* thereof. And if the object is sensible and can be imagined or 'imaged', I may speak of it as homogeneous not only with another sensible particular thereof, but with an image; not, however, with a concept.[1] Of figures imagination, prompted by description, may even precede sense-perception, so that when for the first time I saw St. Peter's I might say that it is very like what I had pictured to myself. But I do not subsume St. Peter's under my 'picture'. There is perhaps a special liability, however, to confuse a geometrical figure with a concept, because we can imagine it fitted to one body after another. A geometrical circle (which Kant calls the pure geometrical concept of a circle[2]) can be imagined fitted or applied to all plates of the same radius in the sense in which Euclid speaks of applying one figure to another. But the concept is not applicable in this sense, and in the sense in which it is applicable, it is so throughout all differences of radius.

---

[1] It is very hard to say how we should describe these images. But when I imagine a circle, there certainly seems to be something before my mind representative of a visible circle, but not it. This is best realized if we consider imagination as it accompanies memory. When I remember how the Matterhorn looked, what I remember is not now before me; but the image is. Sounds again can be vividly imagined by many persons when they see a page of music; there is some resemblance between the melody 'called up in imagination' and what was heard, but they are not the same. Yet colour images and seen colours seem, to me at any rate, less comparable.

[2] *Kr. d. r. V.*, A. 137 = B. 176.

Kant himself observes that 'No image of a triangle could ever be adequate to the concept of a triangle in general. For it would not attain that universality of the concept which makes the concept valid for all triangles, right-angled, acute-angled, &c., but be restricted always to a part of this sphere'[1] (as the image of a circle is to circles of a certain radius). The homogeneity, therefore, which makes a geometrical circle or triangle applicable to part of the sphere of a concept does not exist between that or any other part and the concept under which it may be subsumed.

Hence the difficulty which Kant felt about the pure concepts of the understanding does not arise, as he supposed, from their being heterogeneous with the particulars subsumed under them, whereas other concepts are homogeneous with their particulars. It arises from the fact that what the particular must be in order to be subsumable under any of these concepts is no sensible feature of it. Kant is struggling with the problem with which all philosophers find themselves confronted: how can what is sensed be also thought? what is the relation of the intelligible to the sensible in things? And this problem is not the same with that of the universal and its particular instances, although they seem connected.

The evidence of the distinctness of the two problems is furnished by what we have just been noticing. Mathematical circles or other figures and mathematical units or numbers are not universals: they are instances of circularity, squareness, or whatever spatial form it may be, of unity or of twoness or whatever numerical form it may be. But they are not sensible. On the other hand, particular reds, sweets, shrills, are instances of redness, sweetness, shrillness; and they are sensible. The antithesis of universal and particular is therefore not the antithesis of intelligible and sensible.

[1] Ibid., A. 141 = B. 180.

It may be asked, if there are universals whose particular instances are not sensible, are there also particulars which are instances of universals that are not intelligible? This would be a hard saying. For if the universal is not intelligible, it must, one would suppose, be sensible. But everything sensible can be either seen or heard, smelt, tasted, or felt; can we see, hear, smell, taste, or feel any universal? Rather than say yes, we might be inclined to question whether sensibles like reds and sweets and shrills are instances of any universal. What difference is there between the particular reds, of which I may see 32 on a chess-board, and redness? Their redness is not a 33rd particular visible red; there are no present visibles of this colour except the thirty-two; there are only reds, and not redness. But we shall be driven far if we maintain this. If there are 32 reds, but no redness, similarly there must be 32 squares and no squareness. We shall then have to give some other reason why they are all called by the same name, *squares*, than that they are particulars of one kind. If we say it is because they are members of one class, we must ask what makes them so. A class is a collection. Certain items may be in one collection because I have collected them, but if they are so independently of any collecting, something in them must separate them from the members of other collections, and this cannot be their membership of their own collection. Belonging to a class cannot be the class-characteristic in virtue of which its members belong to it. It is not enough to say that those figures belong to one class, each of which is congruent with every other. For three reasons this fails to define the class of squares. (1) Congruence with any given member of the class would itself be a common character of the rest, and could not in turn be reduced to membership of the same class. (2) It is not strictly congruence that is meant, but capacity for congruence, and therefore we must ask what makes them capable of congruence with one another, and not with members of the class (say) of circles. (3) Not all squares are capable of congruence, but only those of the same size. Mathematicians have tried to meet this difficulty by going back from congruence of lines to one-one correspondence of the points in them. It is impossible to discuss here all the issues raised by the attempt to arithmetize space. But this much may be said. (*a*) In a square, lines meet at right angles; rectangularity is the same in all its instances, and cannot be reduced to a one-one correspondence of points in the lines containing the right angles, even if the congruence of the lines intersecting at right angles and of other lines concerned can. (*b*) There is the same difficulty about correspondence of points as there is about congruence of lines. Lines may have capacity for congruence, but are not congruent of themselves; points may be made to correspond, or correlated, but do not correspond of themselves. Some reason is needed why a given point should be said to correspond with this rather than that other.[1] (*c*) The reduction involves treating the congruent lines as ordered sets of points. Each of these sets of points will have the same form of order, and as our 32 squares were instances of squareness, so the ordered sets of points will be instances of one form of order. The reduction, therefore, fails in that the universal distinct from particulars, which it attempted to abolish, reappears in the identical form of order distinct from the particular ordered sets. (*d*) The distinction of universal from particular also reappears in the consideration of any equally numerous selections of corresponding points that may be made from corresponding ordered sets. These selections will be instances of the same number. At this point the would-be reducer denies the numerical forms to which Plato called attention. Pairs are not instances of twoness, nor dozens of dozenhood. Twoness or dozenhood, or whatever it may be, is not the identical or common numerousness of divers aggregates,

---

[1] Cf. *supra*, p. 235.

but the aggregate of those aggregates. In the language of Frege and Lord Russell, a (cardinal) number is a class of all classes similar to a given class. But 'similar' here means 'capable of being correlated one-one', and again we must ask what makes them so capable; and even if this definition could otherwise be maintained without ultimate circularity, when applied to *one*, so as to abolish the distinction between units and unity, it breaks down at once.[1]

To reject any squareness distinguishable from yet exemplified in all squares involves these difficulties. But if we accept squareness must we not equally accept redness distinguishable from and yet exemplified in all reds? Yet where are we to draw the line? Plato in the *Parmenides*[2] shows himself conscious of this difficulty. It is noticeable that the cases which give him concern are those in which the particulars are sensible—this and that man, fire, water, hair, dirt, clay; where the particulars are this and that likeness, justice, beauty, goodness, he has no hesitation in distinguishing the one form from the many instances of it. It might be said that he seems more ready to admit universals whose instances are not, than whose instances are, sensible.

This fact brings out very clearly the distinctness of the two problems, how the universal is related to its particular instances, and how the intelligible is related to the sensible. Perhaps Croce's separation of concepts from pseudo-concepts and Prof. Whitehead's language about eternal objects and their ingression into actual occasions are both indications at once of the distinctness and of the connexion of the problems. If the universal is the intelligible, then the identity in particulars so far forth as they are sensible is not properly speaking intelligible, nor conceived; hence Croce calls redness or manhood a pseudo-

---

[1] See a paper by me in *Mind*, 1933, 'A Defence of Free-thinking in Logistics Resumed' (N.S. vol. xlii, no. 168, p. 441 *ad fin.*).
[2] 130 b 1–d 9.

concept. On the other hand, if we treat everything that is one in many particulars as a universal, or in Prof. Whitehead's phrase an eternal object, then the difference between what is sensible and what is not in the particular depends not on there being no eternal object ingredient in respect of the sensible, but on the way in which it is received in the process of the actual object's (or actual entity's) concrescence. Another doctrine which may have arisen from the difficulty of clearing up the relation between the universal as what is one in many instances and the intelligible as what is not sensible in a particular instance is Lord Russell's doctrine that there are no instances of relations, but that the similarity (say) of two pennies is numerically the same similarity as that of two shillings. No relations are sensible; if there are instances of a relation, how do they differ from that of which they are instances? But Lord Russell is inclined to deny also that like sensibles are instances of a universal, and to reject universals altogether. There are many like sensibles and no like relations; but sensibles and relations are all of them particulars.

Be this, however, as it may, Kant has not kept distinct the question how what is sensed can be also thought from that of particular and universal. The bodies with which science is concerned are sensible bodies; yet much that we know about them is not sensible. To know anything, however, about a subject is to subsume it under a concept, i.e. to recognize in it what might be also in another subject.

That which is sensible in a given subject might equally be sensible in another, and that which is not sensible in it might equally be in another, and there too not sensible. In a red rose, its red is sensible; that its red has degree is not sensible, but thought or thinkable. The red of another rose would be sensible, and its having degree thinkable. Such red is an instance of redness, the degree of each red is an instance of degree. Kant is puzzled how the thinkable degree is connected with the sensible red. This is a question how, in some individual, two features, one an instance of sensible and the other of thinkable being, are united. He thinks it a question how a particular sensible is connected with a thinkable universal: how to subsume an 'empirical intuition' under a 'pure concept of the understanding'; and that the answer is to be furnished by finding what he calls a transcendental schema to mediate between them, which is 'void of empirical content' and yet sensible. The schema will be subsumable under the concept, and the empirical intuition, the given sensible, under the schema; and thus the empirical intuition, not immediately subsumable under the concept because not homogeneous with it, will be mediately subsumable.

This is surely an impossible solution. If the question were really one of subsuming a particular under a universal, and not of understanding how in the particular instance its sensible and its thinkable being were united, each being equally subsumable, not one subsumed under the other, and if what is subsumed must be homogeneous with the concept under which it is subsumed, then no mediating schema can make subsumable under a pure concept of the understanding an empirical intuition not homogeneous with it. Now Kant accepts the conditions and denies the consequent in this statement. Yet between a concept and an 'empirical intuition' nothing could mediate except another concept that was a determination of the first; and the intuition, if homogeneous with the more determinate, would be homogeneous with the less determinate concept. Kant speaks as if the schema were a determination of the pure concept, and the empirical intuition an instance of the schema, and yet the empirical intuition not an instance of the pure concept. If it be objected that he does not say that the schema is to be subsumed under the pure concept, we may point in reply to the following paragraph as implying it.

'The concept of understanding contains pure synthetic unity of the manifold in general. Time, as the formal condition of the manifold of inner sense, and thereby of the connexion of all presentations, contains a manifold *a priori* in pure intuition. Now a transcendental time-determination is so far homogeneous with the *category* (which produces the unity of the time-determination) as it is universal and rests on a rule *a priori*. On the other hand it is so far homogeneous with the *appearance* as *time* is contained in every empirical presentation of the manifold. An application of the category to appearances therefore becomes possible by means of the transcendental time-determination which, as the schema of the concept of understanding, mediates the subsumption of the latter [sc. the appearances] under the first [sc. the concept].'[1]

In saying that the concept of the understanding contains pure synthetic unity of the manifold *in general*, Kant should mean one of two things. Either (1) that the understanding in all its activity is unifying a manifold; sense provides it, in the pure intuition of time, with a non-empirical manifold; and the schemata are so many forms of relatedness resulting from exercising diversely upon that pure manifold the generically identical activity of synthesis. Or (2) that the understanding, without the pure manifold of time on which to exercise its activity of synthesis, produces its pure concepts, each of which is a distinct form of relatedness in a diversity of non-temporal 'moments'; and that the corresponding schemata exemplify, in a pure manifold of time, these forms of relatedness, which might be exemplified in some other manifold. According to (1), the empirical intuition whose form of relatedness conforms to some schema exemplifies synthetic unity in general; according to (2), it exemplifies the relatedness in some pure concept which exemplifies synthetic unity in general. Either way, it is subsumed under what understanding furnishes, and ought on Kant's principle therefore to be homogeneous with this; yet he says it is not, and that therefore the mediating schema is required.

[1] *Kr. d. r. V.*, A. 138 = B. 177, Kant's italics (except for *a priori*). The interpretation of 'latter' and 'first' must be as above.

Both these interpretations of Kant's statement, however, present difficulties. On (1), the generic identity of the understanding's activity of synthesis diversely applied to the pure manifold of time is to furnish a variety of schemata which reveal the diversity in that identity. The pure concepts could not be distinguished except through the schemata. To this there are two objections. (*a*) It is hard to see how the synthesis could result in anything except the relatedness there is between moments or parts of time; and (*b*) that result is ascribed by Kant to the synthesis of sense, not of understanding. These objections seem fatal. If, then, we accept (2), we must suppose that certain conceived forms of relatedness show themselves in the time-relations of an empirical manifold. Here also two serious difficulties arise. First, without some thought of empirical differences in the manifold, it would be inconceivable how the time-order of the items unified in accordance with the concept should make any difference. For example, if causal nexus is to show itself in regularity of succession, it must be regularity in the succession on different occasions of items of one sort upon items of another.[1] To conceive this, the thought of the different sorts is necessary; a manifold contained *a priori* in pure intuition will not suffice. Secondly, the conceived form of relatedness which is to be recognized in the empirical intuition to which the pure concept must be applicable will be just this relatedness of the empirical manifold in time. It will be, as it were, analysable into this, not a generic identity specified in the schema. To say that the schema of cause consists in the succession of the manifold, in so far as this succession is subject to a rule,[2] will mean that for any A to cause an x is that every A is followed by an x.

At this point we may revert to an observation on p. 270. It was there said that one problem puzzling Kant was in principle the same with Hume's problem about the origin

[1] Cf. *supra*, p. 249.   [2] *Kr. d. r. V.*, A. 144 = B. 183.

of the ideas of 'those relations which do not depend on the ideas which we compare together, but may be changed without any change in the ideas'. According to Hume, to think of anything is to have an idea, ideas are faint replicas of impressions, and impressions are sensible. And this was his stumbling-block with causality, and other relations which do not depend on 'the ideas which we compare together'. As Alice complained to the Dormouse, you cannot make a drawing of a muchness. It is true that no relation is really sensible. T. H. Green very justly said that 'respect for Hume's thoroughness as a philosopher must be qualified by the observation that he does not attempt to meet this difficulty in its generality, but only as it affects the relations of identity and causation'—Green should have added, and of time and place.[1] But where the relation is grounded in sensible qualities of the *relata*, as similarity and dissimilarity and relations of quantity and degree[2] are, the sensibles presented apparently seemed to Hume to serve as impressions from which the idea of the relation, no less than the ideas of the *relata*, could be derived. Ideas of these relations, then, he treated as fundamentally themselves sensible or imaginable, like their terms. And if all relations thus 'depended entirely on the ideas, which we compare together', what there is to be known might be treated as nothing but sensibles. It is true that its unity would disappear if it were this; but Hume declared that the mind is a mere bundle of impressions and ideas, and its objects or content the same; Neutral Monism is of Humian ancestry. The disappearance of unity

---

[1] See Green and Grose's edition of the *Treatise of Human Nature*, General Introduction, vol. i, § 210. It is the same difficulty which makes sensationalists like Herbert Spencer treat relations as momentary feelings: cf. *supra*, p. 232.

[2] Hume writes 'degrees of quality and proportion in quantity or number'. But strictly proportion is a relation, degree a *relatum*. Whether proportion in quantity is the same as relation between numbers we need not here ask. The only difference Hume noticed was that the least differences between numbers can always be perceived, but not between quantities.

puzzled him, but did not shake his confidence in the principles from which it followed; what did threaten to shake
this confidence was to find himself apparently apprehending relations which were not grounded in their terms, and
therefore could not be supposed to be somehow themselves,
like their terms, sensible.[1]

[1] These relations were those of time and place, causation and identity,
and, put briefly, Hume's procedure was this. First he considered relations
of space and time between sensibles. These may vary with no change in
the sensibles; yet any whole of spatially or temporally related sensibles,
like a picture or a tune, would be sensibly different if its qualitatively
differing parts were re-arranged. He therefore regarded what one may
call the patterns of wholes as sensible features from which the ideas of
spatial and temporal relations are derived. Secondly, when precedency
and contiguity had thus been vindicated as equally sensible with similarity,
he resolved the causal relation into like relations of precedency and contiguity
between respectively like sensibles, so that nothing was involved which was
not either a sensible term or a sensible relation. Thirdly, he regarded the
identity of an object as its invariableness and uninterruptedness through a
supposed variation of time. (*Treatise of Human Nature: Of the Understanding*, iv, § ii, ed. Green and Grose, vol. i, p. 490.) 'The idea of time...arises
altogether from the manner in which impressions appear to the mind, without making one of the number. . . . The idea of duration is always derived
from a succession of changeable objects, and can never be convey'd to the
mind by anything stedfast and unchangeable. . . . Since the idea of duration
cannot be deriv'd from such an object, it can never in any propriety or
exactness be apply'd to it, nor can anything unchangeable be ever said to
have duration.' (Ibid. ii, § iii, vol. i, pp. 343–4.) But the idea of time, or
duration, applied to a succession of changeable perceptions is, when an
unchanging perception, to which it is not applicable, accompanies these,
transferred to or associated with that. Belief being a lively idea related to
or associated with an impression, we come to believe that the one (because
unchanging) perception has that duration which consists in a succession of
different perceptions, i.e. is identical in different times. Further, the mind,
when there is a succession of perceptions over which it passes with the
same sense of facility as it feels in having an unchanging perception,
is apt to take the first for the second. Relations of resemblance, and others
that facilitate association of ideas, connecting a series of perceptions make
the mind pass over the series with this sense of facility; and we therefore
come to ascribe identity not only to an unchanging perception associated
with the duration of a succession, but to certain successions of perception
themselves. Consider (it is not Hume's example) our impressions of the
slowly waxing and waning moon; the difference is slight between our
impressions to-day and to-morrow. Hence, the monstrous fiction of an

Now Kant was clear that the mind is no mere bundle, neither is what it knows. The mind is one in knowing a manifold of sense; the condition on which alone this is possible is that the manifold of sense should be brought into unity by relations. The relatedness in it is not sensuous, but it is in it, and we know that in certain respects the relatedness in it conforms to laws, or is of definite pervading types. In saying this we are not recording what we have observed, but what we apprehend to be necessary. That this colour is darker than that, or this field bigger than that, may be learnt from perception; but that everything sensible must have degree is an anticipation of perception, and it is an axiom, not an empirical fact, that what I intuit must be an extensive magnitude, something of a certain quantity in space. That connectedness of the perceived which I express by saying that sensible qualities depend on the existence of permanent substances in mutual interaction, and the changes in any one stand in regular time-relation to changes in some other, is itself in no wise perceived; and yet I know it. None of these characters in things is sensible as red or hot or sour is. Seeing, feeling, tasting acquaint me with these. In Hume's language, that I have the ideas of these can be explained from impressions. To recognize what is seen, or felt, or tasted as *a* red, *a* hot, *a* sour, subsuming the present

unchanging body, i.e. perception, having a permanent existence without the mind, identical through change.

In this way Hume supposed himself to have reduced what is apparently not sensible in the relations of sensibles to what is—or what he treated as if it were—sensible. It would be more surprising that he should have been content with the reduction, if we did not find able men to-day content with doctrines substantially the same. Kant apparently was not acquainted with Hume's *Treatise*. Hume's reminder that causality was not perceivable came to him through the *Enquiry*; but it is an interesting speculation what would have been the effect on him of reading a more thorough-going exposition of empiricism. It is interesting, too, to notice that he also reduces causality to regularity of sequence, though he seeks *a priori* grounds for asserting that there is such regularity.

sensible under an empirical concept, may require help of thought. But if, with Hume, we substitute similarity of particulars for their common nature, since two reds, two hots, two sours are sensibly similar, we may trace to sense the apprehension of what we substitute for the concept. On the other hand, a red, a hot, a sour are not sensibly similar, and if we apprehend them all as qualities we bring them under a concept of which we cannot trace the apprehension to sense. Nor is it because I have classed them together that I call them all qualities; but, because I find in them and in much besides the identity which I call quality, I class them together. I might class together reds and hots and sours, and give to the class of which every member was one or another of these a common name *redotour*, so that a *redotour* would be a member of the class each of whose members was either red or hot or sour. Lord Russell would say that we had a class-concept 'red or hot or sour'. It is not so. And it is not as being each either this *or* that *or* the other that we call reds and hots and sours, and much besides, qualities, but as being all something the same. Yet *what the same* is not manifest to sense; and when Kant asked himself what the same they were, he said 'intensive quantities', i.e. they all have degree; and to have degree, in his view, was to integrate increments of being from zero, be it increments of being red, or of being hot, or of being sour, or of what not else that is strictly sensible.

Here is a concept not abstracted from the sensible (or, in Hume's language, from impressions) as redness is from reds, and the thought of it may be called in that negative sense *a priori*. How Kant held that we come by the thought of it we must consider presently. But we must here notice that if every sensible does thus integrate increments from zero, it should be as directly subsumable under the pure concept *quality* as every red sensible is under the empirical concept *red*. The mediation of a transcendental schema is for this purpose quite uncalled for. Equally, if a sensible is so much, it should be directly subsumable under the pure concept *quantity*.

Why then did Kant think some schema necessary to connect each pure concept with that which is to be subsumed under it, or to which it is to have application? It is generally hazardous to dogmatize upon the causes of an erroneous train of thought; but it may be suggested that the principal reason lay in the relation in which he held the synthesis of understanding to stand to that of sense, particularly in regard to causality, of which the problem filled so large a place in his thought; the interests of his architectonic may have been a subsidiary influence.

The synthesis of sense is primary and fundamental. Though held responsible only for the form of what is sensible, it is thereby responsible for there being any sensible presented, since the matter of sense, or that in the sensible which, so far as we can see, is wholly contingent and to be taken as given, would in the absence of space and time relatedness in it be nothing for us. If we ask what is ordered in space and time, we can give no satisfactory answer, for to name as so orderable what are themselves analysable into parts so ordered is useless. Critics of Kant may treat this as fatal to the whole thesis of the *Transcendental Aesthetic*. We need only notice here that the sensibles whose spatial and temporal arrangement is contingent are themselves spatial and temporal; they are not what Hume treated them as being, *minima sensibilia* at once sensible and yet punctiform and instantaneous; and the contingency of arrangement of sensibles is subject to certain necessities of spatial and temporal relatedness illustrated equally within each of them and in the spatial and temporal wholes which, however arranged, they constitute.

But, this being granted, we have granted what, in Kant's view, is at once all that the synthesis of sense secures and all that merely sensitive consciousness requires, but is not enough to make the sensible understandable, nor to enable experience, which is more than merely sensitive consciousness. To be understandable, what is sensible must exhibit other forms of relatedness than are required for it to be in space and time. It must be capable of being thought as a quality, definite in degree, of some permanent body, or material substance; the body must be capable of being thought as extended in space, or an extensive quantum; and whereas sensibles change, to be understood their changes must be capable of being thought conformable each to some rule connecting a change of one sort with an immediately preceding change of another sort. What that which is to be understood must be conceived to be is strictly speaking not sensible, but thinkable. Yet these concepts are to be applicable to what is sensible, and they all involve some form of relatedness either of one sensible to another, or of the parts within one sensible *inter se*. That a sensible should have degree involves relations of degree between it and other sensibles otherwise like it; to be an extensive quantum involves relations of the parts of what is so *inter se*; to be a sensible *quality* involves relations to that of which it is a quality; to occur in a process of change involves causal relation to other occurrences. What is the condition on which such concepts can be applicable to that which is sensible in space and time?

In the first place, if a concept is or involves[1] a form of relatedness, it can only be applicable to what may be conceived to consist of parts so related. If I say that the extinction of life on the earth is inevitable, I mean that it is connected with other events which I am not specifying, and so I must conceive it and them to form a whole of parts

---

[1] There is no causality where there is no time-relation, but it does not follow that causality is a relation. The phrase 'causal relation', common as it is, may be improper, and belong to the tendency to recognize nothing but terms and relations between them. Cf. *supra*, p. 238, n. 2, and Xenocrates' reduction of the Aristotelian categories to τὰ καθ' αὑτά and τὰ πρός τι.

capable of that kind of relation. I should not say that seven is inevitable, because it is not an event, and the kind of connexion in question is one that I can only conceive among events. But why should that be so, if the concept is nothing sensible in what is to be subsumed under it? Merely to say that events are capable and numbers incapable of a relatedness that does not depend on anything sensible in the related, or (as Hume would say) on the ideas which we compare together, is to be dogmatic. If, however, it involved relatedness in time and space, which is only to be found in the sensible, and were found there because the synthetic activity of sense had imposed it on a sensuous material, then we should have ground for saying that the concept of such relatedness was applicable to events but not to numbers.

That, however, is not enough. Kant maintains not only that events *might* be thus related, and numbers not; events *are* thus related. The concept *mother* is in one sense applicable to Queen Elizabeth and not to her ruff; in another sense it is applicable to Queen Anne and not to Queen Elizabeth. The pure concepts of the understanding or categories are, Kant holds, applicable in this second sense to appearances, though not to things in themselves. And the reason is that appearances are in space and time, that is, have forms of relatedness which the synthesis of sense has given them. And this can only be a reason why the categories are applicable in this second sense, if the synthesis of sense cannot occur without their becoming thereby applicable, or in Kant's language valid for all possible experience. Otherwise, how do we know that through the synthesis there may not come to be presented sensibles ordered indeed in space and time, so that the categories are applicable in the first sense, but not so ordered therein as that they are applicable in the second?

For this purpose sense, in its synthetic activity, must work under the control of understanding. And understanding must control it in accordance with its pure concepts. And these will be concepts of how the manifold of sense must be spatially and temporally ordered it if is to be subsumable under the concepts. The instance in which this line of thought can be made most plausible is causality.

Hume reminded philosophers and indeed the world at large that causality is nothing sensible. Why, then, is the extinction of life on the earth something caused, and the number seven not? If we can substitute for causing or being caused something which, though not strictly itself sensible, can be found only in what is, we shall have an answer. Now that regularity which consists in like antecedents having like consequents can be found only in what is sensible, though mere time-order of what is sensible does not require it. And we do in fact use it as evidence not indeed of events having causes, but of what kinds of events have what causes. It is plausible, therefore, to resolve causality into this regularity in the successive. 'The schema of cause and of the causality of a thing in general is the real whereupon, to whatever date assigned,[1] something else always follows. It consists, therefore, in the succession of the manifold, so far as this is subjected to a rule.'

Kant has not expressed himself very carefully, for mere time-order involves that something else always follows. And the inaccuracy betrays the weakness of his doctrine. It is false that the schema of regularity in succession is a mediating conception between the pure concept of cause and effect and any presented particulars. Whether or not reading Hume was the cause of Kant's abandoning what he came to call dogmatism, to think that his abandoning it was caused is not to think that it was an instance of regularity in the succession of events. For this regularity is that *every* event of a kind *a* is followed by one of a kind *x*; and the sequence upon Kant's reading Hume of his abandoning dogmatism certainly was not an instance of *every*

[1] *wenn es nach Belieben gesetzt wird*: *Kr. d. r. V.*, A. 144 = B. 183.

event of the former nature being followed by one of the latter nature. What I may subsume under a concept must have the conceived character *in it*. That every *a* should be followed by an *x* cannot be a character found in a given *a* or *x*, not yet in the given *a*'s being followed by the given *x*. The reason why the cause of a singular event, like Kant's abandoning dogmatism, cannot be its invariable antecedent is that this event only happens once, and cannot have an invariable antecedent. J. S. Mill thought that, just as whatever illustrates the law (or any instance of the law) that rivers run downhill illustrates the law of hydrostatic pressure, so it illustrates the law of the uniformity of nature. By the uniformity of nature he meant that every event of every kind illustrates some law or other. Some one event, being of its own kind only, cannot be an instance of every event of every kind illustrating some law or other. If nature is uniform in the sense explained, nothing short of the whole of nature illustrates it. So long as the movement of liquids conforms to the law of hydrostatic pressure, the movements of rivers will illustrate the law, and the Thames will run down to the sea; and the movement of gases might be completely random, illustrating no law, without affecting the fact that the fall of the Thames illustrated the law of hydrostatic pressure. Yet on the supposition that the movements of gases were completely random there would be no uniformity of nature, and the fall of the Thames therefore could not illustrate it. It is sometimes said to-day that laws of nature are really no more than statistical averages. If that be so, they have no instances. It may be true that for men who reach sixty the average age of death is seventy-two; but no man who dies at seventy-two can exemplify the truth of this statement.

Causality is an action, not a relation. To be an event is to have time-relations to other events; to be an effect is to have it because of an action. Hume did not think that an event had its time-relation to other events because of anything;[1] but Kant did, and this in two senses. He thought that in nature, or the world of things in space and time, every event was caused. He did not mean to abandon this concept of cause, and substitute regularity in the succession of events. The latter was to mediate the subsumption of an event under the concept of effect or cause, not to serve instead of the concept; though in fact it cannot discharge the function which Kant assigns to it. And, further, he thought there was a cause of the regularity in the succession of events, in the control exercised by understanding over the synthesis of sense. Only because of this control do appearances or phenomena conform in their succession to the schema which mediates the application to them of the concept of cause and effect, i.e. only because of it is the concept valid for all possible experience.

So much for the instance in which the doctrine of the schematism is most plausible. But Kant extends it to explain how the other categories become applicable to sensible phenomena. As the list of them is supposed to be produced systematically from a common principle,[2] so their applicability is supposed to be mediated according to a single method, viz. through 'the transcendental determination of time'.[3] The interest in architectonic may have influenced Kant here. But we may perhaps conjecture why, if there was to be a single method, it should be one involving the synthesis of time. Not only does that seem to fit the important category of causality. Time also is in Kant's language the formal condition of the manifold of

---

[1] This statement needs qualification so far as the occurrence of ideas in a mind is concerned. He thought that their time-relations to impressions or to other ideas preceding them in the same mind are what they are because of certain 'natural relations' of similarity and contiguity which they have thereto; and the statement in the text concerns perceptions as objects of our knowledge, not as composing the mind that knows. It will be seen that Hume's famous argument about causality amounts to explaining what causes us to believe falsely, or at least unwarrantably, that there is causing.

[2] Ibid., A. 80 = B. 106.   [3] Ibid., A. 139 = B. 178.

inner sense. The relevancy of that is, or seemed to Kant to be, this: the pure *a priori* manifold involved in time is as it were to become sensible through there being sensuous material to occupy it, in which temporal relatedness may be intuited; yet it is not necessarily in the sensuous material of what is outside us that the relatedness must appear. My own empirical existence lies in being conscious of many things and thinking this and that about them. The unity which I am is differentiated by what I am conscious of. But what links the differences in which I am one is time-relatedness. The categories have their source in certain dispositions of the human understanding.[1] Yet they are forms of unity in a manifold. If from being latent in the unity of the understanding they are to become explicit to it in their purity, the mind that understands must be no analytic or undifferentiated unity, but hold together in the unity the multiplicity of its own being. This as conscious in time it does. The pure manifold of time, in which the mind as subject of experience exists, furnishes a multiplicity for the category. Each category furnishes a principle according to which to determine the pure manifold of time. The result is a presentation, but pure or having nothing empirical about it; such a presentation is a transcendental schema. But because time-relatedness belongs not only to me as experiencing but also to what I experience, therefore the schema, which is a time-relatedness wherein a conceived unity of a manifold is expressed or developed, may be exemplified in what I experience, and so appearances can be thought under the categories or pure concepts of the understanding.[2]

The foregoing is offered as an attempt to elucidate Kant's thought; but it must be admitted that what he says of schemata and schematism is very obscure. Thus he says that a schema is a product of the imagination, and yet that

[1] Ibid., A. 66 = B. 91.
[2] Cf. Ibid., A. 66 = B. 91 with A. 137–9 = B. 176–8.

the schema of a concept is the presentation (*Vorstellung*) of a general procedure of the imagination, in fashioning its image for a concept.[1] Five dots in a row are an image of the number five, but if I think of number in general, I think of a method for presenting an aggregate in an image in accordance with some definite concept; and the thought of this method is the schema. How is this to be interpreted?

Let us revert to the example of causality. To present to oneself the succession of the manifold, so far as it is subjected to a rule, is to think of a schema for the concept of cause. This must mean that, if a succession in the sensible is to be thought as causal, it must be thought as conforming to a rule of succession. The presentation of a method, therefore, is the presentation of what the sensible must be if it is to exemplify the concept. So I might say that the proper method of planting fruit-trees is in quincunces, where the quincuncial order would belong to the trees when planted, and not to the activity of planting them. But if this is Kant's meaning, to be cause and effect is to conform to a rule of succession. That is what was taken above to be the upshot of his teaching about cause, viz. that causality is resolved into regularity of succession. If the other categories also find their schemata in some transcendental determination of time, should not that mean that a sensible manifold becomes subsumable under one of the categories through some kind of time-relatedness being given to the manifold? And because time-relatedness belongs equally to the mind in its diversity as apprehending a manifold and to what it apprehends, Kant fancied that if in our apprehension of what is to be subsumed under a category there is a synthesis which somehow concerns time, that will make the apprehended, which is also subject to the form of time, subsumable.

Yet a little reflection shows that what may be called a

[1] Ibid., A. 140 = B. 179, *einem Begriff sein Bild zu verschaffen.*

time-pattern depends on the nature not of time but of what is ordered in it. Different airs using the same notes may be called so many different ways of ordering these notes in time; but if we ignore the sensible differences of the notes, and consider only the moments they fill, the difference of order disappears. Now the time-pattern constituted by the regularities of succession between various qualitatively differing events in nature could not be found also in the series of my qualitatively differing presentations. And that our apprehension of some conceivable character in appearances somehow involves time does not show that the character apprehended does so. The method by which the sensible becomes subsumable under the concept, if this means what must be in the sensible for it to be subsumable, need not be a kind of time-relatedness because our coming so to conceive it involves time-relatedness. What belongs to the process of coming to know need not belong to what I come to know. I come to know in time; and what I come to know may be in time. But even then the time-patterns in coming to know and in what I come to know will not be the same, since the sensuous differences between the items in the process of coming to know and those between the items in what I come to know are not the same.

A general consideration, therefore, of the grounds on which Kant seems to have looked to 'transcendental determination of time' for his schemata does not encourage the expectation that the doctrine of schematism will stand examination in detail. And this mistrust, already supported by what has been said about causality, will be confirmed if we turn to other categories and their schemata. We may consider first the schema of quantity.

The plate which I may judge to be round, and so bring under the concept of circularity, I may judge also to be of a certain magnitude, i.e. to be a *quantum*. Quantity may be apprehended, however, in subjects which are not round and indeed which, like a duration, are incapable of shape. The pure schema of quantity as a concept of the understanding, says Kant, is number. Number is a presentation 'which holds together the successive addition of homogeneous units. It is therefore nothing else than the unity of the synthesis of the manifold of a homogeneous intuition in general, arising through my producing time itself, in the apprehension of intuition.'[1] It will be noticed that my producing space itself also in the apprehension of intuition, is neglected. Space is 'the pure image of all magnitudes (*quanta*) before outer sense'.[2]

'Magnitudes before outer sense' merely means spatial magnitudes; and to say that space is their pure image is to call attention to the difference between the objects of geometrical study, μαθηματικά in Plato's sense,[3] and sensibles. The notion of an image which is pure, i.e. non-sensuous, no doubt is difficult, but this difficulty lies in the facts. Images anyhow certainly help us to apprehend the objects of geometrical study. But as Kant held space to be the form of outer sense, or of its objects, so he said that time is the form of inner sense, or of its objects, though an image for temporal magnitudes must be borrowed from spatial; we represent duration to ourselves by a line. Both kinds of magnitude, then, spatial and temporal, may be apprehended. Of both the apprehension involves synthesis. Kant conceives the synthesis as successive addings or unitings of

---

[1] Ibid., A. 142 = B. 182. That 'number is a presentation (*Vorstellung*) which holds together' really means the same as that 'number holds together, &c.' Whatever I apprehend, whether by thinking or sensing, Kant is ready to call a presentation. A presentation is the *esse objectivum* of what is apprehended. What, however, my efforts at thinking fail to make me apprehend, or at imagining to imagine, is not a *Vorstellung*. The words *die Apprehension der Anschauung*, 'the apprehension of intuition', mean, of course, not that intuition is apprehended, but is a way of apprehending.

[2] *vor dem äusseren Sinne*, ibid.; *für den* has been suggested. If *vor dem* is correct, presumably Kant was rather loosely thinking of 'outer sense' as 'looking at' what is seen.

[3] Cf. *supra*, p. 271.

part to part. We might say that this requires time, but he says that it generates time. This generation of time may be called a transcendental determination of time, and is just the same in every synthesis; but the form of relatedness in the manifold synthetized is not always the same, and except when temporal order is that to the apprehension of which we are brought by our time-generating synthesis, it is not the same in the synthesis and in the synthetized.[1] The only reason, therefore, for connecting the schema especially with time must be that Kant is thinking of what is necessary to the generating activity of synthesis, not to the subsumability of the synthetized appearances under pure concepts. The method for presenting an aggregate in an image in accordance with some definite concept, which as thought of the schema is said to be, is the 'transcendental determination of time' in synthetizing, and nothing in the synthetized.

It may perhaps be fairly said that the form of that which through some activity of ours comes to be an object of apprehension must control the activity. By the activity of the form of a statue in the mind of a sculptor the marble, said

---

[1] It is interesting to compare this distinction between time-relations in and generated by the activity of synthesis and those consequently apprehended in appearances with Hume's distinction between natural and philosophical relations. (See *Treatise of Human Nature: Of the Understanding*, i, § v.) The natural relations of resemblance and contiguity (causation he ought never to have added) bring it about that there are ideas as well as impressions presented to us, among which there are relations of resemblance and of contiguity, as well as of other kinds, for us to apprehend, 'particular circumstances', as Hume calls them, 'in which, even upon the arbitrary union of two ideas in the fancy, we may think proper to compare them.' Causation should not have been included among the natural relations, or principles of association, because the theory of Association is that an impression or idea will call up another idea, i.e. cause it to appear in the mind, in virtue of past contiguity or of resemblance (cf. *supra*, p. 290, n. 1); and we cannot add, or in virtue of causing it; no subsequent psychologist, therefore, has reckoned it among the principles of association. These relations are between 'phenomena of inner sense'. But the regularity of succession into which Hume resolves causality is mostly anyhow a matter of time-relations apprehended between 'phenomena of outer sense'.

Aristotle, comes to be of that form. If it be objected that the thought of the form, not the form thought of, is what operates, we must reply that at any rate there need be no conscious thought of it. But the form thought of is what is to be realized in that which will be presented, and if we may speak of it as in the activity which realizes it, it is nevertheless not the form of time in that activity. If the 'method' in question is merely the adding the apprehension of one 'factor' to the apprehension of another factor of what is finally to be apprehended in its entirety, and this addition of apprehensions generates time, then it may be called a transcendental determination of time. But if it is that form of union among the factors of the whole which, when we apprehend the whole in its entirety, we shall recognize as making some concept applicable to it, then it has no title to be so called. Kant confused these two views of it. When he said that the transcendental schema is homogeneous on the one hand with the category and on the other with the appearance, as the empirical concept of a plate is homogeneous with the pure geometrical concept of a circle, he must have been taking rather the second view of it than the first. If we take the first, a transcendental schema would not be less required to make the plate conceivable as round than as a magnitude. For the space-forms which we intuit, no less than the categorial characters which we understand, belong to the appearances in virtue of a synthesis. The synthesis is that of sense and not of understanding, but it is equally an activity of uniting the elements of a manifold, and if that involves and generates time when the understanding is active, it must do so equally when the sensibility is active. Yet where it is a question of the applicability of a geometrical concept, no mediation is required. Therefore the schema should be something in that which is to be subsumed, not in the activity of synthesis whereby that which is to be subsumed comes to be.

Yet that the other view of it, the first of those just distinguished, viz. that it is something in the activity of synthesis, is also in Kant's mind comes out notably again in his treatment of the schema of Quality.

'Reality', we are told, 'is that in the pure concept of the understanding which corresponds in general with sensation—

i.e. I may not merely see a red, or hear a shrill, but think there is something red or shrill—

it is that then whose concept in itself indicates an entity (in time); negation is that whose concept presents a nonentity (in time). The opposition of the two thus arises in the distinction of the same time as a full or an empty time. . . . Now every sensation has a certain degree or magnitude whereby it can fill the same time, i.e. the inner sense in respect of the same presentation of an object, more or less, until it disappears in nothing, $= 0 = negatio$. There is therefore a relation and connexion or rather a transition between reality and negation, which makes every reality presentable as a *quantum*, and the schema of reality, as the schema of the quantity of something so far as it fills time, is precisely this continuous and uniform production of the same in time, in descending in time from a sensation of determinate degree to the vanishing thereof, or gradually mounting from negation to the degree of it.'[1]

Clearly this transition belongs to the activity of synthesis, whereby I build up, in the continuous addition of qualitative infinitesimals from the sensuous manifold, a determinate sensation. This it is supposed I can do because, through the time-relatedness of what belongs to 'inner sense', I am one in these successive addings. It is more difficult to see how Kant supposed that I produce a determinate sensation by diminution; he does not generally suggest that there is a transcendental discerption, as well as a transcendental synthesis, and was probably thinking of how the presented sensible may decrease in intensity, when he ought to have been thinking of the unpresented activity by which there comes or ceases to be a presented sensible.

[1] *Kr. d. r. V.*, A. 143 = B. 182.

But the time in this process is not in the sensible which, in virtue of it, comes to be presented and is thought real. The transcendental determination of time involved in the unconscious transition may bring about the sensible; it does not explain why we should nor how we can think the sensible real, i.e. it does not mediate between the pure concept and the sensible appearance. Neither does it elucidate what we mean by degree. Sensibles of the same kind may form a series in respect of differences in degree, but not a temporal series. If the series of degrees is continuous, it is in that like time, but not therefore temporal. And any intensity of a sensible, though it may continue the same for a longer or a shorter time, does not contain, in what it is at any moment of this time, the time involved (if any was involved) in its generation. Just as, even if there comes to be a determinate magnitude of quantity by addition of infinitesimals, the time of the addition does not belong to the quantity that has come to be, so it is with a determinate degree of quality. Therefore the conception of degree as intensive magnitude,[1] even if it were correct, as it is not, would do nothing to justify Kant's account of the schema of quality.

It is not necessary to say much about the categories of relation and their schemata. Causality has already been discussed at length. Substance and Reciprocity are differently dealt with from Quantity and Quality. We read that 'the schema of substance is the endurance of the real in time, i.e. the presentation of the real (*desselben*) as a substratum of empirical time-determination in general, something which therefore abides while everything else changes'.[2] It is hard to see how this so-called schema is any more homogeneous with the sensible object conceived as substance than the concept of substance is. To be a substance is, we think, to be such a substratum. True, the

---

[1] See the *Anticipations of Perception*, Ibid., A. 166=B. 207.
[2] Ibid., A. 143=B. 183.

substance is thought to endure while the attributes change, and so the thought of time is involved. But this thought of time is not a synthesis in time in the inner sense. And what we should like to understand is the meaning of 'substratum' and the relation of what is so called, in its endurance, to the changing attributes. The schema does not mediate an understanding of this. No doubt, as we may say that a substance endures in time, so on Kant's view may we say that a determinate degree of any sensible has been brought into being by a synthesis in time. But there is no real parallelism; for the first statement tells us what substance is, the second does not tell us what degree is.

The schema of Reciprocity is 'the coexistence of the determinations of one substance with those of others according to a universal rule'.[1] There is no suggestion here of the strange doctrine of the *Third Analogy*, that reversible order in the succession of presentations is the source of the thought that substances coexist.[2] It is the determinations of substances which are said here to coexist. And here again, as in the case of Substance, the schema is something presented and thought of, not, as schemata are said to be and those of Quantity and Quality are described as if they were, something which concerns the determination of inner sense in general.[3] It may be added that, since Kant speaks of 'a universal rule', in the singular, one may question whether he merely means that it is a universal rule that the determinations of all substances coexist, or is making the same mistake as in the *Second Analogy*, and supposing that the thought of conformity to law in general will suffice to settle what determinations of one substance shall coexist with what of others, without the thought of the several laws and therefore of the determinations.[4]

The schemata of the categories of Modality are defined

---

[1] Ibid., A. 144=B. 183. [2] Cf. *supra*, pp. 254-5.
[3] Ibid., A. 142=B. 181. [4] Cf. *supra*, pp. 262-3.

with mention of time, and again the time meant is that thought of as involved in the being of what is thought possible, actual or necessary, not that involved in the transcendental synthesis. Since no category has application to anything not in time and space, it is not difficult to drag in reference to time when saying what that is to which a category is applicable. But the schemata of Possibility and Necessity are so described, like that of Causality, that the concepts are resolved into certain time-relations thought of in the manifold.

The confusion between time-relations supposed to be involved in my coming to apprehend in an appearance what makes it subsumable under a category, and those (if any) involved in its being what makes it so subsumable has been sufficiently illustrated. Two further general remarks may be added.

(1) Kant supposed that arithmetic had the same sort of relation to the *a priori* intuition of time as geometry to that of space. This opinion seems to involve the sort of confusion just mentioned. For we become aware of determinate numbers by addition of units, which takes time; so number is called 'a presentation which holds together the successive addition of homogeneous units'. But what the number thought of is thought to hold together is not the addition of these units, but the units themselves. In order to *become* aware that my fingers are five, I may need to add, but not in order to *be* aware of it. So in order to become aware of a shape I may need to attend successively to different parts of it; but I can then be aware of it all at once; and I think all at once the parts to coexist in the shape, and the units in the number. If, because successive acts of attention are necessary to the grasping of a number, number has special connexion with the *a priori* intuition of time, then because they are necessary to the grasping of a shape, shape should also have special connexion therewith; and the account of the schema of quantity rather suggests this. Yet

Kant's doctrine is that shape has special connexion with the *a priori* intuition of space.

(2) It is tempting to think that there was moving in Kant's mind, without his having brought it fully to consciousness, the thought of a general theory of order such as modern mathematicians have developed. We saw that in his account of the schema of Quality he confused or failed to distinguish the continuity of a series of degrees and that of time. And in making number the schema of quantity, as 'unity of the synthesis of the manifold of a homogeneous intuition in general', he may have been dimly thinking that in such a synthesis we think without appeal to spatial intuition what we intuit in space, the 'pure image of all magnitudes before outer sense'. If so, indeed, the schema would not help us to conceive the seen or felt sensible as a magnitude, but to conceive its magnitude as a special case of what the general theory of order helps us conceive; and it would be so far from mediating between appearance and the pure concept quantity, under which that appearance is subsumed, that the concept of spatial quantity would be itself subsumed under the schema, and the schema would lay bare in general the form of order displayed in the notion of quantity. There are great difficulties about this generalizing of the notion of quantity into something of which space, time, and other *continua* (if there are others) are divers instances. It is enough to observe here that, if Kant was feeling after any such notion, he was unconsciously moving towards what is inconsistent with the whole doctrine of the Transcendental Aesthetic, and with his sharp distinction between forms of sense and of understanding. For he professed that thought without intuition cannot understand either geometry or arithmetic. But the modern general theory of order denies this; it treats mathematics as a development of logic. Nothing could be in greater conflict with Kant's teaching than this.

Whether any such thought was working in Kant's mind

is, however, a question the settlement of which is not necessary to the thesis of the present argument: which is that in the *Schematism of the Categories* Kant is wrestling with different problems without distinguishing them, has no clear notion what the function assigned by him to schemata is, and treats them, now as schemata of the appearances to which the categories apply, now as schemata of the synthesis whereby there come to be these appearances. If this is true, it may be said that the doctrine really only darkens counsel.

XI

THE CONCEPT OF EVOLUTION[1]

WHEN I received the invitation to deliver this year the Lecture founded here in memory of Herbert Spencer, I hesitated for two reasons. The first was this: I admire (as who could not?) the way in which Spencer dedicated himself to the pursuit of truth, and I recognize his great influence on the thought of his time; but I have never been able to think highly of his achievement, and I cannot stand here to praise him as a philosopher. And secondly, the lecturers whom I succeed have been men of note, and generally men from outside, whom those in Oxford might be attracted to see and listen to by the scarcity of the opportunity.

Yet I reflected on the first count, that no post in the University should bind its occupant to accept or praise the views of any particular teacher in the field to which it belongs; and on the second, that it may be a welcome innovation to give from time to time to those whose study and teaching have been carried on in Oxford the chance of addressing not other students in their own subject merely, but some at least whose subjects are not theirs. It should be one of the most valuable parts of the education which a University affords, to converse with those who know matters of which oneself is ignorant. Many of you doubtless remember what Socrates says in the *Apology*,[2] about the life, if there be any life, after death: how the greatest and most wonderful thing in it would be that he should spend his time questioning and examining those there, as he had questioned and examined men on earth, to find who of them was wise, and who thought himself wise but was not ; what would not a man give to question him who

[1] This Essay was delivered as the *Herbert Spencer* Lecture at Oxford in 1924.   [2] 40 e 5–41 c 7.

led the great army against Troy, or Odysseus, or Sisyphus, or ten thousand more that might be named; to talk with whom and be with and examine them would be inconceivable happiness? Something of this sort surely belongs, or should belong, to life in a University. But we are busy, and in spite of the opportunities which College life affords, we tend to know little of what is being thought by those whose studies are not our own.

I ventured, therefore, to accept the chance of discussion which this invitation afforded me, and that the more because there was a subject in which I had long been interested, belonging also to the interests of most educated men, and specially appropriate to the intention of honouring the name of Herbert Spencer. Spencer counted himself, and was accounted, the prophet of evolution; no term is more prominent in his writings, and no writings have done more to disseminate the belief that something called the theory of evolution will provide and is providing the true answer to all riddles about what comes to be. The biologists, and Spencer himself in some measure, but preeminently Darwin, have worked out the theory in the first place for the forms of life; but its application is universal. The evolution of the various kinds of atom, the evolution of the solar system, of mind, of morality, of society, as well as of species should persuade us that we have in evolution the master-key.

Now in all this I am disposed to believe that there is much loose thinking, and many problems are overlooked under the hypnotic influence of a blessed word. Men seldom ask themselves what they mean by evolving, and how it differs from other processes of change, nor therefore whether all these 'evolutions' are processes of the same kind. Still more rarely do they ask themselves what that is which goes through the process of evolving. And even when such questions are asked, the answers found seem to me often profoundly unsatisfactory. Otherwise, we should,

I think, have ceased to look to the history of organisms for
the best and typical examples of evolution, and should look
rather to that of a mind.

Herbert Spencer's own definition of evolution is an
eminent example of what Aristotle calls the empty and
dialectical. It is, he said, 'an integration of matter, and
concomitant dissipation of motion; during which the
matter passes from an indefinite, incoherent homogeneity
to a definite, coherent heterogeneity; and during which
the retained motion undergoes a parallel transformation'.[1]
Now if we regard the world barely as so much matter disposed in space—and that is how he regarded it when he
spoke of the evolution of the solar system—why is it less
definite in one disposition than in another? and how is
there any integration of matter which is not also a dissipation, and what precisely is meant by dissipating motion?
Or if we consider the evolution of species, can we rightly
call a crab more definite and coherent than a crystal, even
though it be more heterogeneous? or is there necessarily
in it any greater integration of matter? and in the evolution
of mind, or morality, or society, or the modern newspaper,
what can the integration of matter or dissipation of motion
mean? It is no sufficient answer to reply that the formula
applies to the material processes with which these evolutions are correlated. Evolution so defined is a key to no
problem, for you must have another key before you can
know in what sense the words are to be taken.

But perhaps no one would defend this definition to-day,
and it is waste of time to slay the slain. I allow that the
ambiguities of the terms in this particular definition have
long since been pointed out clearly enough for it to have
become innocuous. But the vice of which it is an example
has, I think, by no means disappeared in considering this
subject. Let me take an illustration from an essay recently
published by a distinguished biologist. 'Matter, life,

[1] *First Principles*, ch. xvii, § 145, p. 396.

mind,' he writes, 'this is the simplest classification of phenomena. By means of processes analogous to obtaining a resultant by the parallelogram of forces, we can obtain a resultant of material operations in general, vital operations in general, and mental operations in general, numerous and varied in direction though they be.'[1] I venture to say that unless vital operations are of the same nature as those which are studied in dynamics, the deduction of the result of two or more concurrent vital operations in an organism is not analogous to obtaining a resultant by the parallelogram of forces; and that there are results of concurrent mental operations, and those the most characteristic of intelligence, which are fundamentally different from any that conform to that type. Not unless all processes of thinking out how divers factors co-operate to the production of a single result are to be held analogous to the theorem of the parallelogram of forces, on the mere ground that we are tracing in the result the synthesis of its factors, can the statement I have quoted be justified. But to do that is to treat all co-operation of factors as of the same kind, because it is co-operation: to overlook all that distinguishes one form of co-operation from another; and thus to pretend unity of nature in the different processes to which we give the same name is like what Spencer does in his definition of evolution.

In defence of this criticism let me take a later passage from the same essay. 'We incorporate experience in ourselves, and in so doing we alter the original basis of our reactions; a strong emotional experience colours all that is closely associated with it; and so after birth we are continually making our mental microcosm not only larger but qualitatively more complex, in exactly the same way as before birth our body grew not only in size but also in complexity of organization.'[2] Now I do not of course

---

[1] J. S. Huxley, *Essays of a Biologist*, p. 264.
[2] Ibid., pp. 268–9.

dispute the facts in the development of the mind intended to be described, nor those in the growth of the body before birth. I only urge that what is called our mental microcosm cannot be enlarged in the same sense as a body, that qualitative complexity is not of the same nature as complexity of organization, and that a mind most emphatically does not develop in exactly the same way in which a body grows: nay, if the writer's own view of the nature of bodily growth be correct, no two processes amenable to our investigation could be more distinct.

I will return later to this distinction; to emphasize it is one of my principal objects. But it may help to make my general position clearer if I say something first of the place which the science of biology seems to me properly to hold in any general theory of evolution. I take it that what may be called the evolutionary standpoint is properly that of the 'historical method'. There is a history to be given of how what is has come to be. But as we study that history, certain differences reveal themselves, and certain questions. In some respects what is now seems of the same kind as what was at any earlier period of the history. The elements which are now disposed in sun, moon, and planets were also somehow disposed in Laplace's nebula, or in the asteroids by whose aggregation some astronomers have more recently suggested that the solar system has been formed: and if their disposition was different, the laws of their interaction, so far as astronomical physics is concerned, were the same. Again, if the atoms have a history, yet the protons and electrons out of which they came together or into which they may break up are in them all the time. But in other respects what is now seems to display characters which at some earlier time nothing displayed. There was a time when there was no living body; and there were living bodies before anything which we should recognize as intelligence in their behaviour. Now given the elements, and the laws of astro-

nomical physics, we can understand why one phase of the
solar system should pass into another. The history is intelligible. Can we hope, or ought we to think it possible,
to connect with these data, by steps whose succession is
equally necessary, not only the later dispositions and
processes of matter which fall within the province of astro-
nomy, but those which distinguish living things from
non-living, and intelligent from unintelligent? For a long
time this appeared a vain hope. It is true that every great
advance in science has tempted some thinkers to extend
their newly discovered principles of connexion and explanation to other fields than those in which their adequacy
had been shown. Descartes believed that the principles
of mechanics were adequate to explain the history of all
organisms but the human body; Hume that something
like those of Newtonian gravitation would explain the
history of minds. But the differences between the organic
and the inorganic were not really bridged. In particular,
there seemed to be marks of purposiveness in plants and
animals which were absent in the processes of inorganic
nature; and as far back as men could pry, they found no
evidence that the ancestors with which living things were
historically connected in the succession of generations
differed anywise from their descendants alive to-day. But
the problem seemed to scientific minds to have been placed
in a new light, when the evidence for what is called biological evolution was marshalled in so masterly a way by
Darwin. It is true that he did nothing to establish a
transition from non-living to living aggregations of matter.
But he convinced the world of the truth of two propositions: first, that there has been a continuous historical
process linking the growth of plants and animals now
alive with that of ancestors immeasurably remote, very
different from them in form, and to outward appearance
at least vastly less complex: so that the process might be
regarded as one in which something has been really de-

veloped out of that in which it was not originally expressed; and secondly that, although each plant and animal thus produced exhibits the most intricate adaptations of its parts to one another and to its environment, and only thus maintains and reproduces itself, yet, given the facts of growth and reproduction and variation, much of this can be explained without invoking any activity of design. For the innumerable variations out of which a few are accumulated into the adapted structures of animals and plants are mostly rather injurious than beneficial to the individuals in which they arise. They appear to arise as the necessary result of pre-existing conditions, not otherwise in this respect than do the varying shapes of pebbles on the shore; and that some should fit their possessors better than do others to maintain themselves in the 'struggle for existence' is but an inevitable consequence of the situation, and no more remarkable or indicative of design than that the shapes of some pebbles should make them more suitable than others for sling-stones. The differences among the variants conform to the type of a so-called chance distribution; some of these must be more adaptive than others; the more adaptive must upon the whole thrive, where the less so perish; and therefore what thrives at any time must display adaptiveness; yet no purposive guidance has been involved.

These two conclusions being established, the biologist was tempted to think that the same process by which in his science existing species had been connected with their remote ancestors might be shown to connect those ancestors with non-living aggregations of matter, and be found again connecting the most rudimentary manifestations of conscious life in lower animals with its highest manifestations in mankind. Three considerations in particular lent strength to the temptation. First, if the process of biological evolution had linked by continuous transition things so remote as a mammal and a protozoon, it seemed reasonable to think that the gulf between the protozoon and the inorganic could also be bridged. Next, by dispensing with the hypothesis of design, the assimilation of the laws of life to those of chemistry and physics had been made indefinitely more plausible. And lastly, it was seen that the reasoning which accepted variations as given, and accounted for the perpetuation of certain among them by their survival-value, could be extended from purely physical characters like strength or speed or coloration to any psychical endowment which appeared to advantage its possessor. The remoter implications of regarding every psychical endowment as a selected accidental variation were not always appreciated by men whose primary concern was departmental. Thus in the phrase 'biological evolution' the adjective ceased really to qualify the substantive. It was not the name of one species of a process—one perhaps only to be found in the history of organisms—but merely of one instance of a process going on everywhere, through all history. So one might talk of a biological syllogism, not meaning that such a syllogism differed in form from any other, but merely that the identical form was there illustrated in an example belonging to biology. In popularizing then a philosophy of evolution, the influence of biology is capital. And for that very reason it is biological conceptions which need the closest scrutiny. There, if anywhere, the weak places of a philosophy of evolution are likely to be found.

I must not be understood to deny that what is has in some sense evolved, i.e. it has come to be. This after all is not a discovery of science in the nineteenth century. Plato and Aristotle long ago distinguished this scene of γένεσις and φθορά, generation and decay, from the realm of changeless being. It is the relation of these two which is the problem of philosophy. Something, I suppose, must be taken to be and not to come into being: if not atoms, then electrons, and if not any particular combinations of these, yet the laws of their combination. But what must we suppose to be, and what to become? And how are we to conceive the process called becoming?

Now the evolutionary philosophy which the triumphs of biology have helped to popularize, and which will always be associated with the name of Herbert Spencer, takes matter and energy and the laws of their action always to be, and all else to have arisen out of these. Dr. Alexander indeed would go behind matter and energy to a yet more fundamental entity, Space-Time; but I do not think this doctrine draws its support from the sciences. And if all else has arisen out of matter and energy under the laws of their action, is the reality of all that now is anything more than to be some complex mode of matter and energy?

It may be answered, that a philosophy of evolution expressly contends that out of one thing another arises: that what has come to be is not of the same nature with that out of which it has come to be, but has developed. To this I rejoin that those whose primary interest is with biology or other physical sciences do not seem to me to have thought this question out: they often think they contend this, but do not; while those whose primary interest is with philosophy (if I may be allowed to make this distinction here without expounding it) have considered the question, and have arrived not indeed all at the same conclusion, but at conclusions very different from that of the biologist. For either they have concluded, like Hegel and other so-called Absolutists, that development is unintelligible without supposing the eternal reality of the form which comes to be displayed in what develops; or else, like Bergson (and perhaps I might add William James), that something genuinely new comes to be in the process, whose coming is not explicable after the manner of scientific explanation, so that we must allow an *élan vital*, and that evolution is creative. And I think the philosophers are right; but I do not find the biologists agreeing. Let me quote again from the same volume as before. 'New com-

binations and properties thus arise in time. Bergson mis-
calls such evolution "creative". We had better, with Lloyd
Morgan, call it "emergent".[1] Why 'better', unless 'emergent' means something different from 'creative'? Let us
consider then the common uses of the word 'emerge'. A
chick emerges from the egg, but not till it is fully formed;
Athene emerged full-armed from the head of Zeus. But
does an oak thus emerge from an acorn? or a chick from
a fertilized egg-cell? Does not this preference for the term
'emergent' betray some hesitation of thought? If the
properties are really new, why not allow that they are
created? or is only what is material to be dignified by
calling it created, when, not having previously been, it
afterwards is?

Any man of science naturally boggles at the word
'creative', because no change to which it can be applied
is fully amenable to scientific explanation. But neither,
I believe, is any process to which we can properly apply
the terms 'development' and 'evolution'. I take these as
equivalent, because I believe that 'evolution' is meant now
in the sense of 'development', though in pre-Darwinian
times it was applied to the doctrine of pre-formation,
according to which the chick was present fully-formed
in the egg-cell, and its growth was only a getting bigger.
The following passage from Darwin's *Variation of Animals
and Plants under Domestication* is perhaps reminiscent of
this doctrine. 'The term growth', he writes, 'ought strictly
to be confined to mere increase of size, and development
to change of structure. Now, a child is said to grow into
a man, and a foal into a horse, but, as in these cases there
is much change of structure, the process properly belongs
to the order of development.'[2] I doubt if there is any
growth without some change of structure, or whether
Darwin has sufficiently considered what is involved in

[1] J. S. Huxley, *Essays of a Biologist*, p. 242: cf. p. 33.
[2] Vol. ii, p. 389.

that which he calls mere increase of size; but it seems clear that he would regard evolution as a development.

What then do we mean by 'development', or do we mean anything? I think we do mean something, of which we recognize instances, but whose definition is at first sight so paradoxical that we might be inclined to question its occurrence if we were not confronted with instances. For it is a process in which what as yet in some sense is not brings *itself* into being. And this is so contrary to the ordinary conceptions of physical science, that it is important that the instances to be produced should be indubitable, and not capable of being conceived as involving no such development. Though, therefore, I believe that there are instances of development in the field of biology, yet because many biologists seem to me to view their facts in a way inconsistent with so regarding them, I do not take my evidence thence. The one thing which quite manifestly and indisputably develops is a mind, or anything which, like an institution or a society, has its being in mind.

And this brings me back to the distinction, on which I previously insisted, between the development of a mind and the growth of a body. The body is a material aggregate, and there is no component in the grown body which has not been drawn from elsewhere. It grows, and can only grow, at the expense of other aggregates; and the redistribution of matter implied in its growth exemplifies, as we suppose, physical and chemical laws. Nor in all this does anything new come to be. It is commonly believed that if the physical components of the growing body and of the bodies in its environment, and the laws of their interaction, were fully known, and if our powers of calculation were adequate, its growth would be intelligible in the same way as any other complex result of the interaction of divers bodies according to simple laws; perhaps not much otherwise than a resultant obtained by the parallelogram of forces. I do not say that this is so; but if the principles displayed in the evolution of species are really the same with those displayed in the so-called evolution of inorganic compounds, if 'evolution' is really not an equivocal term in its scientific uses, then it is so. But nothing of this is true in the development of a mind. A mind is not an aggregate whose components have been drawn from elsewhere. It does not develop at the expense of that on which it is said metaphorically to feed; for the mind's food is like the oil in the widow's cruse, of which if one partakes, no less is left for others. Attempts indeed have recently been made, in the name partly of a purely descriptive science, to show otherwise: to construct the mind out of neutral stuff, diversely aggregated in so-called minds and bodies. But there can be no purely descriptive science, for the simplest description of what we perceive makes it coherent by connecting it with something not perceived; and the attempts I refer to, such as may be found in Mr. Bertrand Russell's *Analysis of Mind*, will, I am confident, be counted some day among the curiosities of speculation, along with the doctrine that we originally saw everything upside down, and, as Mansel supposed, have come through association of ideas to see it all the right way up, or James Mill's theory that association by similarity, in those cases where the similar things were not previously contiguous in experience, occurs because we are accustomed in other cases to see like things together.[1] The growth of a mind then is not aggregation: there is a real coming to be of that which, in the sense in which it exists when it has come to be, did not exist before. And yet in another sense surely it must have existed; for else the mind has not developed. There is no process of development, unless what develops is all the time that which it comes to be; and again, there is no process of development unless it is not in the same way so in the earlier and later phases. This is not gratuitous

---

[1] *Analysis of the Phenomena of the Human Mind*, vol. I, ch. III, p. 111.

paradox; it is, I am persuaded, the true account of what we
mean by development, as it is the old account, put forward
by Aristotle in the antithesis of Δύναμις and ἐνέργεια, the
potential and the actual. It seems paradoxical only so long
as we take for examples of development what are not such,
and try to assimilate the evolution of species to that of
atoms. For the atom is conceived as merely protons and
electrons in a particular arrangement, and these, which
have not come to be anything which they were not before,
are the unities which suffer process. If biological evolution is really of the same nature with the evolution of the
atom, if 'in so far as we analyse the material aspect of life,
physico-chemical concepts are _adequate_',[1] and the vital is
at bottom mechanical, then the protons and electrons are
still the unities in the process, and still they do not develop.

For consider what other identical subject or subjects it
could be, to which the biologist can ascribe development.
Whether we look at the growth of an individual from
a fertilized egg-cell, or at his evolution from some remote
ancestor of very different form, there is no material unit
or collection of units that is the subject of the process. It
is a mere illusion to suppose that the continuity of the
germ-plasm in any way lightens this problem. For the
germ-plasm which continues is no self-same physical thing.
An electron may be said to continue to be, in all the combinations or isolations into which it enters; but nothing
physical thus continues to be, through all the generations
which make up the history of the germ-plasm. What
continues to be is something immaterial, a form of combination maintained through change, and displayed in an
aggregate of physical units that is never for two moments
the same. But this form of combination itself no more
truly continues the same than it also changes, at least in
scale; else we should not say that an individual grows,
or a species evolves. I have said before that I doubted

[1] J. S. Huxley, op. cit., p. 100.

whether Darwin was right in thinking any growth to be
mere increase of size. Let me ask now whether there is
anything physical which ever increases in size. A crowd
is said to grow, but physically regarded what is bigger is
not the same with what was smaller. In aggregation, no
physical unit and no aggregate of the same physical units
gets any bigger. Even a balloon, which might be said to
grow larger as it is inflated, does not merely increase in
size; a larger volume comes to be enclosed by the envelope
because the parts of it change their disposition in space.
But we do, I think, commonly distinguish aggregation
from growth by this, that in growth there is a unity determining the continuous manifestation of a certain form, but
in aggregation not. We may, however, make a further
distinction which Darwin had in mind when opposing
growth to development. Sometimes the form seems to be
as adequately displayed in one phase of the process as in
another, and the difference to be one of scale only, though
it is perhaps always something more; this is what the word
evolution meant, when used in the theory of pre-formation.
At other times there is what Darwin calls much change of
structure. But it is to be noted that we cannot rightly
regard increase of size as growth unless in the successive
sizes of the structure there is something the same, nor
change of structure as development unless this is more
completely present in the later than in the earlier. What
that something the same is, is a very difficult question.
But it is clear that it is nothing physical—no physical
unit, nor aggregate of physical units. It is clear too that
the more completely in thought we assimilate the organic
to the inorganic, and mean what we say when we speak
(if we do speak) of the mechanism of life, the harder will
it become to find anything the same, which can be said
either to grow or to develop. If nothing is real (to borrow
Plato's phrase) but what we can squeeze with our fingers,
then there are no units but protons and electrons (if indeed

there would be these) and they remain the same through change, and because they do not alter, there is no unit that alters, and so no evolution.

Now in that growth of an individual, in which there is change of structure as well as of scale, the form which comes to be displayed later was not displayed before; and yet unless it is the same form, there is no growth but only substitution, such as might occur in an anagram, when one arrangement of letters replaces another. This is true also of the process through which the individual has evolved from some remote ancestor. But here the problem of development presented by the growth of an individual is complicated with a second problem. For no individual mammal has ever been any of its ancestors; the historical process is continuous only through the mediation of the germ-plasm. Yet we have just seen that the specific form is not fully displayed in the earlier phases of individual growth: least of all, in the mere fertilized egg-cell. In the continuous process, then, by which germ-cells originate one from another, or from a fusion of two others, if they are undeveloped all the time, how can we have the truth of the evolution of species?

I think this difficulty should give pause to any one who is inclined at once to maintain a purely mechanical theory of life, and to be serious with the assertion of evolution. For reasons to which I will come shortly, connected with the fact of intelligence in man, I do not believe that all physical changes in human bodies can be explained purely mechanically, or, let me say, are strictly conformable to physico-chemical laws. But neither do I believe, though here I speak less confidently, that the growth of any organism can be so explained. Much work of the greatest interest has been done in recent years upon what is called the physical basis of heredity. But though heredity doubtless has a physical basis, I do not think that any one would say that the physical basis has been shown adequate to account for it; and what holds for heredity holds for all development in organisms. It may be retorted that this is because our knowledge is incomplete, and that it is a poor thing, and a sign of *ignava ratio*, to preach inexplicabilities. I am not anxious to offer mysteries by way of release from the effort of thought. But I do not think that a mechanical process is uniquely intelligible, and therefore, so far as scientific thought would reduce all processes to these, I do not see that it should have the last word. I mean by a mechanical process one in which the movements of the parts of a material system are severally deducible as resultants of the interaction of each with all the rest according to laws capable of mathematical statement; though the accurate deduction may be beyond the resources of our mathematics. Now the mathematical calculation may be as intelligible as you please; but some of the assumptions about the physical nature of that to which they are applied are by no means so. If I am rightly informed, the particles of molar bodies have to be treated in calculation as without magnitude, in order to avoid the mere multiplication of the same difficulties which analysis is introduced to solve. They are also regarded as mutually exclusive units of matter; but it is hard to see how they are units if they are extended, or material if they are not, and if they are really mutually exclusive, their commerce in interaction, however calculable, is hardly intelligible. Only if there is a real unity within which they belong, and of whose being the changes in their space-relations are phases, can we find, as it seems to me, any way of understanding the connexion between the successive states of a material system; and such a real unity is not a material thing, nor certainly does every unity display its diversity in a system the changes of whose parts are mechanically connected. Therefore I do not hold it obscurantism to think that whatever physical basis there may be for heredity, it is not such as makes heredity a purely mechanical process, or will ever fully explain it. There is a physical basis for sight; but I say with some assurance that no physiologist or psychologist has yet explained thereby, nor will explain, our seeing.[1] What has been done is to connect differences in our seeing in an orderly way with differences in the physical basis; but the connexion remains as unintelligible in the details as it was in the whole. The achievement is indeed of great value, as Bacon would say, for operation; but to know that if you knock a man on the head he loses consciousness does not explain the connexion between body and mind. So I do not expect that the discovery of a physical basis of heredity will enable us to give a completely mechanical explanation of growth and evolution. The cases are indeed not exactly parallel, for in one the connexion is between a physical basis and events in mind, in the other between a physical basis and events in matter. But it serves to illustrate what I believe the extent of the service of these investigations will be found to be. Such great advances have indeed been made in this subject of recent years along Mendelian lines, and their economic applications in breeding have already proved so important, that biologists are naturally inclined in their enthusiasm to think a complete explanation along physical lines is theoretically possible. But as in physics the explanation of a molar problem is sometimes only effected by re-introducing the same problem on a molecular scale (for the elasticity shown by one billiard ball striking another is explained by reference to the behaviour of their molecules, and, unless action takes place at a distance, the same elasticity must be ascribed to the molecules so long as we consider them to have any magnitude at all), so it seems to me that the problem of reproduction, on which the so-called 'mechanism of Mendelian heredity' is to

---

[1] But cf. W. McDougall, *An Outline of Psychology*, p. 226, n. 1: 'Much confusion would be avoided if all philosophers were born blind or were forbidden to refer to visual perception.'

throw light, reappears many times over on a small scale in the explanation. To explain what I mean, may I refer to the chromosome theory of heredity, though this is not at present universally accepted? There are within the nuclear wall of any cell certain more or less thread-like bodies called (from the way they take a stain) chromosomes; their number varies with different species, but in any one species, at least in the same sex, is constant for all its cells. It is even, at least in one sex; and there are supposed to be so many pairs of chromosomes, all derived ultimately from each parental germ-cell, the odd one when it is present being connected with sex. Each chromosome is conceived to be composed of many unit-factors, called genes, and each gene to be concerned in the mechanism of growth with the determination of some definite character or characters in the plant or animal. For each determination of such character there is therefore concerned a pair of genes. Where the character may assume alternative forms, as the stem of a plant may be smooth or hairy, or the colour of a pea green or yellow, it is supposed that the corresponding genes also have alternative forms; and the pair in any cell may be both of one form, or both of the other, or one of each. When in a developing germ-cell there is one of each, the resulting character is often the same as if both had been of one form, and the gene which in these cases determines the character to the exclusion of any perceptible influence from the other gene is called dominant, and its fellow recessive. But even where the resulting character is some sort of blend of the characters which either pure pair would determine, there is never any blending of the genes. They are to be regarded as discrete alternative factors, segregating or combining without fusion, and are said accordingly to be allelomorphic to each other; if any one is confused by a term suggesting the obscure notion of a one-another form, let him call them rather antimorphic, though the word unfortunately has no biologist's authority. In all ordinary cell-division the chromosomes appear to divide, and it is assumed that each gene divides in such a way that the two cells formed by the division of one cell have the same equipment of paired chromosomes as the one had. But in a germ-cell, before ripening, there is an elaborate process, in the course of which the number of chromosomes is finally halved; the conjugation then restores the pairing. It is supposed that in the halving one of each pair of genes is lost, each germ-cell thus bringing to the act of conjugation only one factor for each hereditary character; but after conjugation there are two. These may be each the same antimorph, or different, and upon the basis of the sorting and combination of these antimorphic factors it is shown that innumerable and important facts observed in the inheritance or non-inheritance of characters, when species and varieties are crossed and the hybrids bred with each other or with the parent forms, may be explained. These genes then are regarded as the principal factors in the mechanism by which the inheritance of character is determined. But if the reproduction of the hereditary characters in an organism depends on the provision of all these pairs of genes in the fertilized germ-cell, on what does the process by which they are provided there depend? It is a process of many phases and of astonishing intricacy; in one phase of it chemical substances arranged in a most elaborate structure within the ovum so combine with the not less elaborately arranged substances within the sperm, that a single system is produced, chemically and structurally similar to the two which have been broken up. Afterwards, when the cell divides, two systems are produced similar to the one that has been broken up. Here is another example of reproduction. What is reproduced is not a multicellular organism, but a cell. Yet its reproduction presents a like problem. The hereditary characters of the organism are explained by reference to the characters of the genes in the cell; and these are not less hereditary. The process of reproduction in a cell is doubtless not the same as that of development in an organism. Yet it seems equally to require explanation.

It may be said, however, that the apparent difficulty arises only from the necessary incompleteness of our analysis in a matter so complex; that if we fully understood the physico-chemical composition of the genes and the other substances with which they interact, and could work out the consequences of the forces in play between the ultimate elements concerned, we could deduce all that happens in the reproduction whether of cells or multicellular organisms; and to do this would be to establish completely the mechanical nature of the process. Let me then waive this question and point out another difficulty that seems to me to be involved in the mechanistic assumption. It is often urged that the greater complexity of the human brain is the necessary physiological basis of the greater variety of response to stimulus displayed by man, as compared with what the animals display, which we describe as dominated by instinct. I shall have something to say about this contention presently; but I would have you note this about it now. It implies a mechanism of human behaviour; it holds—rightly, I think—that if there is such a mechanism, the machine must be more intricate, as the varieties of behaviour for which it provides are more numerous. By the same reasoning it seems to me that if there is a real mechanism of heredity, the machine must, upon the theory of biological evolution, have been most intricate in the earliest living cells. For evolution has taken place, at any rate chiefly, through the selection of those variations which, among many others, had at any moment the greatest survival-value. An ample and continuous supply of variations is essential; and every distinct variation pre-supposes, in the cell that varies, a distinct mechanical provision. This is perhaps only the more obvious, if we accept the view that the modification of species has come about through the selection and accumulation not of continuous fluctuations, but of discrete mutations. Now if C_1 and C_2 be variants born of B, and if C_1 produce variants D_1 and D_2, and C_2 produce variants D_3 and D_4, not only must C_1 and C_2 each have contained mechanical provision for two variants, but B must have contained such provision for four; so that the further we recede the more complex must be the heredity-determining machinery in the organisms we reach; and in this respect the present theory of biological evolution will be no better off than that of pre-formation, according to which Cain and Abel were pre-formed in the loins of Adam, and their children in their loins, and so *ad indefinitum*, and Adam was like a nest of boxes with goodness knows how many boxes inside the outermost.

Let me take leave therefore to reject the view that growth and heredity are purely mechanical processes; and let me remind you that there is no more any continuing physical thing or aggregate of physical things throughout the uninterrupted generation of germ-cells one from another than throughout the unbroken growth of an individual organism from a germ-cell. How then, can we speak of development? For this we must find a subject which develops— which is one through a succession of phases, and yet different in these phases; what can this subject be, and how can we reconcile its identity with the difference of the phases?

It is the old problem of the one and the many, of unity in diversity, with which thought has busied itself since the days of the Greeks, though the departmental inquiries of the sciences can be mainly carried on without attention to it. Unity in diversity takes many forms; in some the diversity which the unity holds together is more profound, in others less; in some the unity seems displayed in a manifestation sensibly unchanged; in others, though its sensible manifestations change, yet we are helped by these, or some of them, to an apprehension of it; and in yet others nothing sensible can be taken to manifest it. Let me illustrate these differences.

A moving body is the same in a succession of places; we commonly regard the difference of place as making no difference to the being of the body, and yet it is a diversity; and since it is due to motion, and motion is a state of the body, and bodies affect each other's motions and therefore each other's states, it is hard to deny that every moving body furnishes an example of diversity held together in unity. Yet here the diversity seems relatively unimportant, and what is one—the body—is manifested to sense, or imagined after the analogy of what is sensible. It is with such units that physics deals; and for various reasons physicists are apt to regard their units as absolutely unvarying, like the units of arithmetic; and for this reason there is no place in physics for the notion of development.[1]

Take next a living body; this is accounted the same in the successive stages of its growth, or rather of its growth and decay. Here the unity cannot be conceived as that of a body of unchanging shape. It manifests itself to sense in a succession of different forms. Nevertheless, when we compare the forms successively assumed, we think that some are in a sense incomplete, and that what they, as it were, point to is more adequately revealed in a later form.

---

[1] Those who accept the modern doctrine of the relativity of motion will still have to admit a unity in diversity, though not accepting all that I have just said. By the modern doctrine I mean that which holds that what we call the motion of a body is *nothing but* a change in its space-relations to other bodies, so that we cannot ascribe motion to any body as its state; of course every one allows that the motion of one body *involves* changes in its space-relations to any others that are not moving with the same translatory motion. The modern doctrine may be said to offer us instead of motion a set of successive relations among bodies all satisfying some equation with four variables; and the equation is the unity, the set of successive relations the diversity; but the terms in the relation are treated as having indeed four variable coefficients, but unaffected intrinsically by the variations of these.

It must not of course be supposed that 'form' here means merely shape; it covers all sorts of characters and relations by no means all of them sensible. Now it is this relation among the successive phases in which the unity is manifested that justifies us in speaking of development. So long as we regard a living body in a purely physical way, as an aggregate of the same elements which were differently dispersed and aggregated before coming into the disposition which they hold in the organism, we cannot think of it as developing. At every moment it is just as definite an aggregate as at any other, in the same way as the rain-drops in a cloud, while it shifts and floats, do not make it any more a cloud at one moment than at another. The unity in a living body therefore is immaterial, though more adequately revealed at one time than at another in what is material. Such immaterial unities are found also where there is no development. What is called the universal displayed in many particular instances is such— the circularity in all circles, however they may differ in radius, the colouredness in green and red and blue, the vertebrate structure in a fish, a frog, a bird, and a mammal. I do not forget that some have denied the existence of these unities. I will not here argue the question, but only say that, if we cannot do without acknowledging other forms of unity in diversity, we may hesitate the less to admit this one.

Thirdly, a mind is one in its various thoughts, acts, and feelings, both simultaneous and successive. And here we find both the profoundest diversity, and the most assured unity, as well as the most indisputable development. Yet this unity is never sensibly manifested. Psychologists have pointed to certain elusive sensations, making up what they call the somatic consciousness, any profound disturbance of which seems to break or confuse the consciousness of one's identity. But these sensations do not sensibly manifest the unity of the self, as that of the developing organism is sensibly manifested rather in the adult than in the germ. As Hume complained, there is no impression which can be called an impression of the self, and yet the various attempts to construct the unity of the self out of an aggregate are manifestly ridiculous.

To acknowledge the unity which thus holds together the diversity of a self is not to say that every soul is eternal, nor yet that all its diversity appears in consciousness. There is nothing in what has been urged inconsistent with psycho-analytic theories of the unconscious, but rather much in these that agrees with what reflection upon the nature of mind independently reveals to us. If any one wishes to be convinced that there is in him such a principle of unity, and that he is not a mere aggregate, he should consider above all the activity of intelligence, and more particularly as it is displayed in choice. There is a profound difference between a choice or rational act and action determined by a mere conflict of desires. In the second, the stronger desire prevails, and for a time suppresses the weaker, as when a hungry man insulted forgets his hunger until his desire is satisfied upon his enemy. But if he deliberate whether to risk the loss of his dinner in order to trounce his enemy, or to forgo this in order to appease his hunger, he asks himself which alternative is better. That question implies that he conceives, and desires, what is good; but this is not a third desire co-ordinate with his hunger and his desire to trounce his enemy, since a good alternative to and exclusive of all objects of particular desires would be void, nothing. It is realized in them, or in some selection of them; but it is not a mere sum of them. When a man thus distinguishes himself and his good from all his particular desires and their objects, plainly he and his good are unities displayed, but incompletely displayed, in these. Plainly too his action is comparable to nothing mechanical. When various forces act upon some moving part of a machine, there is nothing that considers by which it is best to be directed. In rational choice, then, we find evidence of a unity that is co-ordinating a diversity of impulses; and no physical analogies can help us to anything but to misconceive the nature of such choice.[1]

But there are other manifestations of intelligence besides choice, and without considering them we do not understand what is meant by calling choice rational. Choice involves the thought of something good; but we all know that the thought of this outruns the articulate determination of its nature. How do we come to know what its nature is? This problem is fundamentally the same as how we discover the answer to many other questions. When we have discovered it, we should not know it to be the answer, unless the thought of that of which we are in search someway accompanied and controlled the activity of the mind whereby we first arrive at the explicit recognition of it. So also in artistic creation some artists have described, and surely it must be so, how an implicit apprehension of what they are reaching after directs them in discarding any suggestion that is amiss, and developing their thought of what they seek. I say developing, because here we seem to have the true notion of development. That which comes to be was there from the beginning; but whereas then it was not developed, now it is. Here again, no physical analogy can help us to understand, because what develops is no physical unit, nor aggregate of such. What develops is the unity that manifests itself in a diversity both of simultaneous detail and of successive modes of such detail, and reaches an adequate manifestation of itself only by passing through the less adequate.

That we do recognize such progress in manifestation must be allowed, if we are to justify the distinction between growth and decay, between development and degeneration. A purely mechanical view of life, which allows no

[1] Cf. *supra*, Essay III.

genuine break between inorganic and organic processes, cannot justify these distinctions. If we are to take seriously the language we use when we talk about the evolution of species, we must hold that something implicit or imperfectly revealed in earlier organisms is more fully revealed in later. There are many difficulties here which I have not time to discuss. There is clearly a difference between the development of the individual, in which one specific nature is gradually revealed, and that which has led to the revelation of all the types of plant and animal that now exist or have existed. Of the latter we shall have to say that what has developed is the generic unity, which requires, for the revelation of all the diversity that it holds together, not the detail of one individual organism, but of countless such.

The undeveloped then is the indeterminate. And since the earliest living cell, physico-chemically regarded, is as determinate and articulate as any present mammal, it is again not this cell, but some unity—some universal—of whose possible forms there is in this but an instance, that has developed. And because the undeveloped is not articulate, we are free from the necessity, incumbent on a mechanical theory, of supposing that what was present in the earliest living cell was the most articulately complex of all living structures. On the other hand, since we cannot explain the process of growth and generation by recourse to the structure of such a pre-existing mechanism, something like what is found in the activity of intelligence must be admitted also in the growth and generation of organisms. That which is to be revealed guides, or shall we say animates, the process through which it comes to be revealed. But it does so not infallibly; as the mind errs, so organisms grow awry.

All this no doubt takes us beyond the concepts and methods of physical science. But at some point in our consideration of the bodily metabolism we must go beyond these. For if there is such a thing as intelligence in men at all, the intelligent action of a man cannot conform at all points to physical laws. In order not to be misunderstood, let me say that even the requirements of the doctrine of the conservation of energy cannot be fully satisfied in the human body, since that doctrine determines the direction not less than the amount of motion to which the transformations of energy give rise. We must face this consequence. While I have been speaking, and in order to express my thought, there have been various movements of my organs of speech. If these movements are to be wholly accounted for by reference to the state of my cerebral centres and other bodily parts, and that state by reference to previous dispositions of what is material, my thought has had nothing to do with my speech. You may regard it as running parallel to my speech, but independent of it, though I do not think that any theory of parallelism can be satisfactorily worked out; or you may regard it as an expression or by-product of what is going on in the brain and body. Either view, however, presents grave difficulties to a biologist, for on neither can he show that intelligence has any survival-value, nor therefore why it has been selected. Biologists are apt to be curiously inconsistent in this matter. They endeavour to bring intelligence within the sweep of evolutionary biology, as something to be accounted for in organisms on the general principles of variation and selection; and while so engaged, they insist upon the advantage which the possession of intelligence gives to an animal in the struggle for existence; the animal confined to a certain number of instinctive responses to stimulus cannot adapt its behaviour to the infinite variety of situations in which it is placed as successfully as one that can remember, generalize, and think, working out in idea the consequences of various actions and their respective advantages before it commits itself in behaviour. But at other times they connect this power with an increase in the size and complexity of the brain, as if there were the same relation between the less highly organized brain of an insect and its fewer and simpler instinctive reactions, for which the organization of its brain accounts, as between the more highly organized brain of a mammal or particularly of man and his intelligent responses to a situation. Thus one writer, who insists how superior in respect of survival-value is the plasticity of intelligence to the fixity of instinct, nevertheless explicitly maintains that to every variety of mental activity corresponds a determinate variety of process in the nervous mechanism;[1] another seems to imply the same by speaking of the increase in brain-size in man 'and consequently in complexity of mode of reaction and behaviour';[2] and those who think that evolutionary psychology is a science of the same nature as evolutionary biology must either deny that the behaviour even of the earliest organisms, whose mind is the most rudimentary, is fully explicable in physical terms, or affirm it to be thus explicable in those organisms in which mind is most fully developed. Now if this be so, the physical structure is capable of acquiring a sufficiently intricate complexity to ensure by mere reflex action that adaptedness of response which is elsewhere said to require intelligence.

There is a further point to be considered. If what we call intelligence is nothing more than a link (or the reflection in consciousness of a link) in the process which leads the organism to respond to stimulus in a way having survival-value, then there is no ground for distinguishing our intelligent judgements as true or false. They will, like any other varieties of behaviour, be merely advantageous or disadvantageous. Such a doctrine cannot of course be consistently defended, because he who maintains it holds his own doctrine, that men's judgements, like other bio-

---

[1] G. Archdall Reid, *The Laws of Heredity*, chs. xix, xx; see, e.g., §§ 603, 608-9.   [2] J. S. Huxley, op. cit., p. 254.

logical peculiarities, differ not in truth but only in survival-value, to be not merely something advantageous to think, but something true. But it is the logical consequence, and therefore the *reductio ad absurdum*, of attempting to bring the mind within the compass of a science that accounts for everything in the life of organisms on those principles of unpurposive variation and elimination of less favourable varieties by which biological evolution, or the modification of species through descent, is held to have come about.[1]

If then we are to believe in the distinction of truth and falsehood, we cannot work merely with these principles in evolutionary psychology. Mind is that in which we most incontestably find development, and in the development of mind what is to be is immanent in, and helps to control the process of, its becoming. This is to say that its development is purposive; an unpurposive process, on the contrary, is one in which each phase is the necessary resultant of the conditions existing the moment before, and nothing else has to be taken into account. Such processes are 'blind and fortuitous':[2] fortuitous not because uncaused, but because without design, and blind because in no sense guided by the result to be. But if really blind and fortuitous, a process is not one of development.

Are we to say then that purpose is present in a developing organism? not in the sense that an organism is conscious of that towards which its development proceeds. But is it therefore necessary to abandon all that has been said about the nature of life, and revert to a purely mechanical theory? I think not. I said that recent psychological theories of the unconscious accorded in some respects with what reflection in quite other directions reveals to us about the mind. All discovery is made unconsciously: we are conscious of it only when we have made it. Solutions come to us; but yet we find them. They are not given, like

---

[1] Cf. my *Some Problems in Ethics*, pp. 14–15.
[2] J. S. Huxley, op. cit., p. 220.

buns to a bear; it is the working of intelligence in us that reaches them. Not wrongly did Socrates compare the mind that thinks to a mother bringing children to the birth; and 'as thou knowest not how the bones do grow in the womb of her that is with child', so the mind works in darkness until it is delivered. It is, as already said, the nature of mind to be a unity displayed in diversity; but for this reason the elements in the diversity are yet one; they are most completely one in their more intelligent and intelligible phases; such phases are the very unity of the mind, a unity present all along in its development, and so guiding the changes by which it comes to be revealed. May not an organism be a unity not wholly dissimilar? There are, if I may repeat myself, many forms of unity in diversity: in some both the diversity is profounder and the reduction to unity completer than in others. Perhaps these forms are not merely juxtaposed in the universe, but themselves progressively manifest the fundamental nature of the universe, for the universe is itself the all-embracing unity, that determines thereout its own diversity. And if this is so, all that has been said about the nature of development forbids us to regard those forms of unity in diversity wherein the diversity is most profound and the reduction to unity most complete as explicable from inferior forms. It was said long ago by Plato that a δύναμις or capacity can only be known by considering on what it is exercised and what it achieves.[1] It cannot even be named except as the capacity *of* something; and that something is the developed and actual. We must therefore explain the undeveloped from the developed, if we can explain it at all. That Herbert Spencer asserted the contrary is the greatest piece of evidence that he had misconceived the true nature of evolution.[2] In a sense indeed we cannot explain the undeveloped. Just because it is undeveloped it is incompletely what it is. Psychologists should remember this when they construct

---

[1] *Republic*, v. 477 c 1–d 5.   [2] *Data of Ethics*, p. 7.

a genetic psychology; for if there really is an evolution of mind, its realized forms cannot be deduced from what is earlier and more rudimentary in the way in which the sciences deduce a complex result from a synthesis of simpler conditions. Notoriously, the field of such explanation is the quantitative, and in the field of quantity we are furthest from any development. But in another sense we may be said to explain the undeveloped when, looking back on it from the vantage-ground of the developed, we see it as a phase in the self-development of the latter. As this is true when we consider the development of an individual mind, so is it when we consider the relations of lower to higher forms of mind. The higher does not differ from the lower as a more complex from a simpler structure of identical elements. We must not therefore conceive the working of what we call the animal mind after the scheme of a physical system, and that of man's mind as merely a more complex example of the same. Neither must we describe the working of the animal mind as if it was fully human. And therefore we cannot adequately describe it, any more than we can adequately describe those states of re-developing intelligence which we sometimes experience when we wake from sleep. But though we cannot adequately describe it, our best clue to it is through its more developed forms. And of the different modes of unity in diversity the same is true; the most indisputable and illuminating examples of unity in diversity are the highest. If then we are to understand this all-pervasive character of the real, we must start from mind, wherein it is most plainly seen, and the domination of diversity by unity reaches its completion. We shall not fully understand organic life without first attending to the life of mind. By all means investigate the range of processes in the living body that conform to the schemes of chemistry and physics; but if you think there is nothing else, do not speak of evolution. Say rather, the modification of species through descent, and be content to stop at that. Above all, if you think there is nothing else, do not hope to bring within your biological scheme any intelligent activity. For what this is we know better than we know what goes on in an organism; the mind is really more intelligible to itself than a system of bodies in motion is to it, however intelligible also numerical and spatial relations may be; and the nature of mind does not conform to that of a system of bodies in motion, in whose ever-shifting phases there is no place for the distinction of more and less evolved, or higher and lower, nor yet for that of true and false.

INDEX

INDEX

PRINTED IN GREAT BRITAIN AT THE UNIVERSITY PRESS, OXFORD
BY JOHN JOHNSON, PRINTER TO THE UNIVERSITY